PENGUIN BOOKS
THE GREAT INDIAN FAMILY

Gitanjali Prasad graduated from Lady Shri Ram College and has a post-graduate diploma in journalism from the Indian Institute of Mass Communication.

She has written on the family for over twenty years. She did research on the subject as a Press Fellow at Wolfson College, Cambridge University in 1999 and later in a study supported by the Dorabji Tata Trust in 2002.

Gitanjali has been a freelance writer and columnist for several major newspapers and magazines, and for seven years she was bureau chief, eastern region, of Magna Publishing Company. Her children's book, *The Sun Is Like a Football* was published by Children's Book Trust and translated into Hindi and Bengali.

She is married and has two sons.

The Great Indian Family

New Roles, Old Responsibilities

GITANJALI PRASAD

PENGUIN BOOKS

An imprint of Penguin Random House

PENGUIN BOOKS

USA | Canada | UK | Ireland | Australia
New Zealand | India | South Africa | China | Singapore

Penguin Books is part of the Penguin Random House group of companies
whose addresses can be found at global.penguinrandomhouse.com

Published by Penguin Random House India Pvt. Ltd
4th Floor, Capital Tower 1, MG Road,
Gurugram 122 002, Haryana, India

First published by Penguin Books India 2006

Copyright © Gitanjali Prasad 2006

ISBN 9780143061823

Typeset in Sabon by InoSoft Systems, Noida

Printed at Repro India Limited

www.penguin.co.in

This is a legitimate digitally printed version of the book and therefore might not
have certain extra finishing on the cover.

For my parents
For Alok, Viraj and Anurag
And for the larger family, mine . . . and yours

who are the inspiration for this book.

Contents

ACKNOWLEDGEMENTS ix

PREFACE xii

INTRODUCTION: CHANGING
PERCEPTIONS 1

THE JOINT FAMILY: TWICE
THE JOY OR DOUBLE THE
TROUBLE? 39

FULL-TIME HOUSEWIVES:
DESPERATE HOUSEWIVES OR
BLISSFUL HOMEMAKERS? 84

WORKING WOMEN:
SUPERWOMEN OR
OVERWORKED DRUDGES? 122

TODAY'S WORKING FATHERS:
BONDING WITH THE FAMILY OR
IN BONDAGE AT WORK? 186

YOUNG SINGLES: LIVING THE
GOOD LIFE OR NO TIME FOR
A LIFE? 223

viii   Contents

TODAY'S WORKPLACE: DREAM
COME TRUE OR LIVING
NIGHTMARE? 271

BIBLIOGRAPHY 321

INDEX 325

Acknowledgements

'A book on the Indian family!' I cannot remember exactly how long I went around with this thought in my head. Growing up in tumultuous times, it seemed the one constant was the family. And then, somewhere along the line, it seemed that even that was not the same any more. As the world was changing, so was the family. Indeed, perhaps it was the family that was changing even more than the world outside. What exactly was happening? And why? Would it be possible to understand the dynamics of the changing family? It was a difficult project but I must confess that I had no idea how difficult till I was well and truly neck deep!

A book so ambitious in scope could never have happened without help from scores of wonderful people. To so many who feature in the book, and have shared with me their life stories, my grateful thanks. With the tape recorder running, I listened to you as you laughed and cried and sometimes raged. Thank you for sharing your thoughts. This book would not have been possible without your very active participation. My thanks also to the organizations that agreed to be interviewed for the chapter on the workplace. You showed courage in daring to speak on a sensitive subject.

I should also like to acknowledge a debt of gratitude to those who helped while I was doing research on the family. I am obliged to the Chevening Fellowship, which enabled me to take a break from the frantic pace of a journalist's life and enjoy the intellectual stimulation of working on a single project for three months. I was fortunate to have Dr Martin Richards, the head of the Centre for Family Research, Cambridge University, as my academic supervisor, and Dr John Naughton as director of the Press Fellowship programme. When I challenged popular views on the family in the UK, Dr Richard's openness to my perspective as an Indian, and as a journalist, was enthusiastic; Dr Naughton, on the other hand, challenged my most cherished beliefs on the family, which pushed me to research more deeply to understand *why*. Both helped clarify my thoughts. In India, the Dorabji Tata Trust supported a project on working women, which provided invaluable material for this book.

I am grateful to Dr Pradip Kumar Bose, of the Centre for Studies in Social Sciences, Kolkata who allowed me the use of the Centre's library and gave excellent suggestions when I was starting my research. Dr Chhaya Datar of the Tata Institute of Social Sciences was again very supportive. I should especially like to thank Dr Leena Chatterjee, of the Indian Institute of Management, Calcutta, who gave freely of her time and knowledge for the five years I worked on this subject. Of course, I own full responsibility for any errors in any part of the research and writing.

Many thanks are also due to friends (including some who are related by blood and marriage!), and colleagues from every stage of my life for their generous help and suggestions.

And finally, to Karthika at Penguin, who was enthusiastic about the book the very first time we met, and shared with me her invaluable experience, to help me give the book form, structure, shape, and to my family at home, who lived with me as I did so, a salute!

Preface

*'Home is where we go when we run out of places to
go to.'*

Home and family. They are what one took for
granted. Always there when needed. A comforting,
comfortable place where one could just be oneself. This
in any case was the popular perception.

How true is the stereotype? What is a family? And
what does it do for us?

On one level, we know it all. Our families shape us.
They nurture us when we are young and when we are
old and in all the times in between. We inherit our
parents' physical characteristics, our family name, or
'title' as we charmingly refer to it. Some of us inherit
property and other assets. But most of all, we get a
sense of 'who' we are. A value system which could be
good or bad and role models in the shape of parents
and other elders who influence us all through our lives.
Families can, and sometimes do, destroy those they
should protect, but for most of us it is to the family
that we turn, to celebrate our success as also to

commiserate with us in failure. In earlier times, you could turn to your family for help and it could not turn its back to you. The family was crèche, university, nursing home, investment bank, all rolled into one. Or so one felt. How far have we travelled from there? How is the urban middle-class family faring today? What shape is the joint family in? What are the problems of a dual-career family? Is life easier for career women who are single? How do today's housewives view their situation? What are the priorities and concerns of young middle-class adults? Are the pressures of the workplace adversely affecting family life? Can organizations be both profitable and family friendly? What may we expect from the future? Since many of the changes we are experiencing such as increasing materialism and greater individualism are changes the family in the West has already had to contend with, will the Indian family follow the path the family in the West has already taken, or will we chart our own course? This book is based primarily on in-depth real life interviews. In the last five years I have also done a Fellowship on the family at Wolfson College, Cambridge under the supervision of Dr Martin Richards of the Centre for Family Research, and another research project in India supported by the Dorabji Tata Trust.

Since I am not a sociologist by profession, it may not be inappropriate to quickly acquaint you with my interest in the field of family and work. I am a woman who began her career fairly early. At fourteen I was in print in the national media. I was creative chief of an advertising agency at the age of twenty-three. After that I got married and had children. And I have spent the last quarter century trying to balance work and family life.

In my case, I was lucky. Being a writer meant I could write about my predicament. There was virtually no discussion on the subject of the family in the mid-1980s when I began writing articles on many aspects of family life. So in the next two-and-a-half decades, my articles appeared in virtually all the national newspapers, the *Hindustan Times*, the *Times of India*, the *Hindu*, and in magazines that ranged from *Business India*, to *GFQ*, *Gentleman*, *Femina*, the erstwhile *Eve's Weekly*, *Young Mother* and *Family Life*, and then *Savvy* and *Cosmopolitan*. I also had a column titled 'Family Matters' on work and family life in the *Economic Times*, Kolkata. I could share my joy, and sometimes my anger, my exhilaration and exhaustion, and later my concern about the many issues regarding work and family life with readers. The interviews I did for the articles and the lively reader feedback gave me a clearer idea of many of the issues I deal with in this book.

As many women do, I moved when my husband did, finding opportunities in whatever city we happened to be in. When my children went to full-day school, I became creative consultant to J. Walter Thompson (JWT), then HTA, Mumbai. And later when we moved to Kolkata, I became bureau chief of Magna Publishing Company, a popular magazine group. I worked from 9.30 a.m. to 12.30 p.m. at JWT and in my last year with the magazine group, my terms were such that while I had to ensure that the output remained the same, I only needed to come to office when I felt I needed to. In a very limited way, then, I am aware of some of the problems as well as some of the solutions that exist. I was both economically and psychologically able to opt out of the job market when I felt it was not possible to do justice to both work and family. Many women cannot do so. Some choose not to.

I know women who are gifted and talented, and have energy, drive and all the skills that would have made them eminently successful at the workplace, who were unable to use their potential. I also know of women and men who have gone on to have very successful careers, but are torn by conflict and anxiety because they believe they have not been able to fulfil their commitments at home. And I know some who have what they consider a good balance between work and family life. I hope to bring to you all their voices.

Writing this book was an extremely difficult exercise. Research on the subject of the family is negligible, and with a large and diverse population, it was apparent that even a lifetime of research by a team of trained sociologists would lead to conclusions that could, and probably would, be challenged. The cliché that India lives in several centuries at the same time is true. Equally true is the other cliché that whatever statement you make about India, the opposite is also true.

This book has been written by a journalist who fully understands her limitations. Based on in-depth interviews with members of joint families, working women, working men and young singles, it seeks to get a representative cross section of the urban middle-

class Indian family. While every effort has been made
to look at relevant research in the area, this book has
been largely shaped by the author's experience and
observation of family life in India and the experience of
two research projects, which studied some aspects of
family life. It attempts to begin an exploration that
will undoubtedly be taken forward by other writers.

Introduction: Changing Perceptions

'You gambled your future on the goodwill of one man, how could you do it?' asked a young working woman about my self-imposed ten-year career break to bring up my children. The answer is, of course, that I did not think of it like that. As a newly-wed wife and then an expectant mother in 1979, I knew that my decision to put my family first would mean sacrifices on the career front when I wished to re-enter the work force, but the thought that my marriage itself could break up did not cross my mind. Divorce was still a rather shocking occurrence. It happened to few people one knew.

Today, many of my close friends are divorced. And when a young woman asks me for advice about career options, we routinely factor in that possibility when she is making her decision. Many young women are not sure if they are ever going to marry. I am both delighted and depressed when I talk to young women in their late teens and twenties and discover that some of them are completely unaware of the joys of motherhood. Since marriage and motherhood were sometimes seen as the most important, if not the only, goals for young women just a generation ago, I think it is wonderful that we have travelled so far from that particular road that this generation of young women can see so many other destinations on life's journey. Yet, it is also sad that motherhood, a role that women have for centuries cherished above all else, has now been so diminished, or is perceived as being so problematic, that it is not even considered an option by some of today's brightest and liveliest young women.

In many ways, much of the comfort one associates with family life in India seems to have vanished leaving behind a new and sometimes unsettling uncertainty. Marriages no longer offer the 'happily ever after' promise they once seem to have done. Elderly parents often have to contend with loneliness and neglect. The self-sacrificing bahu so popular in reel life often appears to be pretty scarce in real life. The extended joint family with its safety net of aunts, uncles and cousins of all ages is now an endangered institution. Children today miss out on family get-togethers because they need to attend coaching classes for entry to nursery school, for music or tennis lessons and certainly for board or university examinations. These take precedence over family time. Young women from the middle class delay marriage or childbirth to fulfil job aspirations. Quite possibly, a young woman today would not have to contend with the very strong message I had in my head that no matter how strong my credentials on the work front, bringing up my children was in some fundamental way my primary responsibility. Full-time housewives and mothers have gone from being deified creatures to being something of a social embarrassment. One child dignified his mother's stay-at-home status by calling it a 'house business'. Working couples sometimes have to live in different cities; single-parent homes are becoming more common. 'New generation' information technology (IT) companies create a campus with a virtual second home at the workplace. What is the likely impact of this?

In the first decade of the twenty-first century, we are in an era where the outside world has changed just as much as has the family. Job security is no longer something one can take for granted. The Indian executive can climb up the corporate ladder at dizzying speed. Unfortunately, he (or she) can slide down even faster. Indeed, the nature of work is increasingly becoming contractual. You are hired for as long as you are needed. And not a day longer. Since there is little social security in our country, the family provided a very useful buffer when times were bad. If one can no longer count on that support, one can, as one management guru told me, 'go from being middle class to being on the streets, just by losing one's job'. The Indian family is our social security. So it should be worth our while to see how it is faring in these tumultuous times. This is especially relevant, because in spite of the bias towards the West, which defines the Indian urban middle class, we, in India, are not really aware of how emotive and controversial the family is in today's Western societies.

Attitudes have changed in the last few decades. We have changed. And so has the family. But which changes have been for the better and which have been for the worse?

A Historical Viewpoint

When I began my research into the family, I constantly heard the refrain that what was today regarded as the traditional family, was nothing more than a romanticized view of the way the family existed briefly in the 1950s. This does not seem to be an accurate assessment. There is considerable evidence to show that in India, even in Vedic times, the family was very much in existence. In the authoritative book, *An Advanced History of India*, it is stated that 'the foundation of the political and social structure of the Rig Vedic age was the family'(Majumdar et al., 2001: 29). The members of the family lived in one house and the description of the house with its sitting room, fireplace, apartments for the ladies shows a fairly sophisticated construction. Though the family was patrilineal, with a few exceptions, the master of the house, *grihapati*, or *dampati* 'was usually kind and affectionate'. Ordinarily a man married but one wife and the wedding took place at the home of the bride. People prayed for an abundance of sons, but daughters were treated kindly (Majumdar et al, 2001).

Again, in A.L. Basham's *The Wonder That Was India*, we are told that a young man was expected to marry after the period of studentship was over, when he was in his early twenties (Basham, 1993). In those days a girl was also 'fully adult' when she was married. The purpose of marriage was threefold—for the promotion of religion by the performance of sacrifices, for the sake of progeny so that the father and his ancestors could be assured of a happy afterlife, and for sexual pleasure. The marriage was arranged by the parents of the couple and the rites described are still followed today!

Indeed, a look at other ancient civilizations shows an approximation of family life that is not too dissimilar to the contemporary Indian family. In Eastern cultures, the family has always had a very important place.

> When there is love in the marriage, there is harmony in the home; when there is contentment in the community there is prosperity in the nation, when there is prosperity in the nation there is peace in the world (Confucius, fifth century BC).

At one time, a loving marriage led in five rather fast and easy steps to world peace, or so the great Chinese philosopher Confucius would have us believe. In neighbouring India, the law-giver, Manu, would be in complete agreement with these sentiments. The rules regarding marriage are clear and unequivocal.

> When a man has learned the Veda, he should enter the householder stage of life . . .
> He should marry a woman who does not lack any part of her body and who has a pleasant name, who walks like a goose or elephant, whose body hair and hair on the head is fine, whose teeth are not big and who has delicate limbs (Manu: 48).

But if Manu set out a rather exacting set of specifications for the bride, he was also clear how the women of the house had to be treated. For while it is true that Manu has shown scant respect for the female gender in many pronouncements, these are more than offset by the many exhortations he has made urging men to respect the women of their family.

> Fathers, brothers, husbands, and brothers-in-law who wish for great good fortune should revere these women [women of the family] and adorn them.
> The deities delight in places where women are revered but where women are not revered all rites are fruitless.
> There is unwavering good fortune in a family where the husband is always satisfied by the wife, and the wife by the husband (ibid: 45, 48, 49).
> Therefore men who wish to prosper should always revere the women with ornaments, clothes and food at celebrations and festivals (ibid: 45, 48, 49).

Echoes of this may be found in a description of the third century BC provided in a chapter on Egyptian women in *Family Life* (Salisbury, 2001).

> If you are prosperous you should establish a household and love your wife as is fitting. Fill her belly, and clothe her back. Oil is the tonic for her body. Make her heart glad as long as you live (Tyldesley, quoted in Salisbury, 2001: 93).

The ancients, across cultures, seem to have been in agreement that a good marriage and a harmonious home were conducive to human happiness. Women were to be pampered, and to be kept busy adorning themselves, looking after the household and overseeing rituals and ceremonies. Interestingly, a home in those times was not too dissimilar to many homes today.

'A typical family unit probably included a husband and wife, their children, a husband's widowed mother and any of his unmarried sisters' (Salisbury, 2001: 93). This would very much conform to the 'supplemental nuclear' that finds mention in the contemporary line-up of the various family types in existence today. The dowry system, was also apparently very much in place, as we are told that: 'A young women left her father's home with all her possessions, the "goods of a woman", which might have included a bed, clothing, jewelry, a musical instrument and other items. She then marched with great ceremony to her new home' (Salisbury, 2001: 93).

The Family in India

Research on the family has always been problematic. Of India's billion plus population (1,027,015,247 according to the 2001 Census) the vast majority live in the rural areas. The urban population is about a quarter of the total. Employment opportunities have seen a shift in population from rural to urban and then, from small towns to the metropolitan cities. All this has altered aspirations, as also attitudes.

Defining a Family

Every one of us is born in a family, most of us grow up in one, and somehow one's own experience of family life always appears to be more real than anything we may read or hear which contradicts our own perceptions and assessments of family life. In addition, we each make choices with regard to family life as adults, and it is but natural to give credence to theories and anecdotal accounts that validate the choices we have made.

> Everyone has experience of family life, and everyone has opinions and feelings on it. It is very hard to pinpoint where commonsense leaves off and academic sociology begins. In this case one feels that the reluctance to address the subject of the Indian family stems not from the unimportance and marginality of the field, but rather from its importance and sensitivity. It is as though critical interrogation of the family might constitute an intrusion into that private domain where the nation's most cherished cultural values are nurtured and reproduced (Uberoi, 1993).

Just to define what a family is, is fairly complicated. Is it a relationship of blood or marriage, or is it a living arrangement? What are the types of families in India and when we look at the urban middle class, which of these forms would have relevance?

In addition, as Dr Kamala Ganesh points out while talking about the evolving family in the twenty-first century, 'The rather loose ways in which household and family have been used in popular discussions have led to enormous confusion in concepts: household that is the residential aspect and family which is an institution not bound by locality. To put it simply the husband and father who is working in Dubai is not part of the household for many months in a year yet he is a member of the family'(Ganesh, 2003).

According to the Census of India (Ministry of Home Affairs, Government of India, 1991), a fifth of total households are joint families, while most are nuclear families. These range from a single-member family, to 'a nuclear pair' which refers to a married couple, to a host of permutations and combinations which includes 'collaterally extended' to 'supplemental lineal collateral joint' and other such descriptions which describe various arrangements of households that we encounter. There is, it turns out, a special nomenclature for each type of family.

The Kinds of Families We Live in, in Real Terms

If we look at the family in India a little more closely, however, it is clear that making generalizations about the family in our country is perhaps more difficult than it is elsewhere. We do not have a uniform civil code with regard to family-related legislation such as marriage, divorce, inheritance and adoption, with laws being different for people belonging to different religions. (According to the 2001 Census, 80.5 per cent of the population was Hindu, 13.4 per cent Muslim, 2.3 per cent Christian, 1.9 per cent Sikh, 0.8 per cent Buddhist, 0.4 per cent Jains and 0.6 per cent comprised others) Indeed, if we look at the country as a geographical entity, we see both matriarchal systems and patriarchal systems. In addition, attitudes and practices vary in cities and rural areas, amongst the rich and the poor and also amongst the English-speaking élite and those from a more traditional milieu.

Though the listing of family types that exist in India is certainly impressive, most of the people I interviewed lived in nuclear families, some lived in joint families and some lived alone because of job compulsions, or because they had never married, or were divorced. There were also instances of families with one or more grandparent, an uncle, an aunt or cousin living with the nuclear family. However, since I was talking to the urban middle class, the respondents were generally quite cosmopolitan in outlook. Differences were much more apparent amongst different income groups than amongst those of different communities. Of course, many people 'belonged' to one state, had grown up in another and were living in yet another state. Others had one parent from one state and the second parent from another, or had a spouse from another state or community. They were reluctant to dwell on this aspect and considered it fairly irrelevant to the interview. Most people were concerned about what they saw as the decline of the family but an equal number believed that women were far better off in contemporary India than they had ever been in the past, and that there was now a new openness with regard to every aspect of family life, which was better for every member of the family.

The Changing Indian Family

At one level, we appear to be working out individual needs for privacy and freedom, with the requirements of the family. Job opportunities now occur on a global canvas, inevitably changing attitudes and lifestyles. Many who work for foreign companies learn to become comfortable with foreign mores. Some of those who work for call centres learn to speak with foreign accents and work according to foreign time schedules. That many should experience feelings of alienation from their own families and communities is hardly unexpected.

Perhaps the most pressing challenge to the urban middle-class family appears to be the new work culture with its unceasing demands on people's time and energy. We are now moving towards an era where not only the wife but also the mother and the mother-in-law may be working. The traditional support system provided by the women of the family, which our society relied upon, but perhaps did not recognize or acknowledge adequately, may therefore no longer be available for a new generation of young people, or indeed a new generation of old people.

I think if we really think about it, the change in the Indian family has come because it was no longer possible for us to live off the land and people had to move away to find jobs. While people were rooted to their homes and their fields, the values and traditions of the community and the family passed down from one generation to another. Every son walked in the footsteps of his father, every daughter-in-law faced the same challenges as her mother-in-law had before her. She had to learn how to adjust to a new environment, gain the confidence and the respect of those in authority, her parents-in-law, husband, perhaps a sister- or brother-in-law, an aunt- and uncle-in-law. Since the rewards for the favoured one would flow from these people it made sense to do whatever could be done to establish oneself as a good daughter-in-law.

A good support system for the individual was a positive outcome of such a situation. And since one lived within and, to some extent, off the family and the community, it provided one with an identity and a role. In such a scenario, it is not at all surprising that marriages, funerals, indeed ceremonies and rituals connected with the family were considered all-important. Attendance was an imperative. One's survival and status flowed from the family one belonged to and one's place in its hierarchy as also in the unofficial pecking order, much as proximity to the boss does for executives in today's corporate world.

The negative aspect of such a situation was a loss of individual freedom and choice. Too often, one's position in the family defined one's existence. For instance, the eldest daughter-in-law was expected to fulfil certain pre-determined roles and duties. And no one really bothered to ask a girl about to be married what she thought about any of this. The head of the house had to run a tight ship and pandering to individual likes and dislikes did not really figure very high on his or her list of priorities. Indeed, since sons too were dependent on the family for both sustenance and status, keeping the elders happy was an imperative for them too.

Worst-case scenarios were pretty depressing, but happily sometimes people liked their family, found companionship and love in the marital bond, and then the family truly was deserving of the respect it demanded.

The moment people started moving away from home and hearth in search of better opportunities, things started changing. In Delhi or Dublin, in Dubai or Dallas, people neither knew nor cared about who or what you were in your hometown. Status, wealth and, indeed, survival now depended on your success at the workplace so you now gave your job precedence over the family. Earlier, even distant relatives who came to your home had to be made welcome. It was important that they carry a good report of you, your home and your hospitality to the relatives at home. In a way, that was the 'headquarters'. Today even close family members must check to see that they do not inconvenience your new and perhaps more important responsibilities at the workplace. With regard to your spouse too, the approval of your family is now no longer as important as the acceptance of your colleagues and peers.

Not only is the approval of your family less important, their disapproval too is of less significance. So now, if a man and woman do not get along, the chances of their marriage breaking up are much higher. In a way, for the woman, the security that marriage offered, always dependent on the approval of her husband and his family, has become even more tenuous. Now even their censure of a marital break-up cannot protect her if the husband wants out. Also, in a more cosmopolitan environment, the requirements and attributes of what makes a woman a good wife have become more complicated. Companionship and compatibility have become more important and marriage today is more of a relationship than an institution. The arranged marriage with its emphasis on caste, community, family background, looks and educational qualifications, often fails to factor in this change. In addition, since the middle-class Indian woman is often educated to exactly the same level as her mate, she too aspires to a career and financial independence. Indeed, in a qualitative research I undertook for the Dorabji Tata Trust involving thirty career women in Kolkata and Mumbai, many of whom faced a multitude of problems in balancing work and family life, the women were clear that no matter how difficult their balancing act, they preferred to face the problems than opt for the 'comfort' of life as a housewife. Overwhelmingly, the women believed that housewives faced as much stress as career women did.

How Good Were the 'Good Old Days'?

Its tempting to believe that there was once a golden age of the family and that the fissures, the break ups, the many complications that the contemporary family has to face are a recent development. This is, of course, only partly true. Marriages are more fragile today than they were a decade ago, and child care and elder care are perhaps more problematic than they have ever been. But if you think of families of the past there are many instances of half brothers and sisters, of siblings who share only one common parent. Generally, it was the man who re-married after having lost a wife at childbirth. Less commonly, a widow re-married after her husband died in battle. Amongst some communities in north India, it is customary for the widow to marry her husband's younger brother. This happened not just in rural homes, but also in urban middle-class homes. In her autobiography, *On Balance*, Justice Leela Seth reveals that her husband, Premo, actually ran away from home because he was asked to marry his elder brother's widow (Seth, 2003). Indeed, till as late as 1956, it was perfectly legal for a Hindu man to have more than one wife!

So, as far as women are concerned, there were no 'good old days'. The fact that a marriage endured did not in any way indicate that it was a good or a happy marriage. Many women stayed in marriages because they could not survive on their own and they simply had nowhere else to go. And this is why the moment women were offered options they chose to opt out of a situation where they were financially dependent on the men in their lives. Also, the moment the idea that a marriage was less than permanent became widespread, women became even less inclined to plan their lives taking their marriages for granted, making the institution even more fragile.

Reforms in the Indian Family

Fortunately, as a society, we continue to question many aspects of family life in India. Issues like domestic violence and sexual abuse of children are being brought into the open after perhaps centuries of an uncomfortable and discomfiting conspiracy of silence. And when a television commercial for a popular talcum powder shows a girl calling off her wedding to protest against a demand for dowry, we know that we are making progress!

Though surveys consistently show that Indians as a people are very proud of their culture, most Indians also accept that for all its strengths, ours is a very imperfect society. And if the family is the heart of our society, then obviously it is not time to give up on the ECGs. For who can deny that there are grave issues regarding gender justice within the family, which are still to be sorted out. How else does one explain the fact that chilling problems such as female infanticide, sexual abuse of children and dowry deaths are still with us? However, the positive feature here is that amongst the thinking sections of our society, there is for the most part almost universal agreement about what the problems are in our society, and indeed, where the solutions may lie. There is, for instance, government legislation, which makes sex-determination tests at hospitals and clinics illegal and increasingly, women's groups and non-governmental organizations (NGOs) are getting involved in these areas. While it is undeniable that the urban family in India is witnessing unprecedented change, most seem to be agreed upon which changes are for the better and which changes are for the worse. Indeed, though in some instances, some minority groups have been, for a variety of reasons, somewhat resistant to change, as far as the majority is concerned, there have been reforms with legislation to aid implementation of reforms from the beginning of the nineteenth century. From bills to abolish sati, to legislation to allow Hindu widows to re-marry, from raising the age of consent to giving women the right to property and inheritance, the state has often intervened to bring in much needed reform. Sadly, not all legislation has been successful. Though female infanticide was abolished in 1870 and the Dowry Prohibition Act, which prohibits the giving and taking of dowry, was passed in 1961, we know that these two evils are still very much with us. However, it is undeniable that though the abominable practices remain because of human weakness, and perhaps human greed, there is general agreement that they are wrong. As a society, we know where we want to be. We just have to get there.

In India, support for the family is fairly widespread. For the most part, people are in agreement that:

> The family is the first line of defence, especially for children and a major factor in their survival, health, education, development and protection. It is also a major source of nurturance, emotional bonding and socialization, and a link between continuity and change (Sonawat, 2001).

Indeed, Sonawat goes on to list some negative changes that contemporary society in India is undergoing. And it is clear that Sonawat sees divorce and marital separation as problems of perhaps as great a magnitude as drug abuse, juvenile delinquency and domestic violence. These are seen as 'society's inability to cope with the pressures of modern life'. But Sonawat is sanguine about the family's long-term prospects and believes that on balance 'the majority seem to have survived and are able to modify, adjust, and adapt to changing social norms, values and structures, and have demonstrated a unique strength in keeping together despite the growing stress and strain'.

Attitudes to the Family

There are few countries in the world where there isn't intense discussion about sexual equality, the regulation of sexuality and the future of the family. And where there isn't open debate, this is mostly because it is actively repressed by authoritarian governments or fundamentalist groups (Giddens, 1999).

This is not entirely true. Debate about the family in India is fairly tangential, occurring mostly when social evils such as the dowry problem, domestic violence and sexual abuse of children are addressed. But what is true is that marriage and the traditional family are the subject of intense scrutiny and fierce debate in the United Kingdom (UK) and the United States (US) today.

The family has become an issue of acute political debate. Shifts and transformations [in the family] can easily be taken up and used as data in support of highly ideological and crudely partisan/ political positions (Smart and Neale, 1988: 4).

The patriarchal family has, of course, been responsible for a great deal of gender discrimination. Not surprisingly, then, it has been attacked by feminists worldwide. As Carol Smart and Bren Neale point out in *Family Fragments*, at one time, feminists like R.D. Laing challenged 'the mythic harmony' of family life and feminists saw the family as a 'core site for women's oppression'. After the 1990s, however, feminist theorizing moved on to questions of identity, sexuality and the very concept of women having a core site of oppression began to be thought of as questionable, as was the concept that the family could have the same significance for all women, or indeed that women could be viewed as a unitary category.

Governments all over the world invariably support the family. One reason why they do so is because in countries which have social security for those who are in need of assistance, governments end up supporting those who would otherwise have been taken care of by the family. As one heard repeatedly in the UK of single mothers, 'if a woman doesn't marry a man, she effectively marries the state, which must provide her with accommodation and other amenities'.

> Families are the heart of our society. Most of us live in families and we value them because they provide love, support and care. They educate us, and they teach us right from wrong. Our future depends on their success in bringing up our children. That is why we are committed to strengthening family life (Supporting Families, UK Government, 1999: 4).

Many are, however, in unequivocal disagreement. They see the family as an exploitative institution and an anachronism in a modern era.

> The persistence of the traditional family—or aspects of it— in many parts of the world is more worrisome than its decline. For what are the most important forces promoting democracy and economic development in poorer countries? Well, they are equality and education of women. And what must be changed to make it possible? Most importantly,

what must be changed is the traditional family (Giddens, 1999).

Giddens goes on to say that in the traditional family, it was not only women who lacked rights—children did too: 'It wasn't that parents didn't love their children, but they cared about them more for the contribution they made to the common economic task than for themselves'(Giddens, 1999).

The belief that the family as an entity fulfilled an economic necessity rather than an emotional one had votaries even in the past.

The earliest form of the family in human history was the 'patriarchal family'. This was not so much a collection of individuals bound by ties of blood and marriage, as it later came to be conceived, but more a 'corporation' existing in perpetuity . . . Corporations never die. The increase of individual members makes no difference to the collective existence of the aggregate body (Henry Summer Maine, quoted in Uberoi, 1993: 11).

The fact that families do fulfil an economic role can scarcely be denied. It certainly is very apparent in the joint family system. Indeed, if we consider how so many of our biggest business houses are also family concerns, we see how successful and efficient a family unit can be at its best.

But, after talking to hundreds of men and women for interviews for this book, it becomes clear that while we have much in common with Western societies in the way the pressures of work impact the family, we continue to have very fundamental differences in our approach to many issues that concern the family in many other spheres. While it is true that in the absence of any real state-supported social welfare organizations, the family is seen as the primary source of support for the individual, this is not the only reason families are valued. Even as family ties have weakened in the recent past, there is still a substantial amount of emotional bonding between not just members of the nuclear family, but also amongst members of the extended family.

The Family in Perspective

In the West, the position is markedly different. In 1999, I went on a Chevening Fellowship to study the British family. I was interested in the British family because on one level, there seemed to be a great deal of commonality between the changes that the British family had undergone and the changes the urban middle-class Indian family was experiencing. The industrial revolution and the advent of capitalism had seen job-induced mobility and a consequent weakening of the extended family, traditional norms were weakening and marriages no longer had the longevity they were once thought to have had. Materialism and individualism were becoming increasingly important and the dual-career family with its attendant opportunities and problems had created new and disturbing complications with regard to childcare as also the care of the elderly. I made the assumption that if I saw where the British family was in 1999, I would perhaps be able to anticipate where the Indian family may be in twenty-five years time.

My research project became infinitely more interesting because of the advice given to me by my academic supervisor, Dr Martin Richards, the head of the Centre of Family Research, Cambridge University. 'Don't read books', he said, 'go and meet the people who write the books'. In personal interviews one hears views and theories that may not have found their way into print. And so I went, and profited immensely, from meeting experts in the field of the family such as Dr Charlie Lewis, who has researched fathers and fatherhood, Penny Mansfield of the One Plus One Partnership Research Charity, Ceridwen Roberts of the Family Policy Study Centre. I attended the 'Supporting Families' seminar, which was addressed by Home Secretary Jack Straw, concerned parents and experts in the field, such as Adrienne Burgess. I met David Gamble, Chair of Barnado's and actively involved with issues regarding the family, the Reverend Richard Harries and journalists from every spectrum of the political divide from the editor-in-chief of the *Reader's Digest*, to the left-leaning columnist Polly Toynbee of the *Guardian* and the social affairs journalists of the *Times*. I also made a quick trip to the school of Business Studies at Edinburgh University and to INSEAD, the European management school at Fontainebleau, France. It gave me a picture of the British family that was quite unexpected.

'Which family have you come to study', the first academic I was introduced to at Cambridge University, asked me, 'the single-parent family, or the same-sex family, for the nuclear family is dead'. This was, of course, a gross exaggeration. But it did alert me to how highly controversial a subject the family is today in the UK. Cohabitation is common in contemporary Britain and to many people the institution of marriage appears to be an anachronism. The term 'partner' rather than spouse was increasingly used when referring to couples and the Bishop of Oxford, Richard Harries, confided that the children of many bishops actually chose cohabitation over marriage. One was struck by the extreme timidity with which even men of the Church chose to soft-pedal potentially contentious issues such as the government supplying contraceptives to under-age school-going teenage girls without informing their parents. There is a great wariness in passing judgement on any kind of living arrangement people may choose to enter into. And even parents are reluctant to 'interfere' in the personal lives of their children.

In the US, candidates may win or lose elections because of their stand on subjects such as abortion. Indeed, in the 2004 elections, George Bush is supposed to have won, despite mixed feelings on his handling of the Iraq war because the majority of the electorate shared his reservations on same-sex marriages! In the UK, too, attitudes to the family are very sharply drawn. To a large extent, opinions are divided along political lines. There is the conservative viewpoint, which is seen to be pro-nuclear family and therefore anti-gay (a small but highly vocal minority), anti-poor, anti-single mother and so on. Then there is the liberal viewpoint, which is deeply suspicious of anyone who espouses the cause of marriage, and on most issues takes a stand diametrically opposite to that of the conservatives. The newspapers by and large have taken well-defined positions with the *Telegraph* being seen as extreme right while the *Guardian* is regarded as liberal. The *Times* is 'conservative with a small c', said John Harlow, its then social affairs editor. Articles on the family tend to follow a predictable pattern. It is hardly surprising then, that you need only ask a Briton the name of his daily newspaper to be able to predict his views on many matters regarding the family very accurately. And depending on his political affiliations, the person's opinion on the record of the Conservative Party and the current Labour Government on the support they have offered to the family would also differ.

To come back to the state of the family, however, it was certainly a shock to see how very different the attitudes are from those prevalent in India. In the UK even as religious traditionalists decry the 'secularization' of present-day life and mourn the loss of faith among an increasing number of people, they are very worried about seeming to appear to moralize or sermonize.

The Contemporary Family in the West

You are witnessing the most important revolution of our time. This is more important than the Russian revolution or any battle that has ever been fought because it is a revolution about people's lives (Polly Toynbee of the *Guardian* in a personal interview about the changing British family in 1999).

This captures the frenzy that surrounds the contemporary family in Britain.

In a personal interview, undertaken for the Chevening Fellowship, on the family, Ceridwen Roberts, director of the Family Studies Centre, said that though the Blair government recognizes the need to support the family, it does not wish to seem to support the institution of marriage, ignoring all research on the subject which is unequivocal about the fact that the needs of men, women and children are best protected in a stable marriage. Penny Mansfield of One Plus One, The Marriage and Partnership Research Charity, agreed with this view. Both also stated that most people have a very distorted picture of the contemporary British family because journalists, academics and researchers tend to be interested in the atypical, rather than the average, family.

Traditional values are clearly under siege in contemporary Britain. And yet, interest in the family is very great indeed. There is considerable debate on how the government can intervene to support the family. The government is in favour of nuclear families and uses statistics to illustrate that this is not only what most people desire, but also the system that has proved to be most beneficial for children (government statistics available in *Supporting Families*, UK Government, 1999). Liberals are displeased with this stand. The conservative lobby, on the other hand, sees increased support for single-parent families as further weakening the case for marriage. They also fear that as a consequence of support for single mothers and same-sex marriages, young men in the UK have been left without a role. This in turn angers liberals who complain: 'Thus it is argued, women cause crime by rejecting men as potential breadwinners and blocking their transition into responsible adulthood' (Smart and Neale, 1988: 5).

What independent research says is impossible to tell because neither side is willing to accept the findings the other side puts out. For instance, Carol Smart and Bren Neale follow up the statement given earlier with this:

> The point about the tenacity and popularity of accounts such as these is that they have no real opposition. Because most of the available empirical work has been used as the bedrock of precisely these explanations, it cannot alone also refute such analyses (ibid.: 5).

In my study of the British family done under the supervision of Dr Martin Richards, the head of the Family Research Centre, Cambridge University, I came to this conclusion: Statistics are complicated at the best of times but especially so if they relate to an area like the family. There are so many variables when you are examining human beings that you can discount whatever does not suit the viewpoint you wish to propagate. In addition, people find fault with the techniques, as well as the conclusions reached by various research bodies. If you wish to make the case that the institution of marriage is dead in contemporary Britain you could say that less than one per cent of British brides are virgins when they marry. Marriage rates have fallen sharply and in 1995, the rate was actually half the rate in 1970 (statistics of the Family Policies Study Centre, UK). If you wish to take the opposite view, you can say that marriage is still popular in Britain. Over 300,000 marriages take place every year and 80 per cent of young people plan to marry, according to government statistics (Supporting Families, UK Government, 1999). Also, over 60 per cent of married couples actually remain married to the same partner all their lives. However, if one looks at trends, it is clear that even as the marriage rates have fallen amongst the young, divorce rates have risen. So the institution of marriage is certainly in decline though it is far from being obsolete at the present time.

How the Changing Family is Affecting Individuals

By the year 2010 there will be more stepfamilies than birth families, says Polly Toynbee. She describes how this works out in an article 'Happy Step Christmas'

> I come from a multiple stepfamily. Back when I was at school I was one of only two children in the class with divorced parents and was spoken of in hushed tones. I was marked out by teachers for pity and shame—a product of a broken home. But I liked my half-siblings on both sides, while my parents continued to get on amicably. I liked my stepfather and father, my stepmother and my mother. When my stepfather married yet again and he and his new wife had a daughter the same age as my youngest child, we gave up trying to describe the nature of that relationship (Toynbee, 2001: 108).

Though this journalist seems to have adjusted well to these changes, the research on the re-constituted family is not as encouraging. The UK-based marriage and partnership organization, One Plus One, in its study of

remarriage and stepfamilies, while pointing out that
children are resilient creatures, who will for the most
part fare extremely well in any stable family, irrespective
of whether one or more partner has been married before,
has listed some of the likely outcomes which children in
stepfamilies will have to contend with. Compared with
those who live with both their natural parents, children
in a stepfamily are more likely to go through adult
transitions early. For example, girls are twice as likely
to become teenage mothers; children are three times more
likely to leave home before their eighteenth birthday
because of disagreements and ill-feeling; boys are five
times more likely to cohabit with a partner before they
are twenty-one and girls are four times more likely to
marry before they are twenty. Children in stepfamilies
are also twice as likely to leave school and start a job
at the age of sixteen. These types of early transitions are
statistically associated with other types of disadvantage
such as low income and marital breakdown.

Are the Interests of the Woman Better Served Within a Marriage or Outside of It?

Because if you look closely at the definition of 'marriage'
you'll see it splits into two distinct parts. One celebrates the
'institution whereby a man and woman are joined in a
special kind of social and legal dependence', and that's not
what my husband and I signed up for; and the other
celebrates 'an intimate and close union . . .'
Because if the only kind of marriage we're willing to
sanction is marriage for the sake of propagating the human
race or as a way to ratify a man's rights over the property

that is a woman's body, same-sex marriage is a wake up call telling us that there are other ways of looking at the institution (Roy, 2004: 3).

Attitudes in India are changing, and the discourse on marriage in the West is reflected here in some quarters. Whether two consenting adults who choose to live together have religious sanction or state sanction for their union is immaterial, but before we rubbish the institution of marriage, it would perhaps not be inappropriate to see whether the interests of individuals are better served within or outside of marriage.

As we see in a later chapter on working mothers, even as men's attitudes have improved, most marriages continue to be fairly inequitable when it comes to sharing of power. Women continue to be subordinate to their spouses in greater or lesser degree. In India, and the developing world, and also in advanced countries such as Sweden, women still do more housework than men do, they continue to make more sacrifices on the work front and are likely to be more involved with taking care of both the children and the elderly. However, a woman who chooses to cohabit rather than marry is placed in an even more disadvantaged position, as she does not always get the benefit of alimony or child support if the couple should separate after the children are born. Indeed, fathers in cohabitational relationships that break up also discover that their rights as fathers are not protected, says Ceridwen Roberts of the Family Policy Study Centre, UK.

For many young people in the West these days, the first relationship is a cohabitational one. For the most part, cohabitation is still regarded as a transitional phase in a relationship, says Ceridwen Roberts. Preliminary analyses of the British Household Panel Survey quoted in *High Divorce Rates: The State of the Evidence on Reasons and Remedies* brought out by One Plus One show shows that cohabiting couples are between three times more likely to split up than their married counterparts. Similar findings have come in from France, Sweden and the US. In Norway, cohabiting couples have a two or three times higher risk of breakdown even taking into account other factors which could affect the relationship.

In the event of parents separating, the woman is left, quite literally, holding the baby and has to face all the problems a divorced mother has to face and often more serious problems than a woman who was 'protected' by a legal marriage.

The UK government document *Supporting Families* is categorical that:

> There are more children being brought up in single parent households, and there is more child poverty, often as a direct consequence of family breakdown. Rising crime and drug abuse are indirect symptoms of problems in the family (UK Government, 1999).

In other studies we read that the incidence of child abuse is also higher for children in broken or re-constituted homes.

In the chapter 'Good Relations' from the book *The Good Life*, Penny Mansfield of One Plus One says 'On average, married people have better health, longer life, more and better sex, greater wealth and better outcomes for their children. Married people engage in less risky behaviour (they smoke less, drink less, have less unsafe sex)' (Mansfield, 1998: 40). Using as reference studies such as *Marriage and Co-habitation in Contemporary Society* (Eekelaar and Katz, 1980) and *Marriage, Divorce and Re-marriage* (Cherlin, 1981), she points out the essential difference between marriage and cohabitation: 'Co-habitation is a declaration of an existing state of affairs with no implications for future conduct, whereas marriage assumes permanence. That presumption encourages . . . the building of assets both emotional and economic' (Mansfield, 1998).

Penny Mansfield would like to see more support for marriage and points out that its interesting that in the 1970s feminists were loud in decrying marriage and supporting gays and lesbians who were not at that time thinking of marriage. Today, feminists and liberals are vocal in demanding marriage for gays and lesbians!

Mansfield states that in the 1970s it was believed that marriage was good for men but not as good for women, but the latest research shows that marriage is equally good for women. 'Both married men and married women seem to be more contented than unmarried people who cohabit' (ibid: 40). The data for Penny Mansfield's study was based on the data from the General Social Survey, Washington DC, a cross-sectional survey of about 1500 adults done almost every year between 1972 and 1996.

If one looks at all the data, and not the opinion, on the subject, there is no reason not to support marriage.

Facts Regarding Marriage: The Paradox

In an interview discussing marriage in times past, and in the present, the Reverend Richard Harries, Bishop of Oxford, pointed out how in earlier times, one or the other partner usually died, so that the average marriage lasted for about fifteen years. That is about the length a marriage in the UK lasts today.

Increasing longevity is one aspect that has had a major impact on marriage. Now, with increased life expectancies, a couple may be expected to live together for sixty years. Obviously, they would need a far stronger bond to survive for so long. 'It's amazing, how many marriages break up after the children leave home', Harries points out. Speaking on the same subject, Reverend David Gamble said that the difference was that earlier the dissolution took place because of death, now it would more likely be due to divorce.

Today's Work Culture: The Impact of Long Working Hours on the Family

I was interested in this area because in urban middle-class India this has the potential to be a major cause for family stress and breakdown. Of course, to use a catchphrase of our times, we too have a work rich and a work poor division within our populace. I intended to study the small minority of upper-income professionals because this seemed to be the direction much of the service and communication industries, which we are led to believe are the growth areas of the future, are likely to follow.

In India, American multinational companies (MNCs), which pay the best salaries and offer the greatest opportunities for growth, make executives work very punishing hours. And well-established British companies in India have given up the very family-friendly work culture they were respected for to do exactly the same. Was this to be an irreversible worldwide trend, I wondered, and why was it proving to be so popular when the long-term effects were clearly likely to be very negative for the employee, the family and society as a whole. For this part of the study, I prepared a questionnaire, which I used on international students and a faculty member of Stanford University at INSEAD, France, and on Dr Findlay of the School of Business Studies, Edinburgh University.

On the surface, the situation for high flyers in Britain was very similar to what the situation was like for their counterparts in India. Some weeks after I embarked on my project, there was an article in the *London Times*, which stated that 'men give 15 minutes a day to children' and this attracted considerable media attention. However, at INSEAD, I discovered, that even as the long work hours and more competitive work culture of American companies were followed by some British companies, the trend in Europe was exactly the opposite. 'I expect to work far fewer hours than my father did', a young management school student from Germany confided, and statistics certainly bore him out.

The Scandinavian countries are introducing not only shorter hours but also concepts like a month's paternity leave in addition to emergency leave, which may be used for the family. Falling birth rates in much of the developed world and the prospect of an increasing elderly population with not enough young people to support them is forcing governments to think about measures that will make the workplace more family friendly. In Australia, there is a great emphasis on work-family balance, and even countries like the Philippines are exploring the four-day work week, though the Philippine experiment is inspired more from a desire to cut down on traffic congestion!

The Impact of Technology

One development that may have a profound influence on the question of work culture and working hours is the impact of information technology. As the Internet and innovations like e-mail become even more commonplace, men and women may find themselves acquiring a new control over their lives. If it was the industrial revolution that led to job-induced mobility which led to the break up of the extended family and the traditional bonds of the local community, one could argue that with the new technology, the need to physically go to a workplace, or relocate to new cities for the sake of a job, may be considerably reduced. It should be possible then, to regain a sense of being rooted, of belonging to a community, it may become easier to nurture relationships and have more stable families. There is, of course, the danger that an over reliance on technology may further erode the ability to form human relationships and connect with other people, but if the human species is intelligent and can show the survival and evolutionary skills it has demonstrated in the past, then there is indeed a great opportunity for the future of the family.

And What of the Future?

Predictions in the West suggest that in the near future, the woman is likely to be the major breadwinner. There are also signs that there will be a return to a multigenerational family living under one roof, with work and living areas demarcated by an upstairs and downstairs division, and some studies believe there will be domestic help to take care of the cooking and cleaning!

Finally, I am fully conscious of the many limitations of this book. This is not a scholarly treatise but a popular book, the account of an informed journalist. I see it as the beginning and not the end of the debate on the family.

Appendix 1.1

Statistics on the Indian Family

1. Single member households (a man or woman in one household).
2. Nuclear pair (only married couple).
3. Nuclear family (a married couple with or without children).
4. Forms of nuclear family, e.g., (broken nuclear-a fragment of a former nuclear family, e.g., a widow with unmarried children living together.
5. Supplemental nuclear family (a nuclear family plus one or more unmarried/separated/widowed relatives of the parents, other than married children).
6. Collaterally extended family (two or more married couples among whom there is a sibling bond, normally brothers plus their unmarried children).
7. Supplemental collateral joint family (a collateral joint family with unmarried, divorced, widowed relatives, typically such supplemental relatives are the widowed mother or widowed father or an unmarried sibling),
8. Lineal extended (two couples between whom there is a lineal link, usually between married son or married daughter).
9. Supplemental lineal joint (a lineal joint family plus unmarried, divorced or widowed relatives, their married sons plus the unmarried children of the couple).
10. Supplemental lineal collateral joint (a lineal collateral joint family plus unmarried, widowed, separated relatives who belong to none of the nuclear families lineally and collaterally linked) and an unclassified category.

Table 1.1

Household Type	Total %	Rural %	Urban %
1. Single member	5.80	5.15	7.91
2. Nuclear pair	4.98	4.91	5.20
3. Nuclear	38.74	37.88	41.57
4. Broken Nuclear	4.50	4.58	4.28
5. Supplemental Nuclear	16.48	16.81	15.44
6. Supplemental Broken Nuclear	5.61	5.76	5.13
7. Lineally Extended	16.62	17.65	13.23
8. Collaterally Extended	0.17	0.11	0.36

Source: Gulati (1995: 134-54).

Appendix 1.2

Year	Legislation	Purpose
1829	Sati legislation	A regulation declaring the practice of sati or burning or burying of Hindu widows illegal and punishable by criminal courts.
1856	The Hindu Widow Re-marriage Act	Legalized the re-marriage of Hindus of all castes
1870	Abolition of female infanticide	
1891	Age of Consent Act	Raising the age of consent from 10 years to 12 years.
1929	Sarada Act: Child marriage restraint Act	Minimum age at marriage for girls raised to 14 years.
1937	The Hindu Women's Rights to Property Act	Gave the Hindu widow the right to intestate succession equal to a son's share in regard to her husband's

Year	Legislation	Purpose
		property liable to devolution by succession.
1955	The Hindu Marriage Act	Minimum age of marriage as 18 for boys and 15 for girls. Until the passage of this act, every male, in theory, was free to marry a number of times. The Act of 1955 allows women to divorce if they are married to men who are insane, afflicted with leprosy or venereal diseases. Legalizes marriage between members of the same gotra. Provides that a marriage may be solemnized between any two Hindus if neither has a spouse living.
1956	The Hindu Succession Act	Converted the limited life estate of a Hindu female to full and absolute owner.
1956	The Hindu Maintenance Act	Invested certain rights of adoption which she had not enjoyed before.
1956	The Hindu Minority and Guardianship Act	Hindu women are empowered under this Act to choose guardians for the adopted children.
1956	Hindu Succession Act	Rights to per capita partition was extended to matrilineal families in Malabar also.
1961	Dowry Prohibition Act	Prohibits the giving or taking of dowry.

Source: Gulati (1995: 134-54).

2

The Joint Family: Twice the Joy or Double the Trouble?

The joint family. Some of us have lived in one and indeed still do. Others remember going to the ancestral home which had grandparents and what seemed like hordes of relatives, sleeping in beds lined up in verandahs, or out in the open, sharing meals and confidences with cousins, being pampered by indulgent grandparents and perhaps being disciplined by concerned uncles and aunts. But not everyone's recollections are so pleasant. If the patriarchal family has features that are oppressive, it is the joint family where individual members encountered the most repression. So inevitably some men and many more women have unhappy memories and view their time in the joint family as 'soul destroying'. This is most apparent where, as a daughter-in-law, one was in conflict with the mores that prevailed in the family one had married into, or where as a daughter or son, another sibling was seen to have received preferential treatment. However, for most, the irritation of constantly having to conform to rules and regulations, which they may not have been in agreement with at the time, are forgotten in the haze of nostalgia that clings to the past.

A whole genre of television serials has re-created the joint family as a hotbed of conniving intrigue, peopled with women who are either long-suffering Bharatiya naris, or diabolical vamps. And the joint family has also inspired photo essays and films, which showcase an institution that appears to be on the endangered list.

Though the 1991 Census describes a fifth of all households to be joint families, the picture is very different across income groups and in different communities. Job-related mobility obviously turns many families nuclear, while those who are in family-owned business, for instance, are much more likely to be in joint families. Since India is a country where there are actually 'business communities', and where there were till very recently 'martial races', it is possible to see more joint families in some areas rather than others.

What is it like to actually live in an urban joint family today? If we look at the traditional joint family and include in this category families in which married couples live with one set of parents, and possibly other adult siblings and their children, what do we find? How happy are the people who live together, sharing a roof, and both emotional as also physical space? Is this the perfect arrangement for the dual-career family? Does the joint family have a role to play in circumstances where childcare is not a primary issue? Is its emphasis on the common good at total variance with today's individualistic mindset? Does the perspective change depending on what stage of life you are at? How do those who live in such families view them? And what are the prospects for the future?

The joint family the urban middle class remembers was largely a creation of and for the privileged class. It was the large land holdings that made it possible, and indeed profitable, for many members of a family to live together. It was also financial prosperity that enabled them to have the extended family congregate at the ancestral home to celebrate marriages or observe funerals. It was not possible for those who were financially less secure to do this.

> The traditional family was above all an economic unit. Agricultural production normally involved the whole family group, while among the gentry and aristocracy, transmission of property was the main basis of marriage (Giddens, 1999).

When people lived on (and off) the land, the joint family, an inter-generational unit that lived under one roof and shared familial and work responsibilities as also the produce and other proceeds of the land, was quite simply a system that made excellent sense. Every member contributed in some measure, either directly in agricultural activity, or in looking after the household, as also in taking care of the family, including the children and the elderly.

> The ideal family is one consisting of a man and wife and their married sons living in a single household, in harmony. Brothers should remain together; people say united brothers

are like the fingers of a single hand, strong and powerful. The extended family, with married sons remaining in the household of their fathers, has obvious advantages in an agricultural community: fathers with land live with sons who labour. Access to the results of the labour of more than one adult member of a household, whether in the form of agricultural produce or wage labour, improves the living standard of the household. This is true in an urban as well as a rural setting.

At the same time, people are very aware that this causes problems: people fight. Even in a rural setting, land is almost invariably divided on the death of the father. In an urban setting, without land, and possibly with disparities in salary among individual sons, there is even less economic impetus for families to remain in a single household (Laslett, 1972).

The father was normally the head of the house but the mother also played an important role and each enjoyed considerable influence in his or her sphere of activity. Children were inducted into helping the elders as soon as they were able to be of assistance and were therefore seen as an asset and not a liability as they are often now perceived. Today's matrimonial advertisements, for instance, routinely refer to children as 'encumbrances'. And though we do not have such specific studies in India, research in the West clearly shows that the cost of raising a child is constantly rising.

In the traditional joint family, elderly relatives had a definite role to play. Male relatives were often consulted when taking important decisions and often proved to be extremely useful when networking was required. Each family member provided access to additional people, which facilitated social intercourse and may have been useful in forging deals and alliances. Female relatives provided help with childcare and sometimes also elder care, were knowledgeable about the family's traditions, and helped see that rituals and ceremonies were conducted in accordance with that particular family's norms. In an era when the community was considerably more close-knit than it now is, every milestone of an individual's life would be celebrated in a manner which was befitting of the family's status and position in society. These events included birth, marriage, death, but stretched to others such as the naming ceremony of a newborn, the sixtieth birthday of senior family member and, of course, a host of other festivals, both seasonal and religious, where much of the activity centred around fasts and feasts. As multifarious activities called for a wide variety of skills, and much effort, the contribution of every individual member of the family was invaluable.

> In modern nuclear societies there is only one relationship of intimacy and importance and that is the relationship between the spouses. If that does not work the family must be jettisoned . . . (Greer, 1991: 64).

In the traditional joint family on the other hand, a girl married the family and not just the man, and excessive intimacy between a husband and wife was viewed with suspicion. If a man was too deeply attached to his wife, it was feared he would be less committed to the larger family. The show of overt affection for one's own child was therefore also frowned upon. Some books evoke the flavour of the times with remarkable felicity. In industrialist B.K.Birla's engaging auto-biography, *Swant Sukhaya* there is a passage describing the birth of his son, Aditya Vikram, in which he gives a humorous account of how he would, with the active connivance of his bhabhi, sneak up the servant's staircase to wife Sarala Birla's bedroom to see his first-born child because 'Bari Ma' did not approve of husbands going into their wives' rooms! And he states in forthright fashion that he did not approve of this attitude of his 'Bari Ma'(Birla, 1991: 108).

This account conjures up a picture of the joint family that is fairly traditional. There is ample evidence to show that such families and such traditions endure. But the joint family has also metamorphosed into all kinds of new arrangements.

Some families still have grandparents, a Dadaji, a Dadiji, a host of uncles, aunts and young people of all ages who sit and eat at the same table. Or more importantly, who still share the same kitchen and draw money from a common fund. Amongst others, in many wealthy business families, for instance, individual units comprising adult sons with their wives and children live in a large house with separate living areas and fairly independent lifestyles with varying degrees of contact. Some may have one meal of the day with the head of the house, the children may be playmates and the women may share cars, common facilities and staff. Others actually live like neighbours rather than family and may be unaware of each other's programmes on a day-to-day basis. 'We stay in the same house because if you move out, you risk being left out when important business decisions are being informally discussed', a scion of one such family confesses. At the other end of the financial spectrum, one finds similar family units living in cramped two-bedroom tenements. The authority the head of the house wields is total. Sons are sometimes required to pool all their earnings into a common kitty and are not encouraged to keep a tab on the amount they have brought in. Sons and daughters-in-law may have to ask the head of the house for money for even day-to-day necessities. There is absolutely no room for individual programmes or the pursuit of any hobby or activity that is not related to the family as a whole. The lack of space, both physical space and emotional space, takes a heavy toll on those who have to live in such oppressive confinement. A deeply-entrenched sense of duty and the lack of options on how to deal with the 'problem' of elderly parents along with the inability to afford separate accommodation are some of the factors that keep such arrangements going.

Though in purely sociological terms we may have terms like 'supplemental nuclear' to 'supplemental collateral joint' to describe a nuclear family with one or more elderly relative, in this book, I call a family that has parents living with their married children, and perhaps grandchildren, a joint family.

There is, as yet, very little research on the Indian joint family, so this chapter is based on in-depth interviews with people from varied parts of the country. I often interviewed different members of the family individually, and not surprisingly, got a slightly different viewpoint from every member that reflected the reality from a different perspective.

Predictably, when older members of joint families talk about the joint family they refer to an altogether different era. They refer to a time when caste permeated virtually every aspect of life in India, when the authority of the head of the house was absolute and respect for those senior in the hierarchy was not in question. The gender equation was also weighted heavily in favour of the male sex. Their recollections of the joint family therefore conjure up an environment that was circumscribed by some or all of these realities.

The primacy of the needs of the family over the desires of the individual was an integral part of the make-up of yesterday's joint family. Even younger members who would, in all likelihood, find adhering to this very demanding code of conduct difficult in today's more permissive environment, report the passing, of this seemingly more altruistic, somewhat nobler era, with regret. For most families, the times have changed fairly drastically. But it is interesting that even in middle-class homes in the metropolitan cities, there are still families where the parents exercise stifling control over their adult children. And perhaps a smaller number of families where the adult son and the daughter-in-law treat the parents as unpaid child minders and domestic help.

While it is easy to fall for the idea of an idyllic past where elders were treated with reverence and love, and this undoubtedly must have been the case in many families, it is also true, that the old Indian ethos also had the idea that after the grihast or householder stage of life, the man, perhaps accompanied by his wife, should take sanyas.

> After he has lived in the householder's stage of life in accordance with the rules in this way, a twice-born Vedic graduate should live in the forest, properly restrained and with his sensory powers conquered. But when a householder sees that he is wrinkled and grey, and (when he sees the children of his children), then he should hand his wife over to his sons and go to the forest or take her along (Manu: 117).

In addition, there can be little doubt that Indian society has always been somewhat ambivalent in its treatment of widows. While many stayed on in the joint family home as respected members of the family, it is undeniable that our society has also tolerated widows being driven out of their homes to end up as beggars at pilgrim centres such as Varanasi. It is therefore the widowed mother who is most vulnerable in the modern joint family, especially if she is financially dependent on her sons. She may be more welcome in the homes of her daughters, but there remains a strong bias in the patriarchal society that is prevalent in most parts of the country against a mother staying at her daughter's marital home. This is especially true if the daughter is living in a joint family. Interestingly, adult daughters still believe that in some way, they have a greater responsibility to their husband's parents than to their own, for they expect that their own parents will be looked after by their brothers. Women, who do not have brothers, own greater responsibility for their parents. But increasingly such traditional views are changing. In homes where the women are working and earning their own money, they often provide financial and other assistance to their parents.

When several generations live together under one roof, differences of opinion due to differing mindsets are not uncommon. However, even where the relationship between adults in a joint family are strained, the children living together in a joint family home often forge warm and lasting relationships. And in the homes of children of dual-career couples, the grandchild–grandparent relationship is often loving and harmonious, though the equation between the adults may be fairly problematic. Children brought up in the more complex milieu of a joint family may not only develop a degree of selflessness, but also an ability to manage relationships, which helps them later in life. One MBA student who had been brought up in a nuclear family actually said somewhat wistfully that he wished he had experienced life in a joint family only for this reason!

A Glimpse of the Past

> After the large joint family, the caste provided social security, helping destitute members and providing for widows and orphans (Basham, 1993: 151).

A. Padminimurty is a bright, active mother-in-law and grandmother in her seventies. She remembers life in Rajamundhry in the late 1940s where she lived with her husband at the home of her parents-in-law. This house exemplified the traditional joint family for under the same roof, lived not only her husband's two brothers and their families, but also her husband's two widowed sisters and her mother-in-law's mother's sister. 'The caste system was very strong at that time', Mrs. Murty remembers 'and if a lower-caste servant even entered the room where the elders were eating, they would immediately get up and go. They were very rigid, their utensils and dishes had to be freshly washed and could not be wiped dry, they had to be dried in the sun. If it rained, they would dress in wet clothes and eat off wet dishes.' It could not have been an easy life for the young bride who had spent her early childhood in Chennai (then Madras) and had gone on to live all over the country, on transfers with her brothers who were in the railways. But she adapted and was happy with her lot.

With the passage of time, the hardships of keeping house in such difficult conditions were forgotten and the value system that was inculcated in her at the time is what she remembers, and what she has passed down to her grandchildren. 'Never let money matters come into your mind. Some relatives may be rich, some may be poor, but everyone has to be treated alike.' This dictum captures the very essence of a joint family. It calls for a sensibility where material benefits are always secondary to family unity. Most people confess that the high degree of unselfishness that living in such an arrangement calls for, is becoming scarce. And yet, a sense of filial duty is still fairly strong.

Today's Joint Family

*Most Women Have Internalized Society's
Patriarchal Diktats*

As one spoke to women across the country, one saw
that even at the present time, most women have, in
some way, internalized most of a patriarchal society's
diktats of what the 'duties' of a traditional wife, mother
and daughter-in-law were. Not that these were
necessarily adhered to, but they did set a standard that
at some level, women did aspire to reach. It was as if
women would ideally like to fulfil the traditional
expectations, even as they worked to enlarge their roles.

In a nuclear family you don't have to think. You can do
whatever you feel like. You can eat what you want, if you
want to eat a pizza, you can do that, '*manmani puri kar
sakte ho*'. In a joint family, your sorrows are shared, so is
your joy. You are never alone. If you are successful, you
have to share your good fortune, but if you are struck by
ill fortune, if your business should collapse, if you should
be widowed, you are not on the streets (Anshu Modi, a
Kolkata-based fashion designer and businesswoman).

It is interesting that with the passage of time,
adjustments became easier. As women entered middle
age many strictures that caused resentment and
heartburn in the early years were seen in quite a
different perspective. Thus, being forced to get up early,
bathe, do morning puja, take care of elderly relatives
who were less than lovable, were seen to have been
helpful in the long run and were now perceived to have

contributed to the development of a strong character and to personal growth. The sharing of these familial duties appear to also forge an empathy and emotional bonding amongst the sons, but more especially the daughters-in-law who live within the joint family home.

> Though there were fourteen servants in our joint family home, the daughters-in-law were expected to be in the kitchen to supervise the cooking. We actually used to make twenty-eight parathas for the servants. So now, though I hate to even enter the kitchen, I share a really close bond with my sisters-in-law. My sisters-in-law, my *jethanis* and *nands*, are like my friends. We have a fantastic relationship! I now appreciate that my mother-in-law meant not to torture us but to groom us in what she thought was the family tradition. When I was newly married, if I had been given me a choice of staying in a joint or nuclear family, I would have chosen the nuclear family, but today, I am glad I lived in a joint family. I have a far greater respect for my mother-in-law and the joint family system (Pammi Suri, a Punjabi who grew up in Delhi).

The Culture Clash

It Has Always Been Difficult to Adjust to the Husband's Family

Changing values and differing ideas about the woman's role exacerbate relationships between parents and adult sons, and even more between mothers-in-law and daughters-in-law in a joint family. The need to be sensitive to everyone's needs means that everyone's individual freedoms are compromised to a greater or lesser degree, but it many ways it is most difficult for the daughter-in-law who often has to bear the brunt of a patriarchal society's greatest excesses. Daughters-in-law often feel that they are always being tested: 'What time do I wake up in the morning, how long do I sleep in the afternoon all this is conveyed to my parents.' Many homes still circumscribe whether the daughter-in-law may wear a salwar kameez or trousers. Many do not allow the daughter-in-law to wear her hair short. While all adjustments of this sort are difficult, they are most galling when, as is sometimes the case, there is a different standard for the daughter-in-law and a more relaxed code for the daughter of the house. Moving into such a joint family home is, as one woman put it, 'moving from a comfort zone into a zone of acute discomfort'. Nowadays there is often a very great variation in lifestyles even amongst people of the same caste and the same class. This increases possible points of conflict. But there is reason to believe that this was always a problematic relationship.

O river Ganges, all I now want /is to go with your waters that flow gently to the sea; /that never again by my father- and mother -in-law/ I may at every turn be scolded and abused (translation from the Chinese of a Buddhist verse in Fa Hsien's manuscript, thought to have been sung in India between the codification of the Pali cannon from 1 BC and 5 AD, in Basham, 1993: 479).

Living in a Joint Family: The Score Card

Indeed, as women try to forge a new role for themselves as career women in addition to the familiar ones of wife and mother, they often opt for the joint family, which makes housekeeping and childcare easier. However, in many joint families, attitudes remain fairly traditional which does lead to conflict. This may or may not be overtly expressed. Then, women have to do a trade off.

> The joint family is the cause of most of my stress. My father-in-law tortured me by constantly suggesting that I did not know how to bring up my children because I came from a broken home. My mother-in-law also undermined my self-confidence by her unfavourable comparisons to the amount of time my sister-in-law who was a full-time housewife and mother could spend with her children (Sheema Rizvi, a successful Mumbai-based journalist).

And as we talk, Sheema changes from being a cool, very in-control journalist to a woman who appears almost anguished as she gives vent to the guilt of a woman who was trying to do her best by two conflicting roles: that of a housewife and mother on the one hand and a committed professional on the other. This was a fairly typical response. But even as Sheema blames the joint family for causing her unbearable stress, she acknowledges that it also provided much needed support in another area. 'I was secure that my children were not alone in the house. And whatever my problems, I don't deny that my children share a very close relationship with their grandparents.'

When there is a clash of lifestyle and of mores, many believe that it is easier to move from a more conservative, more authoritarian family to a more liberal family. While this is often the case for girls who have been brought up in a fairly gender-neutral environment who would have had to learn to adjust to all sorts of retrograde practices in their marital home, girls who were brought up believing that their destiny was to marry and do whatever it took to keep their husbands and parents-in-law happy, experience great stress in having to adjust to a home where they have to take on more responsibility and be more active in the outside world. Some degree of commonality between the two environments makes for the best fit!

Sometimes, it appeared that a fit between people who belonged to a similar work environment and similar class was easier than between children of a similar caste group. Children of those brought up in business families found it easier to adjust to such an environment; children whose parents were in the defence services found a sense of belonging in that environment. There is it turns out, a 'steel city culture' that prevails in industrial townships such as Jamshedpur, Bokaro, Ranchi or Kharagpur. There is an MNC culture, a government service culture, especially applicable for entities such as the railways, and, quite often, children brought up in such an environment found it congenial and experienced a sense of 'belongingness' in it even as adults. Some people whose parents had had transferable jobs said that they were most comfortable with people like themselves who had lived all over the country and did not 'belong' to any particular region. Of course, personalities, education and occupation were also powerful factors in influencing and contributing to a sense of comfort in adjusting to environments or individuals. And in an era where the job is consuming more and more of a person's time, in the future adjustments to one's own and one's spouse's job environment may take precedence over all else.

The Case of the Dominating Mother-in-Law

Of course it is true that some young women who are in joint families are living with parents-in-law, especially mothers-in-law, who are both selfish and dominating. The old joint family functioned on a spirit of give and take, especially give. 'You have to consider how every action that you take would affect the sensibilities of every member of the family', as one daughter-in-law states. Too strong a bond between husband and wife was discouraged because it could prevent the couple from fulfilling other more compelling responsibilities to other members of the family. In the new truncated joint family, which may just have the husband's parents or even just the husband's mother as an additional member, there may be little need to prevent the strengthening of the husband–wife bond. However, the traditional friction between the mother-in-law and the daughter-in-law, the saas and the bahu, has not completely disappeared. A mother-in-law, especially a widowed mother-in-law, may view a strengthening emotional bond between the couple with some degree of insecurity, as a sign that her own tie to her son has become less important. The wife may wish for her husband to demonstrate the primacy of the husband–wife bond above all else for exactly the same reason. Though women with careers or strong interests of their own seem to be more comfortable with their own achievements and therefore less in need of reassurance on this score, this remains a difficult relationship for both women.

The interviews conducted for this book, and interviews conducted in the past for numerous magazine articles on the subject, can at best be illustrative, but I believe they capture a flavour of our current reality. Many daughters-in-law began by saying that they shared a very good relationship with their mother-in-law and that they credit any success they had achieved partly to her support. However, two hours down the line they would express a real sense of suffocation (some used the word *ghutan*) for the many ways in which they were humiliated and controlled by their mothers-in-law. Even self-confident working women reported incidents that would be ludicrous if they were not also tragic. In Kolkata, I came across 'the piece of fish' story, which seemed to surface with uncanny regularity when one was deep into an interview. 'Every day', Suchismita says, 'my mother-in-law would give my husband the best piece of fish and give me the worst piece of fish. I am not so fond of fish, actually, so I didn't mind missing out on the fish, but what really burned me up was the underlying reminder of my status in the house. It is this that really bothered me. One day, I told my husband about it. The next day at breakfast, he saw my thali and then took a look at his own thali. "Oh, Suchismita, I'm not very hungry today, so why don't you take my thali and give me yours. I don't want such a big piece of fish today". With this he switched thalis and you should have seen the agitation on my mother-in-law's face. She was devastated that her beloved son would be eating the terrible piece of fish that was so suitable for her daughter-in-law', Suchismita said, still smarting at the recollection! Every time I interviewed a daughter-in-law in Kolkata and repeated this story there was an immediate gasp of recognition. This clearly was fairly commonplace. If it had not happened to the woman in question, it had happened to a close friend. So, are Bengalis more chauvinistic than other communities? I do not think so, because when I mentioned this to women of other communities many expressed astonishment that I was surprised by this trait. 'A Punjabi mother-in-law would always see that her son got the biggest dollop of desi ghee, the tallest glass of lassi!' And the response of the Tamil, Maharastrian and Oriya daughter-in-law was identical with only the food items changing. But happily, some women of every community said that they had never experienced it.

Was a Whole Generation of Women Robbed of a Role?

Why are some mothers-in-law so very difficult? The daughters-in-law sum it up in one word, 'ego'. Their problems, the daughters-in-law believe, are due to 'nothing but ego and the desire to dominate'. And why should 'happily married, educated women' turn into such terrible control freaks, who seem almost sadistic in their treatment of their daughters-in-law? If you see it from their point of view, these women have had the worst of both worlds. When they entered their marital homes as daughters-in-law, the power structure of the traditional joint family was very much in place. The parents-in-law were very much at the top of the hierarchy, and in a typical joint family the mother-in-law wielded considerable clout. While the father-in-law as the head of the family took decisions regarding virtually every action taken by the male members of the family, or decisions that concerned the public or outer sphere, the mother-in-law had considerable influence with regard to the goings on in the home. Winning her trust and approval was important to any daughter-in-law if she wanted to influence key decisions in her favour. Anshu conjures up the flavour of those days with the simple observation that, 'In our times, you had to think ten times before you did anything. If someone asked you whether you were free, you couldn't say yes or no, your family would tell you whether you were free or not.'

I heard more than one mother-in-law crib, sometimes good-humouredly, sometimes less happily, that 'when we were young, we were led to believe that the most important person in the house was the mother-in-law, "you must do this because your mother-in-law will like it, you mustn't do that, your mother-in-law, won't like that". Now when it is our turn, the emphasis has changed. Now it is, "you mustn't say this, your daughter-in-law won't like it!"' When we look at middle-class India, as we moved from the family home where the main income came from the family property and its offshoots, to an era where most people looked for jobs in the cities, and ones advancement both financial as well as social depended more on success at the workplace rather than popularity at home, it became less and less important to be the perfect daughter-in-law. Today, very often the daughter-in-law has a career of her own, and balancing work and family life, getting ahead in her career, being involved with her husband's advancement in his career, has become more important than being a good bahu! As more and more couples opt for nuclear families, or even joint families that have only the parents living with the couple, the husband–wife bond has strengthened. Suddenly the age-old axiom that sons' mothers in the West used to fear, 'your son is your son till he gets himself a wife', is becoming true of India as well. This is still not the norm; most of the working women interviewed still tried very hard to do their best by their jobs as also their families. But the world is changing and this is the direction that the Indian family is heading toward.

So when the present-day mother-in-law believes that somehow, somewhere, she has been shortchanged, she has ample cause to think so! There is a real dissonance between the world she grew up in and the world she has now to live in. There is unease that the old realities no longer ring true.

Nowadays fifty-year-old women who respected their mothers and nursed their grandmothers find themselves without honour, and left to the care of strangers. They have been caught in the transition from one kind of system, a system identified with the self-help networks of the working class or the ghetto, to another, generally considered better and more progressive. At worst, the woman who grew up in a house with her gran and her mother and her aunts and did her bit to help out for them will eventually find herself in an inadequately heated council flat that she is too frightened to leave because old women are easy pickings for the muggers on the streets outside (Greer, 1991: 64).

And obviously, the fall-out will be greatest for those daughters-in-law who come from fairly conservative families but go on to become successful in fields that keep them in the public eye. Quite unwittingly, these women challenge some of society's most deeply held tenets that a woman should play second fiddle to her husband.

Suchismita, from Kolkata, a woman we shall meet again in the chapter on working women, squeezes her career aspirations into very small pockets of time so that she can fulfil a demanding role of caregiver to elderly parents-in-law who need constant attention. She feels (as did Sheema, the Mumbai-based journalist) that the treatment meted out to her by them could qualify as torture. Why does she put up with it? 'I love my husband', she says unequivocally, 'and after all, it is my duty'. There is also a realization that with the passage of time, she may well be in need of the service she is giving to her parents-in-law from her own children.

Some of the things that so enrage Suchismita are clearly only examples of misplaced enthusiasm from a mother-in-law who wishes to emerge as the mother-in-law with the best daughter-in-law. 'My mother-in-law would constantly cook delicacies and send them to our relatives telling them that I had cooked them. It used to really embarrass me to be thanked for things I had not done. I repeatedly asked my mother-in-law not to do this, but she just wouldn't listen. So once when my aunt-in-law praised me for something I hadn't cooked I just said that not only had I not sent that dish, I hadn't ever sent her a dish, and that what with managing the home, looking after my parents-in-law, taking care of my child as also my part-time job, I just had no time to cook! My mother-in-law was furious and felt I had publicly humiliated her but I was fed up and past caring.' This is a classic case of how change has affected our behaviour and reactions. The mother-in-law, who had grown up in an era where there was a clear role for the daughter-in-law to follow, took on the extra effort required to make her daughter-in-law look good in the eyes of the other family members. She did this without even telling her daughter-in-law about it. In an earlier age, this would have been taken as a thoughtful gesture, evidence of a truly loving mother-in-law. However, with the change in attitudes, the daughter-in-law seeks to prove herself in her career where she is proud of the recognition that she has been able to get in spite of her many other responsibilities. She belongs to a more frank and forthright generation and is tired of taking part in the charade her mother-in-law would like to play out!

In addition, these women have been robbed of a role. When these women were growing up, in the 1940s and 1950s, there was a sense of family and community.

Religious festivals ranging from Holi and Diwali, to Pongal, Durga Puja and Ganesh Chaturthi, from Id to Christmas, called for weeks of planning and the involvement of all the women of the family. With large close-knit families, there was a marriage to organize almost every year and births in the family were even more frequent. Chattis and annaprasans, not to mention the many rituals connected to a wedding meant that the knowledge that these women had imbibed made them precious repositories of culture. They were much sought after and their intimate knowledge of the family's particular customs, the exact sequence of events, the relevant songs to be sung at various ceremonies, the people to be invited, the gifts to be given to various members of the family, the amounts to be paid to the pundit, the menu and the quantities of various foodstuffs required for both feasting and fasting (anybody who imagines fasts were nothing but a starvation diet is, of course, quite innocent of our customs!) meant that the experience and expertise of the senior ladies of the house made them irreplaceable. Gradually, the weakening of the bonds of the extended family, the compulsions of the modern age because of which ceremonies and processes had to be both simplified and compressed meant that this age-old knowledge held little value.

On a day-to-day basis too, young parents are more likely to turn to the paediatrician rather than to granny for advice! It is not surprising then that many mothers-in-law feel irrelevant to their families and indeed to the world. They now need to find a vocation or an interest of their own to retain a sense of self and to keep themselves busy. 'I took to learning Sanskrit and teaching young girls to dance', says A. Padminimurty. Another matriarch makes homemade jams and pickle for her grandchildren. One grandmother used to help her family stay connected by making albums of family events and reminding her children and grandchildren about family birthdays and anniversaries. She is now taking computer classes to better communicate with the younger generation of her family! 'If I didn't have a strong interest of my own, I would have got on my children's nerves', says one mother. She is probably right.

The Difficult Daughter-in-Law

It is also true, however, that no matter what some mothers-in-law may do they are still going to have a difficult time. Today, when there is a sizeable number of families that have elderly parents staying with their children, there are also stories of neglect and sometimes even abuse of the old couple. While there is really little that can be done about meeting their need of companionship, when the adult children are in jobs that require long hours, old parents sometimes report needless acts of indignity. Even children who are in high-income jobs resort to petty acts of mindless cruelty, locking the STD code on the telephone, giving instructions that the air-conditioner must not be switched on for the elderly couple and even locking the fridge. And sometimes, if a couple has more than one adult son, the wife of one will act in so objectionable a manner, she ensures that no one comes to live with her at all. Contrary to the stereotypical picture portrayed by the multitudes of family sagas on television, it is not the more assertive and Westernized bahu who will be most averse to offering the parents-in-law refuge. While, it is true that the sense of family, of duty, may be stronger in a girl brought up in a more traditional 'Indian' home, the actual behaviour pattern is dictated by the norms prevailing in the community outside the four walls of the house. In the city, where you are in a sense almost anonymous, where few know or even care about the goings on in your house, the situation is quite different. While it is perfectly true that many Westernized career-oriented women are both selfish and uncaring, it is not at all uncommon to find that it is this daughter-in-law who will provide the most congenial home, if only because she is likely to be earning better than her more provincial sisters, and may be living in a larger apartment, and perhaps able to afford a nurse. Also, it is she who may be able to stand up for her rights and lay down some boundaries within which she will operate. Often the daughter-in-law who comes from a small town feels more threatened and less able to protect her rights. She may get away from her 'duties' as she sees them, by escaping to her mother's home, or getting caught in an emotional battle with her husband, throwing tantrums and even threatening suicide if she does not have her way. The training programmes that all employees, which includes women employees, undergo at a good organization, help an individual deal not just with interpersonal relationships at the office, but also the home. While they do not guarantee harmony, they certainly may help bring much needed perspective to petty problems that sometimes seem to grow to gargantuan proportions. The daughter-in-law who has no access to anyone or anything outside the four walls of her house, is sometimes caught in a web of pettiness, which negatively affects her and those around her.

Does the Turf Matter? The Problems of Proximity

Sometimes adult children live with their parents. At other times, parents live with adult children. Does it matter which it is? Most women believe that it does.

> If you live with your parents-in-law in their home, obviously you have to fit into their schedules and their way of life. You have to adjust to their eating habits and their timings. You have to fit into their social circle. If they come and live with you, they have to adjust to your way of life (Neeta Patankar, whose parents-in-law came to stay with her after her father-in-law suffered a massive heart attack).

Feeling a little irrelevant in the busy schedules their son and working daughter-in-law had to follow, Neeta's in-laws soon packed their bags and returned to their life in Pune where they had their own circle of friends and their own life. Many parents find that the convenience of being taken care of is not sufficient compensation for the changes they must effect in their way of life to fit into their children's homes and lifestyles.

In a more individualistic era, there appears to be no ready-made formula that will ensure harmony. If you talk to adult offspring they express their own difficulties.

We lived as a nuclear family for so long and we got used to our space and our own way of doing things. Now when my mother-in-law expects everything to be done in a different way, it's really very difficult (Ratna Saxena, a daughter-in-law whose mother-in-law now lives with her).

The contemporary daughter-in-law also chafes at being boxed into a traditional role. 'When we have a party my mother-in-law will tell people "Oh, Ratna has been at it since the morning, poor thing, she has taken no rest at all." But I really don't want that particular set of guests to feel that I have given them so much importance. I feel like saying, "No, I haven't gone to any such lengths for this evening". It's really quite frustrating!'

Most women are able to overcome the petty irritations the older generation's desire to conform to traditional roles engenders. In the chapter on working women, we shall come across many women, especially those who have young children in the house, who feel a real sense of relief that a senior family member is there to help keep an eye on the children, but some are unable to see things in perspective. In such cases, good equations between the generations are destroyed by proximity.

The Man in the Middle

If a man's wife and mother do not get along, he is going to get caught in some very unpleasant crossfire. If he takes his mother's side he gets labelled a 'mamma's boy', if he speaks up for his wife, he is taunted as a 'joru ka ghulam', a wimp, or a henpecked husband. In earlier times, the patriarchal nature of society and the fact that one married into one's own caste, creed and community meant that the adjustments required were far fewer. Marriage in the days gone by may not have been a meeting of minds and hearts, but it was high on comfort! Today, a man may fall in love, or find compatible a woman he meets at the workplace, one with whom he finds he has shared goals and aspirations, a similar sense of humour, common hobbies, in other words, a 'soul mate'. However, the pheromones neglect to alert the couple to the many differences that also exist. To some extent, the region you belong to, the caste you were born into, dictate lifestyle. And while it is sometimes possible to create a new way of life in a nuclear home, the adjustments that are called for if parents or other relatives live with the couple simply prove to be a huge strain. However, many men said that though friction between mother-in-law and daughter-in-law continue to be problematic, what makes it easier to cope with is that it is now more acceptable for the couple to move out if the situation becomes really unpleasant. Also, attitudes today are far more tolerant of things like the husband helping the wife in the kitchen, or with housework, so in some ways stress points have been reduced.

No Easy Solution

Ironically, when as sometimes happens, the woman tries to please the man by changing her whole personality to conform, there may be less stress at home, but the man ends up feeling frustrated that his wife no longer remains the woman he chose to marry.

If I had wanted to marry a typical Punjabi girl, I would have done that, wouldn't I? I chose to marry you because you were different from all the women I know and all the women in my family. So what do you do the moment we get married? Try to become as much like the women in my family, and as little as the woman you were, as you can! (Sunil Bhatia, an ad executive complains good humouredly to his Kannadiga wife).

It is not a common occurrence, and yet one woman I spoke to actually believed that her marriage was in trouble because she was trying to bridge the huge chasm that existed between the roles she was trying to blend, of the ideal daughter-in-law on the one hand and the perfect wife on the other. They are not always compatible. Sometimes, the husband may want his wife to entertain his office colleagues in a certain way, to serve non-vegetarian food at home, join him for a drink. He may wish that she accompany him to official parties, or even to the disco. His mother, on the other hand, may feel very uncomfortable about a daughter-in-law who does all or any of these things. Those brought up in large families with diverse cultures are better able to manage the contradictions and can walk this tightrope, many others find doing so an unbearable strain. Some simply do not wish to do so.

When the Family has Two Sets of Parents that Need Care

The dual-career family often settles for a single child. This is likely to create additional pressures on adult offspring as their parents age. Women often tend to be apologetic about taking care of their parents.

My husband is an only child, so his parents are always with us. In fact, as his grandfather is alive, he too stays with us. Then, since I am one of two sisters, my parents often stay with us too. In our case, I think I am fortunate that we are Tamilians. At least our food habits are simple. I cook the food for the whole day in one pressure cooker and since we're not so fussy about hot food, my cooking for the entire day is over by 8.30 a.m. However, old people do tend to fall sick and I often have to take my parents or parents-in-law to the doctor or to nurse them when they are sick. It is at these times that I notice a subtle change in my husband's attitude. If my parents need attention, he exerts subtle pressure on me to accompany him to his official engagements. But if it his parents who need care he wants me to stay back and look after them. He will say, 'Don't worry I will make your excuses for you, they'll understand' (Sandhya, who often has two sets of parents staying with her).

As divorce rates rise, the situation is likely to get even more complicated. Couples who both have divorced parents living have a really difficult task of being there for them when they are ill or need attention. Instead of a number of adult offspring having to take responsibility for two sets of parents who would be living in two homes, the younger generation may have to take care of four individuals in four different establishments in what may very well be four different cities!

Moving from a Joint Family to a Nuclear Family

Shifting into a nuclear family suddenly makes you feel desolate, it is very lonely. In a joint family there is a lot of fun and frolic, a festive atmosphere at all times. There is never a moment of boredom as there are so many people to talk to. Housework is simplified as everyone shares work equally. And there is a lot of unity and bonding among the family members. Little things you need never bother about while living in a joint family suddenly look like huge responsibilities when you are in a nuclear family (Twenty-five-year old Annapoorna Ramnath from Bangalore who moved from a joint family to a nuclear family).

Those who have enjoyed living in a joint family miss the bonhomie and the sense of support they find there when they move to a nuclear family. However, most couples who have experience of both arrangements discover that in a joint family it is much more difficult for the couple to make independent decisions as many more people are involved in the decision-making process. It is also more difficult for a couple to spend quality time together, so it becomes more difficult for them to bond. In comparison, settling down into a nuclear family, though not entirely free from problems, is fairly smooth. Those who have made the journey in the other direction have found the transition far more difficult.

Where the Joint Family Scores

The joint family calls for a continual effort from all its members.

As Anshu Modi says, 'I am a businesswoman earning lakhs, but in the home, I don't do anything without consulting others. In a joint family, there is caring, sharing, It's where you see the good Indian values of self-sacrifice at their best. On a more practical level, you can leave the house whenever you feel like, you never have to lock up and if there are children, there is always someone at home for them, they don't have to be left solely with the servants.' In an earlier age, the level of empathy that was exhibited was far greater: 'In the old days, if any one in the family had diabetes, then mithai didn't come to the table', Anshu Modi reminisces. Putting the common interest before one's personal desires became second nature to those who lived together.

However, as we look ahead, there are compelling reasons to believe that the joint family can perhaps be the only thing that can help us cope with the family of the future. As we move into an age when a sizeable percentage of our population is going to be old, it may prove to be the best solution to taking care of the elderly. For if any member of the family is sick, a joint family ensures that there is a family member around to keep an eye on the patient and on paid nurses, in case they have been employed.

How Attitudes have Changed with Time

Many middle-aged women have spent years selflessly taking care of their parents-in-law, and more specifically their mothers-in-law, through prolonged illnesses. Interestingly, not all these women believe that they were welcomed very warmly into their marital homes by the women they later took care of, but they saw this as their duty and did it, or so they believe, uncomplainingly. And do they expect that they will, in turn, receive the care and attention they lavished on their elders from their own children? They would rather not speculate, saying that times have changed and one can only be happy if one does whatever one does without any such expectation! At some level, a very contemporary pragmatism combines with a very ancient philosophy at least at the cerebral level. One would have to fast forward to a decade or more into the future to check whether reality bears out these pronouncements!

We can also already envision a world where not only the mother, but also the mother-in-law may be working. It is inarguable that as far as middle-class India is concerned, the full-time housewife and mother is going to become extinct sooner rather than later. There may not be a female relative to help out with childcare, illness and other family emergencies. Living together with various degrees of independence and interdependence will be one way to deal with the situation.

Mothers-in-Law-in-Waiting: How Do They See Their Role?

Will things be different for the younger generation of women who are waiting in the wings, so to speak, to become mothers-in-law in their own right? They certainly believe so! Women who are now in their forties and fifties, have already seen the changed equation and are comfortable with it. 'Earlier old ladies were very rigid, we are not so rigid', says Anshu Modi. 'I don't do housework, myself, so how can I expect my daughter-in-law to do housework?' Mothers of adult sons say that though they would be flattered and very happy if their sons chose to live with them after they marry as it would give them a chance to be with their grandchildren and have a real connection with them, but they would accept their sons' decision even if they chose to live separately. They hope to try and guide their daughters-in-law without overpowering them with their affection. 'I think today's daughter-in-law is very suspicious of too much affection. They want a little distance.' The modern mother-in-law will try and give it to her. They remember the problems they themselves faced when they first stepped into a joint family and are firm in their resolve that another generation of women not have to relive those experiences. 'I would not like my daughter-in-law to feel she has been put in chains, that's really how we sometimes felt.'

Today's parents accept the reality that these days the joint family exists because of practical considerations. If young couples had to make a choice, they would choose to live on their own. The patience to adjust is diminishing. They believe that this generation of mothers-in-law will be far more accommodating than the previous one.

Prita Singhal belongs to a joint family that has two brothers and their wives and families, which includes the married son and daughter-in-law of the elder son and his infant child. There are, therefore, twelve

members and three generations. This joint family exists
in a form that Prita believes is no longer very common.
'In most joint families today, they merely live under
one roof, they normally have different kitchens and live
life fairly independently. In our house we all eat together,
everyone is expected to be down at the same time, so
that the system runs smoothly. We also have a common
kitty from which funds are dispensed according to the
needs of various members.' Prita, who comes to a joint
family from a nuclear family, says, 'I spent twenty years
in a nuclear family and then the next twenty in a joint
family. In a nuclear family, you tend to take your
parents for granted, in a joint family in some ways the
reverse is true; you have to build rapport and
understanding through effort, work and compromise. If
you do this, then in your time of crisis, the joint family
will be there for you.' Without even being aware of it,
Prita addresses the problem some of the younger women
interviewed were confronted with and so deeply
unhappy about, the power equation of family dynamics.
'In a joint family', Prita says, 'as a younger member,
you should do work without taking away the
responsibility of the person whom you are helping. A
daughter-in-law should see that her mother-in-law
continues to feel in control. You have entered her house
and she should never feel that you have taken over.'
Prita conjures up memories of the era that is slowly
slipping away. And she reminds us that there is more
than one way for a woman to assert herself. 'When I
got married', Prita explains, 'my mother-in-law's friend
told me something I never forgot. "Listen for some

years, understand the family"' the old lady advised, '"and then you can rule them for the rest of your life!"'

Today's young woman will treat this piece of advice with derision. There is undeniably an element of scheming manipulation in pursuing such a course of action taken with the prospect of future benefit. It is, however, perhaps not very dissimilar to how even an ambitious young woman will first try to win her boss's trust before she begins asserting herself. Of course, I do not deny that this analogy is not completely fair. For the working person employs strategy in the workplace and then comes home to relax. If the daughter-in-law of a joint family has to strategize at home, then when and where does she relax?

But as Prita is discovering, as she grows older and more senior in her own joint family, and observes the situation in other families, the adjustments tend not to be a one way process, 'With every new entrant to the family, the whole dynamics of the family changes.'

The NRI Syndrome

In the beginning I used to dread answering the phone because I couldn't follow the American accent. Moving into a joint family with parents–in–law and a brother-in-law, all living in the same house, was a lifesaver (twenty-year-old Nandana Prasad, who went to California from Jamshedpur).

For many brides such as Nandana, who are moving to a foreign environment, where the culture and lifestyle is completely different, the joint family is a safety net. The mother-in-law is a reassuring role model in a new and sometimes confusing world. The familiar food and customs are a comforting security blanket that cushions, for some time, the shock of stepping into a world where every tenet one was brought up with is questioned and sometimes brushed aside. And it is important to understand that this holds as true for a move from Chennai to Kolkata, or Delhi to Mumbai, as it does for a move from Ludhiana to London, or from Bangalore to Bangkok!

However, it's interesting that after an initial settling down period, the norms that the joint family may impose upon the new entrant are sometimes as distressingly restrictive as they would be in India. While some families embrace the new culture, some get locked in the norms and mores that were prevalent in the home country when they migrated, something that a girl who has chosen to live in the West may be very unprepared for.

Generation Next and the Joint Family

In a nuclear family you become extremely attached to your parents, in a joint family there are so many people you have to adjust to it can be quite bewildering
(Anitha A., a Bangalore-based working woman in her early thirties who has moved from a nuclear family to a joint family).

Anitha believes that initially being in a joint family could be difficult for a young couple, as they will not have the space they may wish for, and would have to put up with interference with regard to every single decision. However, she thinks that in the long run, a joint family is beneficial. Indeed, after three years in a joint family, the person Anitha feels closest to in her family is her mother-in-law!

Though there were some exceptions, overwhelmingly, those who lived in joint families believe that the joint family was a good place for children to learn correct values. Anitha, for instance, believes that a joint family is an ideal place for young children to grow up in. 'I think personality and character will develop better surrounded by so many people of diverse traits.' Indeed, most mothers believe that if young people can adjust to a joint family, they will benefit, as they are so many people to guide them in making choices in what is increasingly becoming a very complicated world. In middle-class homes, where parents tend to be focussed on giving their children the very best start they can, a joint family offers role models and in-house expert advice on a wide range of career options!

Anshu Modi, the designer, also points out that in a world where people are so aware of networking, young couples may actually enjoy the reach afforded by the superior status of the senior members of the family. 'If you are a senior journalist, you will have so many contacts, you could pick up the phone and get your interviews, if your daughter-in-law is in the same line, she may just decide that it would make sense to stay in the same house so she can also take advantage of this. Or if you are a designer, or a senior bureaucrat or executive, you would again have a reach and an access that a young person could never have. Young people today would like a mother-in-law's help, if they do not need her as a babysitter, then they may like to make use of her power and status!'

However, a contrary viewpoint holds that it is easier for a personality to flower in a nuclear family where choices are dictated by an individual's own inclinations and interests rather than in a joint family, where too much time and energy goes in managing relationships. 'Some of the softness in my personality died after I began to live in a joint family', says one woman a little wistfully. Perhaps the joint family works better for the individual who has or acquires good people skills and is able to persuade family members to his or her own viewpoint. It also works better for those who are able to balance personal desires with family responsibilities. Indeed such a person is likely to develop communication and leadership skills that would be useful in any field of endeavour!

One factor that people across generations mentioned was that the present generation was so selfish, materialistic and impatient, that it would be very difficult for them to adjust to the very exacting demands of the joint family. They believe that young people may go in for the joint family because of the convenience it appears to offer. Many young working women admit freely that the only reason that they put up with the many adjustments living in a joint family, which in today's urban concept often means living with the man's parents, entail is because it frees them from the tedium and the problems of housekeeping.

However, there were those who enjoyed life in a joint family:

I like having people around. If you can adjust to one person, you can adjust to ten. Some people feel overwhelmed by large family gatherings. I enjoy them (Twenty-four-year-old Pallavi, who has grown up in a home with paternal grandparents, working parents and a younger brother).

The notion of young people with individual rooms and locked doors is still an alien concept in India. As of now, visits from uncles and aunts have young people moving out of their rooms without question to camp in the living room or in verandahs or balconies. The Indian mother still would not think of knocking or asking permission to enter the room of unmarried adult children who live in the family home. But as families get wealthier, and homes get larger, sharing is required less and less and people get used to their own space. It then becomes that much more difficult to live in the cheerful commune atmosphere that was once considered so enjoyable. In marriages where young girls have to move from a nuclear family to a joint family, or from a more modern to a more conservative environment, adjustments are inevitably called for. Some young people are happy following the norms and mores of an earlier time. Others have learnt to manage the contradictions that inevitably surface between the outside and the inside world.

Today's mother-in-law is trying very hard to break the mould. Women who are in their forties and fifties want more than anything to be a friend to their daughter-in-law. 'They will even take up cudgels with their son to ensure that their relationship with the daughter-in-law is not affected in the event of a quarrel', says one forty-year-old woman with adult sons.

For the joint family of the twenty-first century is certainly quite different in form and spirit from the joint family that today's grandmothers remember. Today, one may no longer rely on family members to take on a hands-on role in looking after those who need extra attention. Sons and daughters-in-law who have children who need looking after are much more likely to employ a maid and then expect that the presence of family members in the house will act as check on her.

But if the younger generation is changing, it appears that so is the older generation. Observing her peers, A. Padminimurty says that 'nowadays even grandparents want to enjoy their independence, they don't want to be tied down to look after their grandchildren. "We have done our bit, why get tied down again", they say. They do not realize that tomorrow they too may need assistance. Who will look after them then?'

Even as they claimed that they may choose to make the adjustments required to live in a joint family to enjoy the benefits of having someone to help with the housekeeping or, if they were working women, the childcare, many of those interviewed believe that the whole concept of a joint family required such a loss of privacy, of space and freedom, that it could only exist if there was a marked shift in the attitude of the older generation.

In many ways, the joint family emerges as a particularly rigorous training ground. It seems to flourish, as any organization would, if the head, whether that is the father-in-law, the mother-in-law, or an elder brother-in-law, is perceived to be fair and willing if not to put the family's interests before his or her own desires to not do the reverse. In such a scenario, even if the daughter-in-law finds the adjustments difficult at first, as time goes on she appreciates that there has been a purpose behind the many unwritten rules the family enforced, and in retrospect, she can view them without rancour. However, if the head of the family is perceived to be selfish, then if the finances allow independent living the family will soon splinter apart, with bitterness and resentment completely burying family feelings and making brothers and their wives strangers who come together only for family functions such as weddings.

Pammi Suri had a difficult time with her mother-in-law at first. She resented being forced to fit into her mother-in-law's idea of what a daughter-in-law should be. Today, however, she believes that she learnt a lot from her mother-in-law 'I think my mother-in-law taught me the importance of treating every human being, no matter how lowly, with equal respect. She made me touch the feet of an elderly retainer's wife. You can't imagine the goodwill this generated for me. Little things like this have really made a difference to my life. It is something I have tried to pass on to my own children', Pammi says.

In some cases, I have interviewed three generations of a single family. These interviews were fascinating. They were like snapshots of the same object taken from different angles. A. Padminimurty's granddaughter, for instance, confided that since they had been virtually brought up by their grandparents, both she and her brother felt closest to them. So, how does daughter-in-law Lakshmi Murthy react to this development? Quite well, as it turns out. She sees it as a necessary and not too difficult a price to pay for being able to pursue a career without too much conflict.

It is interesting that recent research in the West shows that societies there are now more open to adult children living in the same house as them, and indeed, projections for the future actually see a return to the model of the multi-generational family living under one roof. In India, too, the joint family may survive out of sheer necessity. Surveys show that young people like the idea of living in a joint family, as they believe living with grandparents would be good for their children. According to a survey mentioned in the *India Today* (31 January 2005, p.70), 70 per cent of young people would like to live in a joint family and 28 per cent in a nuclear family. The Grey Survey of young women mentioned in Chapter 6 of this book states that 62 per cent of young women would like to live in a joint family because they believe that the grandparents would have a healthy influence on their children. While the older generation often believes the younger generation does not have the patience and the selflessness required to make a joint family work, the younger members believe that though it is extremely difficult to adjust to living with others after having got used to living alone, there may not be any alternative in the future. It will perhaps be the only way in which they can take care of their parents. And it will probably be one way in which their children can be taken care of. It may also perhaps be the best way for the families of the future, which are most likely to be dual-career families to take care of household responsibilities.

In the chapter on working women, many of the women did say that the joint family was a major cause of stress in their lives. They encountered disapproval for not playing the stereotypical gender role and challenging the norms of a traditional society.

Interestingly, while the older members of the joint family talk about how they were expected to adjust and adapt to the joint family, the young singles I interviewed expected the joint family to change to accommodate their special needs and requirements. The elder members of the family were aware of this and for the most part were quite prepared to do so. How well the generations succeed in managing this conflict will determine the nature of the joint family of the future. The joint family is likely to survive. It is however going to be a very different joint family from the joint family as we know it today.

3

Full-time Housewives: Desperate
Housewives or Blissful Homemakers?

The reason the family seems to be coming apart at the seams is that women are no longer content being housewives. Children are neglected because there is no mother at home. The same is true for old people. Families reach crisis point when one member falls ill. And why, because there is no one at home to take care of them. If only women could get over this nonsense of trying to compete with men at the workplace and be happy with hearth and home, as is 'nature's law', all would be well. After all, were women not content looking after the home for millennia? This is still a popular argument. And one hears it in drawing rooms and in office canteens, in trains and on buses through the length and breadth of our country. At one level, there is no denying, that without a woman to look after the home and family, the family is facing unprecedented challenges.

One can also understand how it is difficult, for many people, to understand why what appeared to be the natural order, which remained unquestioned for so long and enjoyed social sanction for millennia, is somehow not working any more. Why is the modern woman challenging traditional gender roles and equations?

Gender roles all over the world, but especially in more traditional societies such as India, are based on role models that show the man as provider and protector, and the woman as nurturer and carer. Every major religion reinforces this stereotype, as do mythology, literature, art, music and dance. The image of a fiery Durga astride a lion, and of Shakti, the very embodiment of strength, do exist, but much more compelling are the iconic Ruth who stands in the alien corn forsaking her own home for that of her husband, or of Sita, who sacrifices all for the sake of her husband, Rama. In Islam, too, women are expected and encouraged to conform to fairly traditional ideas of what men and women must do.

Young girls often grow up with the idea that docility, fidelity, self-sacrifice are the most desirable attributes for women. The ability to run a home and care for the family are indeed often seen as the very greatest qualities a woman could have.

Fairly predictably, researchers find a shift from these stereotypical roles to far more equal gender roles amongst urban, higher-income, better-educated, dual-earner families. My own research showed a similar shift even in single-income families in this segment, at least as far as attitudes were concerned. This means that though the woman who is a full-time housewife may still take responsibility for most of the housework, she is more likely to have a husband who will pitch in both with childcare and housework when the need arises. But as we shall see, this slight amelioration in the woman's role has not improved her life in any real way. For even as her husband may have personally become more sensitized to her predicament and sympathetic to her many problems, his working hours and preoccupation with work-related activities may make him behave in a way that is less than helpful.

The question is, of course, that if women were genuinely happy being housewives just a generation ago, why are their daughters so very reluctant to play that role today? What is the message today's young woman has received from her mother, both overtly and covertly? How is life for the contemporary housewife when one compares it with the life of housewives earlier? The women I spoke to were almost unanimous in their belief that the life their mothers and grandmothers led was far from enviable. They do not buy the myth of the all-sacrificing Bharatiya nari, whose greatest joy was looking after the well-being of her family, no matter at what cost to the woman herself. And most women are unequivocal that at some point of time they would like to be financially independent. They are aware of the status of the woman who is not. They have seen it in the many examples of subservience they saw in their grandmothers, mothers, aunts and other female relatives. Many of these women acknowledge that their experiences of childhood were happier because their mothers had so completely devoted themselves to the family. But, for themselves, they wish to make this sacrifice only while they have really young children.

In the West, in the post-feminism era, first-person accounts from women with no ideological baggage are now becoming increasingly common. These allow a new generation a chance to review the past in its own way. In an article in the *New Statesman* (18 August 2003), Lauren Booth discusses research that finds that the contemporary woman eats more and does less housework than her grandmother did and goes on to comment:

> With astounding predictability, this information is being used to make us feel guilty about our lives. Guilty that we eat well, guilty that we go to the gym, guilty that we leave the house at all while a single one of our husband's socks remains undarned or the scullery floor unmopped . . .
> In the 1950s, it seems all mothers looked like Doris Day or Betty Grable. If my Nan had been buried instead of cremated, she'd be turning in her grave. For 50 years, she was a housewife who fought a daily battle against dirt without any labour-saving devices—and she hated it . . . I moved in with her when I was 16 and remember being shocked by how hard she worked . . . I glimpsed a womanhood that frightened me half to death.

Conditions in India are not identical to conditions in the UK, and indeed conditions in each home vary, but it does seem to appear that this writer's reaction is far from unique. So though men may never have guessed, many women were far from happy about the role they had to play and passed this on to their daughters.

In a domestic management programme run by a major corporate house, which had been designed to help the wives of supervisors and workers better appreciate the work-related demands on their husbands, I asked the women attending the programme about their response to the many changes the Indian family had undergone. Had they been for the better or for the worse? It was interesting that though the women agreed that many changes such as the increasing break-up of marriages, the decline of the extended family, and the 'lack of respect' young people seemed to show to their elders were cause for concern, on balance they felt the changes were for the better. 'Women too have a voice now', 'women are no longer treated like animals', 'women have choices, they don't have to put up with all sorts of nonsense', were some of the comments. Each and every woman present felt the emerging problems could be tackled, the betterment in the status of women was worth the new complications that had arisen. The education of the urban middle-class woman and the fact that she is capable of holding a job has changed the male–female equation irrevocably. The woman is now unlikely to accept a position of subservience in the early days of the marriage. However, if the woman is unable to work outside the home, over the years, being housebound takes its toll. She may lose confidence in her own abilities and with every passing year her qualifications become further devalued. This happens even to those women who were once achievers in their own right. Rachna, a woman who had a promising career in the hotel industry and is married to the general manger of a popular hotel group, had to give up her job as she was not able to make adequate childcare arrangements for her young child.

This is how she describes her predicament:

Though I am unable to take on a regular job, I do have time hanging on my hands in the mornings and wish I had something constructive to do. I find I am beginning to lose confidence in myself. Just the thought of looking for something [job-related] is very daunting. I find I am getting lethargic and am not interested in anything.

It is difficult to believe this of the vital, vivacious person seated in front of me, but Rachna's description of her current predicament outlines copybook symptoms of what being a housewife does to a woman. Indeed, Rachna also gives vent to the feelings many women, who have formerly worked experience, when she recounts the many ways in which her life has changed after becoming a housewife. 'I was always financially independent', Rachna says, 'suddenly we're on one salary and so I've changed my spending habits. No longer will I buy something spontaneously, on the spur of the moment'.

For a woman who has been part of an exciting and demanding workplace in her own right, it is difficult to suddenly become the traditional wife who necessarily spends much of her time waiting for her husband to come home. Though she understands the pressures her husband has to deal with, it does not really make the situation very much easier to deal with. 'I've been there, I know about the long hours of work, the lack of family time, but still it does bother me that quite often my husband will return my call after I've dialled his number six times!'

So even if women like Rachna understand their husbands' long hours of work as also the very intensive nature of their jobs, they mourn the loss of their own identities and the sense of importance their jobs gave them. The first time these women hear themselves being introduced as somebody's wife, instead of as individuals in their own right, they feel a sense of hurt, which endures.

In another era, the man was judged by his performance at the workplace, the woman by her appearance and her skills as a housewife and mother. This has changed. While looks certainly matter and housekeeping skills are not yet irrelevant, in today's world, a woman's designation and salary also define her status, as they have always done for a man.

So in this new world order, not only does the housewife have to contend with being stuck with an unequal gender equation within the home, she also feels that she is getting less respect than the working woman in the outside world. The position is exacerbated because of the comparison that is inevitably drawn between the housewife in a nuclear family, who may find it more difficult to fill her days with something she finds truly fulfilling or rewarding at a time when the children are growing up and need her less, and her counterpart at the workplace who may be reaching a senior level, just as the housewife feels most uncertain about her role.

Jaideep Majumdar addressed this problem in an article in the *Hindustan Times*:

Manjula Mishra should have been a happy housewife, with a doting husband, caring in-laws and an adorable three-year-old son. But five years after her marriage with Siddharth, an affluent businessman, she went into acute depression. What was lacking was a sense of self-fulfilment. Women like Manjula need no longer despair. Come July, the city will play host to an interactive workshop to help bring out the best in women, particularly housewives.

Christened Dahleez (Urdu for threshold), the workshop is the brainchild of Raj Sethia, an educational psychologist and motivator. 'Most home managers have little or no interaction with the rest of the world. Their desires and ambitions remain suppressed leading to deep sorrow. This has a profound effect on their children and family.'

Sethia said the popular perception that women from affluent households have a fair degree of self-fulfilment is a myth: the picture is the same across the social spectrum. (Majumdar, 2004: 12)

In an environment, where work is consuming most of our time and more and more of our energies, the housewife is placed in a peculiar position. A consumerist, achievement-driven society effectively devalues her contribution, as so far no monetary value is attached to her contribution to the family. In many ways, then, the housewife's job has become more difficult than ever. As 'working people' spend less and less time at home, her many contributions to the home and family are now less appreciated than ever before

In many ways, I have personal experience of many of the issues the contemporary housewife has to contend with. I was the first professionally-qualified woman from my family. As I mention in the introduction, I had got off to a good start professionally and I fully expected to be an ambitious career woman. However, after I got married I realized that nobody had told me how hard it is to leave an infant and go to work. Having a baby changes one. It changes one's priorities much more dramatically than one can imagine. And while it is indisputable that some women feel the maternal tug much less strongly than others, the demands on the job front are so inflexible and there is so little provision for childcare in our country that all too often women who had always seen themselves as career women find themselves playing the role of full-time housewife and mother for at least some part of their lives.

Impact of Being Housebound on a Housewife Who Has Worked Previously

It's not a good job. If people define themselves by what they do, doctor, engineer, graphic designer, then yes, I too am doing a job. Full-time housewife and mother. It's one where I don't get paid. There are no increments, no days off, no recognition, no rewards (a twenty-nine-year-old housewife, who has given up her job to take care of her young children and elderly parents-in-law).

While many housewives are fulfilled with the routine of a housewife's life, increasingly, many urban, middle-class women who are educated and have the qualifications to land good jobs, are not. They miss their financial independence, but equally, they miss not being able to use their potential, they miss getting out of the house and the stimulation of a different environment, of going to a workplace where one has colleagues who open a whole new world that is different from the narrow circumscribed world at home.

In cities and small towns across India, many housewives are coping with a far harsher reality. Educated to post-graduate level, they find themselves playing roles that are unchanged and unchanging from very ancient times. Indeed, it often seems that as far as the contemporary housewife is concerned, no option is a good option. While the housewife in the nuclear family, especially one who is married to a man in a transferable job, may often have to contend with loneliness and boredom, the housewife in a joint family may be faced with problems that are different, but are often even more difficult to handle.

In modern nuclear families, the children only know their parents as family. That's wrong. But then some importance should also be given to the couple. I have to look after my parents-in-law almost entirely by myself. Because my sister-in-law works, I have to take care of her child as well. I can never cook what my husband or my child wants to eat because so many people's preferences have to be taken into consideration. Then, we have to ask my father-in-law for money for every expense, even to buy a cake of soap! (Rupa Kumar, thirty-four, an economics honours graduate and full-time housewife and mother who lives with her husband and son (aged five), her parents-in-law and a married brother-in-law, his wife and their son in a two-roomed house in a congested locality in Delhi).

Rupa is less affluent than many of the women I have spoken to. Her husband is a modestly successful event manager. Rupa is not unhappy or discontented with her lot. She has married a good man and he is clearly fond of her. Her parents-in-law are fond of her too. 'I make no difference between her and my daughter', her mother-in-law tells me and Rupa does not disagree with this statement.

But there are problems. The fact that so many people live together in such a small space means that Rupa cannot afford to have another child. Indeed, her bedroom is so cramped there is barely space for a study table for her child. The couple cannot buy their son a computer as there is simply no place in the house for it. Then, even though people always surround her, she longs for friends, for companions of her own age. Rupa was born and brought up in Varanasi. She knows no one in Delhi and is completely housebound looking after her parents-in-law, her son and her nephew.

Rupa has been brought up with very traditional values. She sees her most important job as 'looking after my parents-in-law'. Her father-in-law has been ailing for some years and is a dominating head of the family. Family finances, as also attitudes, dictate that Rupa do a substantial amount of housework, and this she does cheerfully enough, commenting only that housekeeping is difficult with so many family members to cater to as accommodating individual preferences can be problematic. She would have preferred having only her parents-in-law to look after.

Rupa is troubled with the changes the consumerist ethos of the capital city has brought into her home. Her five-year-old son is 'stubborn' and insists that his parents buy him jeans, shoes and even food items of brands advertised on TV. Rupa finds it increasingly difficult to discipline him and her husband's long and erratic work hours make it difficult for him to help very much.

Sometimes it seems Rupa is caught between two worlds. On the one hand, she believes that it is terribly sad that in the modern nuclear family no one bothers about anyone except the spouse and the child or children. 'No one else exists', she says disapprovingly. On the other hand, her face lights up when you ask her if she would like to be financially independent. 'YES!' she says, 'that would be so nice'. And if you ask her whether she has any suggestions on how the housewife's life could be made easier, she has very small, very simple suggestions. 'She should be given a day off from housework and sometimes people should compliment her on something she's done', she offers.

Rupa would qualify for the epithet 'happily married woman'. But as we talk, woman-to-woman, Rupa confides that she often suffers from headaches and migraines. She does not know what causes them.

The Impact of a Transferable Job

Due to the transferable nature of most jobs today, women are transplanted from their homes into cities or towns where they have no roots. Being housebound, there are few opportunities to get to know new people. Growing up in the 1960s and 1970s one listened with fascinated horror when friends settled in the West recounted how one did not even know one's neighbour in the fast-paced cities of the developed world. We were smug that we Indians were different. Here, your business was everybody's business. And the demands of the community could become tiresome, but surely there could never be a time when they would cease? By 1979, when I came to Calcutta as a bride, I realized exactly how lonely life in a city could be. When the door shut after my husband left for work, I was all alone till he came back late in the evening. All day, every day. Finding a friend was a major challenge. My husband's colleagues had working wives and I was completely housebound. It was then that I realized exactly how difficult life was for the housewife and mother in our contemporary world.

Being a journalist helped. I let out steam by writing an article called 'Under House Arrest', in a national newspaper. It obviously touched a chord, because the article was published unedited and drew letters to the editor till correspondence on the subject was declared closed. Once I became tuned into the problem, I learnt of others whose plight was very much worse than mine. In the Greater Kailash I locality we lived in, when we were in Delhi, a friend from college lived in another block. She had two girls roughly the same age as my two sons at the time. One day, when I had gone to visit her, I found her lying on the couch in the drawing room while her three-year-old was wailing for milk. 'Open the fridge and get it yourself', she said flatly to the toddler. 'She's three', I said in remonstration. And suddenly it seemed that a dam had burst. 'I'm not feeling well, my husband is away on tour and the maid hasn't shown up in days. I am so tired I can't get up, if you feel so full of energy, go heat the milk up', she snapped.

And then I learnt that this young mother had not had a break in years. Traditionally, most young mothers went to their 'maike' or mother's home for a respite. My friend's mother lived in a tiny apartment in Mumbai. She suffered from problems related to the heart and the children's natural boisterousness in a confined space could set off a heart attack, so my friend was always on tenterhooks when she went to her maternal home, and often returned from there even more stressed.

If you do not have family members to baby-sit occasionally, or reliable hired help, then life can become very difficult indeed. It is exhausting bringing up a baby. This is why, in 'the good old days', the nurturing of a child was not just the mother's responsibility. Grandparents, uncles and aunts, brothers and sisters would vie with each other to play with and look after the baby. 'It takes a village to raise a child' goes an African proverb that inspired the name of Hilary Clinton's best-selling book, *It Takes a Village*. Unfortunately, in our urban villages, increasingly, it is not a village, nor a family and not even a couple that is rearing a child. Too often, it is just one woman. And the toll it extracts is often considerable.

Interestingly, we in India are now thinking about these issues just as the Western world is actually seeing what could be the beginning of a trend in the reverse direction. Some women apparently are now seeking to become housewives. However, one report states that these women wish to avail of the services of nannies and au pairs so that they do not need to do housework. Men have apparently not taken kindly to this development. They do not enjoy carrying the financial burden single-handedly!

NoMarriage.com
Women aspire to be housewives—without any of the housework.

Mothers are rejecting equality in the workplace and prefer the idea of becoming full-time housewives — but not ones who actually do housework . . . This is the overall conclusion of research among 2,100 British adults that says women are happy to abandon the workplace but not if it means spending all day at home cooking, cleaning and looking after children.

The report, by Marian Salzman, chief strategic officer of Euro RSCG Worldwide, the world's fifth largest advertising agency, describes these women as princess-style 'domestic divas' who effectively exploit their husbands. 'Today, "women's lib" means wanting to be liberated from the intense pressures of the modern-day working mum", she said. 'And what we're seeing is a serious gender divide regarding women in the workplace. This time around, it is the women who want to stay at home and the men who want to keep them in the offices and factories.'

Miss Salzman, 45, who does not have children, is well known in the United States for spotting trends before they go mainstream . . . (from the website www.Nomarriage. com).

As is to be expected, this view is fiercely contested. The article goes on to say:

Holly Hamilton-Bleakley, of Full Time Mothers, a lobbying organization, said she abhorred the idea of women buying in childcare so that they could simply sit in a coffee shop, but she did not believe this was an accurate picture.

Hamilton-Bleakley is of the view that 'The dual income, two-career family is becoming outdated. Parents are finally recognizing that children need time with them. Time spent with children is well spent and makes a major difference to a child's life' (from the website www.Nomarriage.com).

Many housewives will tell you that they are glad to be in India rather than in the UK or the US because of the availability of affordable domestic help in the country. However, when you go to a housewife's house, nine times out of ten you will have to listen to her problems with the self-same domestic help. Working women too will talk disparagingly of the housewife's preoccupation with 'servant problems'. After listening to account after account of the acute stress generated by the domestic help's unreliability, ingratitude, not to mention dishonesty, the problem becomes crystal clear. Middle-class housewives who are struggling to cope with roles that they consider joyless themselves, expect women who are more disadvantaged to fulfil a small or greater number of these jobs with a degree of efficiency and a sense of reliability that is clearly unrealistic. They expect women who live in appalling conditions, or live-in help who provide for families that are battling for survival every day of their lives, to bring in an element of order and chaos in the lives of their middle-class employers who are privileged in ways the domestic help can only dream of. Predictably, such relationships are highly problematic. The employers believe that since they are providing the domestic help with a much better standard of living than they could afford on their own, they should be grateful. In return, they expect the same level of responsibility that they themselves provide their employers. However, the domestics work under vastly different conditions, with completely different job prospects and therefore see little impetus for making too many sacrifices on the personal front to accommodate the employer's needs. While the employer need only pick up a telephone to inform the workplace of a possible delay or absence, the domestic help would have to put in far greater effort to do the same thing. Aside from this, in an uncertain job scenario, with no real tradition of a notice period before termination of job, no real provision for sick leave, or pension, domestic staff have got used to living by their wits and taking full advantage of every opportunity that presents itself for bettering their lot. So the housewife gifts the maid a sari that she knows the maid would never have been able to afford on her own and expects gratitude. However, we live today in a more egalitarian environment, where the opportunity for upward mobility does exist, even if it is severely circumscribed. A maid who has worked for even a short time becomes aware that this gift, generous though it is, falls far short of what her employer would herself wear, or gift a friend, or relative. So, far from being cheered by the gift, she may feel dissatisfied and even resentful that she is not treated at par with the family. Not surprising then, that a great amount of stress housewives face is because of their reliance on domestic help. We need solutions for work-family conflict that are equitable and accessible to all classes of women. So, if the contemporary Englishwoman indeed aspires to be a housewife who is looking at nannies and au pairs to provide her with comfort, it should be interesting to see how that experiment works out.

The debate over the role of the housewife in society is an extremely emotive issue everywhere in the world. Any change in traditional gender roles is understandably disturbing for many who see it as an attack on their belief system and culture. On the other hand, the role of the housewife has been deeply politicized. In *The Origin of the Family, Private Property and the State* (1884), Fredrich Engels puts forward the argument that the oppression of women in the nuclear family could be traced back to the emergence of the capitalist system which led to men's labour being transferred from the home to the farm or factory. The few women who worked received less pay than their male counterparts for women were relegated to 'the roles of breeding, maintaining men, and buying consumer goods. Mothers provided the next and appropriately indoctrinated generation of laborers for the capitalists; housewives maintained the male workforce by cleaning and cooking; housekeepers enriched the capitalist structure by consuming the products it produced.'

In the 1960s and 1970s, there were feminists like Kate Millet whose book, *Sexual Politics*, led to the widespread acceptance of the idea that politics was not confined to the outside world, and indeed that the personal was political. In 1963, Betty Freidan wrote *The Feminine Mystique*. This book is widely credited with inspiring a second wave of feminism. A whole generation of housewives identified with the book's description of domesticity as a dehumanizing experience which denied women a chance to develop their potential and indeed reduced them to becoming 'dependent, passive, childlike' creatures who lived at a 'lower human level'. The 1950s family, which is often taken to symbolize an idyllic entity, was described by Friedan as a 'comfortable concentration camp'! Some upper middle-class Indian women who are now in their forties and fifties have also been influenced by these theories, but many more would find some degree of resonance in what she said because conditions for that class of women in India today have many similarities with conditions that prevailed in the West in the 1950s and 1960s with regard to society and the family. In our metropolitan cities today, neighbour does not know neighbour, and with some exceptions, there is a dwindling sense of community. The mohalla, and the para, the neighbourhood by whatever name it is called, is much less important than it once was.

It is inarguable that the family has lost much of its earlier importance in contemporary India. The Indian executive is working longer hours and far more intensively than ever before. And unlike the US and the UK, over here, the weekend has little sanctity. New job opportunities such as in the call centres require employees to work to US and UK time. Children and young adults are also focussed on school and college activities. Less and less time is spent at home. A consumerist economy is beaming messages exhorting people to buy electronic items, holiday at exotic locations, and do a wide variety of things with their time and money. Indeed, 'hanging out' at malls is now rated as amongst the most popular recreational activities for young people!

On the one hand, technology has taken the grind out of housework. The upper middle-class or upper-class housewife, who grew up in a house full of servants and still employs domestic help of every kind, may not notice the change very sharply. But the housewife from a less affluent household is better off, in that she does not have to actually do the back-breaking jobs, such as grinding masalas, washing clothes by hand, or say even darning old clothes, which her mother may have had to contend with. On the other hand, research has shown that by providing conveniences to take care of a vast variety of household chores, jobs which were earlier outsourced to the dhobi or laundry, or given out to specialists, are now handled by the housewife herself, making the load the contemporary housewife carries actually heavier.

But even as everyday household jobs have moved from the outside specialists to the housewife, perhaps the most pivotal job of the housewife, to get food onto the table, is gradually losing its importance. There is an interesting little theory that monogamy dates back to the time when human beings started cooking tubers. Apparently, it was when men discovered that culinary skills were not equal, that some women's tubers were more appetizing than those of others, that they decided that it made sense to stick to the woman whose tubers one fancied. Voila, monogamy! Whether this theory is rooted in history or pop psychology is a moot point, but it is undeniable that the belief that the way to a man's heart is through his stomach has many adherents all over the world. The practice of eating out at restaurants, of ordering from takeaways, or eating packaged foods, may have eased the life of today's housewife, but it has also taken away a major source of satisfaction, of looking after the nutritional needs of those one loves.

In her book, *The Whole Woman*, feminist Germaine Greer decries the passing away of this gendered activity that has apparently left many women with a sense of loss.

> When the family was required to gather around the table, for meals at least once a day and snack foods were unknown, the food-provider was directly responsible for her family's quality of life. She could display both authority and skill and express her love for the family by the effort that she put into the dishes she brought to the table. That female role has now disappeared (Greer, 1999: 57).

In addition, in an era of increased outsourcing, many of the more interesting ceremonial jobs have moved from the housewife to the outside specialist. Where a marriage in the family would have meant the energies of all the women of the house would have been engaged for months, today, designers will take charge of the trousseau, the local beautician will offer an all-inclusive bridal package for the bride and her friends, caterers and event mangers will take care of the wedding. Even the traditional 'kohbar' or 'first night', takes place in a hotel with decorators taking charge of every last detail.

This not only makes the housewife miss out on what used to be a welcome break from the monotony of her day-to-day life, it also prevents her bonding with other women, both within and outside the family, that followed taking part in shared activities. In addition, there are now fewer avenues for the superior housewife to show off her skills. A woman who has an eye for the aesthetic and can do up her home attractively now has to compete with the professional interior designer. Similarly, a woman who has a talent for arranging flowers, for cooking, for stitching, or even making an intricate rangoli cannot now expect that her talents will get the recognition that they would have once got. All these women must now compete with professionals, and they must face the reality that all the knowledge, which was so lovingly acquired, can now be bought without too much trouble.

It doesn't matter if you can't tell a rose from a lotus or parsley from coriander, if you have money, you can get a caterer, a florist, an interior designer and no one will be the wiser. I think this has really reduced the importance of the superior hostess and homemaker. I think it's quite sad, really, and yes, sometimes it is a little worrying too. With my husband life is all about cruises to the Antarctic, wild life safaris in Africa. I try to do my bit by taking care of everything inside the house. I try to be the perfect housewife. But let's face it he has a lot more to offer a woman than I have to offer a man. especially at this stage of my life, so I would be a fool if I were smug or complacent about my position (forty-year-old Sita Narain, third wife of a Bangalore-based businessman who lives life in the fast lane).

Insecurity and inadequacy about doing her fair share may be one result of this option to 'outsource' skills and services only a skilled housewife could normally provide earlier. Another likely outcome is boredom. Without the involvement and the preparation required for big events, the housewife's job has been diminished. So there are fewer highs and lows in a housewives existence, just a never-ending series of small chores, which no one notices except when they are not done. All is not well on the home front. Instead of the full-time housewife being a relaxed, stress-free woman who enjoys the joys of domesticity, it appears that being at home is fairly taxing.

It is taxing because of the very nature of housework, which is both 'endless and thankless' to use a cliché, which many housewives employed, but also because of the underlying reason for this problem. If housewives are not given recognition or appreciation for many of the jobs they do, it is possible that the family is insensitive and boorish, which may sometimes be the case. But it is also possible that her husband and children really do not wish her to take on many of the tiring jobs she does take on. Why then does she feel compelled to do them?

One possible explanation could lie in what social scientists would call 'situated social power', says US-based family historian Stephanie Coontz in her book, *Coming to Terms with America's Changing Families*.

[What Social Science Tells Us About Male-Female Conflicts]. Following one of my talks, a couple stood up and described a conflict they were having in their marriage. She complained about how unappreciative he was of the effort she took in making gourmet dinners and keeping the house clean. He said: 'Hang on a minute. I never asked her to do any of those things. I can't help it if she has higher standards than I do. I don't *care* what we have for dinner. I don't *care* if the floor gets mopped twice a week.' They wanted me to comment on their situation.

The author analysed the problem thus:

Perhaps the problem we have here lies in what social scientists call your 'situated social power' . . . I reminded the couple that men have different options in our society, outside and independent of their personal relationships . . . A wife may feel, especially if she jeopardized her earning power by taking time off to raise children that she can't give up the domestic services she performs, because if her husband does get dissatisfied she has fewer options than he does in the work world, and will be far worse off after a divorce (Coontz, 1997: 18-20).

Consciously or not, the wife in this particular marriage seemed to be assessing the risk of not keeping a nice house or putting delicious meals on the table, and finding it too high to just relax and let the housework go. But she was also resenting her husband's unwillingness to help out. This very common pattern of seemingly voluntary sacrifice by the woman, followed by the the man's failure to reciprocate, originates outside the individual relationship. The man was probably completely sincere in not caring if the work got done, but he was missing the point. His wife had looked around, seen what happened to wives who failed to please their husbands and tried extra hard to make her husband happy. He could not understand her compulsion and resented being asked to participate in what he saw as unnecessary work. Counselling and better communication might help, but would probably not remove the kernel of fear in the wife's heart that stems from her perfectly reasonable assessment of the unequal social and economic options for men and women.

When it comes to domestic chores, I came across some families where it was customary for the women of the house to be saddled with all the kitchen work, something that the contemporary housewife resented. But I also met women, who clung on to doing fairly menial jobs, even when the family was eager that they be left to the domestic help. It was almost as if the women, intelligent, educated women, who had been confined to the home, by chance or by choice, now sought to validate their own decision by making themselves believe that somehow what they were doing in the home was of consequence. 'I have to dust the cabinet myself because the servants can never do it properly', or 'I always chop the potatoes for the bhujiya myself, as the servants do it very unevenly'. If the only person who shares her view is she herself, then frustration and resentment step in, sooner rather than later.

In addition, there is the whole problem of adjustment. Arranged marriages worked well when the home one married into was not too dissimilar to the home one grew up in. Today, many small-town women marry young men from similar family backgrounds, who happen to be working in MNCs or the new IT companies and find themselves quite unprepared for their world changing as much as it has. Postings to Europe, to Africa and south east Asia, a lifestyle that is far removed from what they are used to, engender a deep sense of alienation. It becomes easy to tune out, to blame the husband and even more specifically, the husband's family for the sense of inadequacy one experiences. And many women caught in such a situation, chose to strengthen their position by cutting the man off from his own family

Indeed, when I exhorted young mothers (and readers) to take responsibility for their own happiness rather than blaming their husbands or their families for their problems, because that really was the only positive action that was open to them, in a column 'The Tears and Joys Of Motherhood', in the magazine, *Young Mother* (1992), I was overwhelmed with responses from readers which seemed to suggest that I had indeed struck a chord!

Of course this is not to deny the reality of the many women who marry and discover that they have landed into homes where they face any number of problems ranging from being treated as glorified domestics, to actual spousal abuse. But problems of compatibility are not always related to ill treatment, they may just be pointers to the far greater complexity of our times.

Working women often imagine that while the work environment is dynamic, the housewife's environment is static. The truth is that the changing work environment profoundly affects the environment at home.

The Change in the Work Environment Affects the Home

My father's colleagues were my 'uncles'; our families did everything together. Movies at the club, potluck at each other's homes, we were really close knit. Now I hardly know my husband's colleagues, everyone works such long hours that we see each other a couple of times a year. It is really difficult to plan a dinner party because one never knows people's touring schedules, and let's face it, with today's competitive work environment, my husband discourages too much interaction with office colleagues. 'Why bring the heartburn home?' he says (a thirty-eight-year-old housewife, whose husband works in a public sector undertaking).

Army wives who had previously been 'army daughters' and wives of executives who work for MNCs who had grown up in such environments all reported significant differences between 'then' and 'now'. The way in which the importance of the workplace has risen, accompanied by a corresponding decline in the importance of the home and the community has led to new problems of loneliness and of self-esteem amongst stay-at-home wives and mothers.

The Skills Housewives Acquire

'Running a house is a complex task requiring high levels of managerial skills, if men did it, the domestic sphere would be invested with prestige and value', Germaine Greer points out in *The Whole Woman* (Greer, 1999: 62).

So, though many housewives go through a 'low period' because of a variety of reasons, at some time of their lives, there are plenty of success stories. Many housewives attempt to find something to do when the children are old enough to require less attention, and most are able to find some opportunity or another. A good housewife develops many skills, which could be useful in a number of jobs. She learns to budget, to manage time. She learns man-management and if she is a mother she may, in fact, become quite an expert in crisis management. She often becomes quite proficient in interior design and cooking. Some or all of these skills may prove useful when she is ready to step out of the house. I remember while living in Bangalore in the early 1990s seeing an advertisement for housekeeping staff for a five star hotel especially seeking wives of defence services officers over the age of forty! Even the trendier BPOs worried by the high attrition rates amongst the young are finding that older people, retired men and housewives are a better option.

So, though the jobs that a housewife may get when she is ready to re-enter the job force may be inferior in every way to the job and the position she would have held if she had devoted herself to her career, it is heartening for some women just to know that a second chance is possible. Some women choose to start their own venture and then they surprise themselves and their families with the success they make of it!

The real challenge for the housewife is to keep her self-confidence, and stay abreast with the world outside and her area of interest, through her years of confinement in the home. This is not to justify the argument for women staying in the home, but only to reassure women who have done so that there are indeed second chances.

As far as the work environment is concerned, the rise of contractual work and the increasing emphasis for knowledge and skills rather than appropriate years of service in an organized office are positive developments as far as housewives are concerned. However, the bias toward youth and against age is a formidable barrier, which she may not be able to overcome. Some women in the teaching profession told me that in the Union Territory of Delhi, while teachers may serve till the age of fifty-eight, a new teacher over the age of forty is not employed even though she may be trained and have experience. In some states, they said, women over the age of thirty-five may not train for the B.Ed course. If such rules exist, either overtly or covertly, it is truly unfortunate.

One never ceases to be a parent; a mother is a mother all her life. In some way she will never cease to feel connected to her children, to think, plan and hope for them, and to hurt for them when they are going through tough times. But in many ways, motherhood is now a part-time job. As Gail Sheehy had observed in her book *Passages,* over two decades ago, 'Motherhood is a phase' (Sheehy, 1976: 314). The middle-class housewife is likely to have no more than two children. The younger child is likely to be going to regular school while the mother is still only thirty-five. After this, the child's active need for her will begin to wane. And by the time the children are in their teens, they will get busy with their own lives and want less rather than more maternal supervision. What then does the housewife who has devoted her whole life to taking care of others do with herself and the rest of her life?

Sheehy discusses the either–or choice most women face: 'Either I put off any strenuous career efforts while I marry and start a family, in exchange for the dependable affection of a mate. Or I stick faithfully to outfitting myself for a career, postpone marriage and motherhood, and resign myself for the time being to scraps of attention. At some point most women feel required to choose either love or children or work and accomplishment' (ibid.: 311). Sheehy then goes on to ask that tantalizing question, 'If a man were presented with such a choice, would there be any husbands?' (ibid.: 312).

The Pressures Mothers of Special Children Face

I used to work in a BPO. I gave up my job when my son was diagnosed as autistic and mentally retarded. He goes to an integrated school. I go to my son's school everyday. I sit with him, as it is not possible for the teacher to accommodate his special needs and also teach the rest of the class. He is making slow progress, but every day is a new and difficult challenge (Anita Bewoor, forty-two, happily married to an executive with a major Indian group and mother of a special child).

The lack of awareness and of facilities for children with special needs makes the lives of mothers of such children a daily tryst with courage. Because of the transferable nature of many jobs, women like Anita cannot avail of family support. With globalization and the increasing pressure on her husband, Anita finds the pressure on her family has increased. 'Today, one has to show results every quarter, such great differences in pay and perks now happen with differences in performance. It is difficult for families such as ours, where the needs on the home front are also intense.' In an era of increasing job insecurity, families like the Bewoors, who are dependent on a single income, are uncomfortably aware of the total dependence on the husband's employer. This makes them unable to refuse transfers even to places where there are no facilities for their son.

Anita's husband, whose presence at home would provide welcome relief for his wife, feels considerable pressure to put in the long hours and do whatever it takes to strengthen his position at the workplace.

If Marriage is Your Only Security, What Happens When the Marriage Crumbles?

Sushmita is a Kolkata-based housewife. Thirty-six-year old Sushmita appears to be a fairly typical happy, harried housewife, coping with housework, a child and elderly parents who live in an adjacent flat. But Sushmita is also coping with the scars of an earlier marriage that ended in divorce some years ago. She is therefore now very conscious of how fragile the institution of marriage really is.

Sushmita had a love marriage at the age of twenty-three. Her husband was a marketing representative of a major multinational company and his job involved extensive travel. On one occasion, while her husband was away on tour, both her children, a son aged three-and-a-half and another aged four months fell ill. Sushmita telephoned her husband to hurry home as she was finding it difficult to handle both the children on her own. He promised to return in a few days. However, there was no sign of him for two weeks and a common friend broke the unpleasant news that her husband was having an affair with a woman he had met in Orissa and so she better get used to the idea that she had lost him. Sushmita's world crumbled in a second. In a bid to get her to leave, her husband started torturing her and withholding money. Though Sushmita had a degree in mass communication, she was forced to get whatever job she could. She worked as a sales girl in an exhibition to earn Rs 100 a day to look after her financial needs. 'I couldn't even afford cereal for my child!' she exclaims, describing her condition at that time.

Sushmita got help and advice from women's groups, foremost amongst whom she mentions Kolkata's Swayam. But though their support helped her cope with her situation, she was forced to give up custody of her older son to her husband, 'My son is asthmatic', she explains, 'and I didn't want to involve him in a bitter custody battle which would cause him too much stress and emotional trauma'. It is a decision that causes her much pain.

Today, Sushmita's first husband is married to the woman with whom he had the extra-marital affair and Sushmita is herself remarried to a 'man who is very sweet and kind' whom a friend introduced her to. But she says, 'after my experience, it is difficult for me to be completely at ease being financially dependent on a husband. Otherwise also, I would like to lighten my husband's financial burden, I would like to send my parents who are in their late sixties on a holiday, but I simply can't put that burden on my husband.'

Sushmita's story brings out the extreme vulnerability of the housewife and mother who effectively hands over her security, and indeed her very self, to her husband. If he betrays her, she must seek refuge with her parents, or brothers and sisters from her natal family. If she cannot do this, as Sushmita could not, she is forced to get a job far below what she may have got if she had not sacrificed her career for marriage.

Coping with Job Related Separation

Having to deal with terrorism on a day-to-day basis, putting your life on the line everyday, that's really what's hard. The problems and tensions I face are minor in comparison. One has to see things in perspective (an army wife, twenty-six, who is bringing up two young children on her own in family accommodations provided to officers who are stationed at the border).

Other women who have to cope with long separations are wives of merchant navy officers who often have to remain alone for the course of a voyage which could last for months, and wives of consultants who go abroad for assignments of about six to nine months duration, not long enough to allow for the family to be re-located and yet a very long time for a mother to manage the home and children on her own. Though all women find separations difficult, their responses are coloured by how they perceive the reasons for the separation. An army wife is most accepting, recognizing that it is an integral part of the job, other wives are more likely to assess how the family is likely to benefit from this, how fair the organization has been in dealing with the sacrifices asked for and the payoffs delivered.

An Overview of What Housewives Feel

Most of the women I spoke to had qualifications that equipped them for a job. However, they were at home because they were unable to achieve a satisfactory balance between work and home. Young children were the primary reason for a mother to content herself with being a housewife. 'A stay-at-home mother's children are safe, they need not fear anything from servants, they are well looked after', as a housewife from Bangalore states.

Are a full-time housewife's children better off than a working woman's children? This is the crucial issue that divides what could best be described as opposing camps. Full-time mothers believe that 'quality time' is a fancy concept dreamed up by those who are unable to accept that their children just do not get the love, attention and care that the full-time mother can give her child. A Kolkata-based housewife and mother of two, says 'I notice my ten-year-old son's friends will often come over at meal times, probably because there is no one at home to attend to their meals. They also like talking to me on the phone, something I never find my son doing with his friends' mothers, I think the children of working mothers just miss out on the full-time attention that the children of full-time homemakers get.' Amongst working mothers on the other hand, though some do believe that their children miss out on a mother's time and attention, many point out that the children of working mothers grow up to be more responsible and independent. Most interesting is the response of full-time mothers who were working women earlier. These women often claim that they actually did more for their children when they were working mothers. 'Even a full-time mother can't spend all her time with her children', is one response. 'Full-time mothers have a good time. I don't see them spending a great deal of time at home. Most of their time goes in shopping, seeing movies, having kitty parties etc.' Women appear to be grappling with some degree of internal conflict on this highly emotive issue. Mothers who have given up their jobs because of their children are reluctant to accept that they may have caused their childern irrevocable damage because of their working status. They believe that a full-time mother wants to validate her non-working status by attributing all the problems children of working mothers have, to their mother's employment status, when they may be completely unrelated to whether the mother is working or not.

Predictably, the long working hours the husbands worked, along with the lack of control over their time, is a major irritant for housewives. Sruty Ghosh, who is married to a professional photographer who has to work to the schedules decided by advertising agencies says, 'My husband will often come back close to midnight and then want to play with the children. They may finally sleep at around 2 a.m. which means that they may not be able to get to school the next day.' Perhaps because a photographer's profession does not require one to be highly qualified academically, her husband is comfortable with this, but it upsets Sruty greatly.

Many housewives believe that in today's competitive society, the father's help is needed to help the child cope, especially when it comes to academic performance. Others find disciplining a child in today's complex society difficult to handle single-handedly. Most are agreed that long hours are harmful for the health of both the partners, as stress levels go up as husbands are unable to meet commitments at home and wives fret waiting endlessly for men who just can't keep to time.

A few wives, however, are not angry with their husbands but feel a deep sense of regret that their husbands are missing out on what is, after all, a fairly brief period and a precious time of life, their children's childhood.

Not Having a Life of Her Own

'It seems to be that everyone else has a life but the housewife', was a common complaint. 'I have to schedule every activity keeping in mind the children's school timings, my husband's office timings, the part-time maid's timings. I'm constantly watching the clock and yet every little chore is given to me, because I'm the only one who is supposed to be having time on her hands!' says more than one housewife wryly.

Lack of Spending Money

Even the most traditional housewife I spoke to was acutely conscious of the total financial dependence on others. Women who had been financially independent till they had to give up their jobs were obviously most irked by this. Neera, a housewife who was earlier a working woman, says, 'My entire spending behaviour has changed. Earlier, when I went shopping, I would pick up a tablecloth for the house, a book for my daughter, a shirt for my husband, or even a piece of jewellery for myself without thinking. Now, it's as if my purse strings have been knotted twice over. I won't buy anything unless it's absolutely necessary. I wait for sales. My husband makes fun of my anxiety but even though I know he earns well, the loss of the second income has had a huge impact both financially as well as psychologically.'

What most galls women is 'Buying a present for my husband with his own money! It just makes me feel ridiculous.' The lack of a personal income also affects the way a woman feels about buying a gift for her parents, or just providing them financial support.

After talking to scores of housewives, it is clear that this is a role that most are playing because of circumstance and not because of choice. Caring for young children and moving with husbands in transferable jobs were the most common reasons why housewives were unemployed outside the home. Also, in a country with so many qualified people available for virtually every job, a career break often makes it impossible for the woman to re-enter the job market. In a later chapter on the workplace, there is research to show that the home is, in fact, an excellent training ground for managerial skills and innovative thinking.

When the workplace becomes more flexible, perhaps the options for women, who are today full-time housewives, to resume their careers, may improve.

4

Working Women: Superwomen or Overworked Drudges?

This chapter has been both the easiest and the most difficult chapter of all. Since it is women's entry into the workforce that has really brought the problems of work–family balance into focus, the interviews and the findings of this chapter are crucial to the book. Indeed, since they are part of the study I did supported by the Dorabji Tata Trust before I started the book, I already had this chapter written out in my head, when the rest of the book had still to be worked out. However, as the predicament of the working woman receives continual media attention today, there is the possibility of reader fatigue. Many problems are well known. However, as virtually nothing has been done to address these problems, I feel they could do with reiteration. Finally, though I am a journalist who has been writing about these issues for over two decades, I was moved by the stories the women interviewed had to tell. Even as I 'knew' the problems, I was quite unaware of the magnitude of the challenges so many working women have to contend with every day of their lives.

Why should educated women going to work cause quite so much social upheaval?

The answer is quite simple. Though, 'buy one, get one free', seems a recent marketing gimmick, organizations have, quite unconsciously perhaps, always been guided by it. In many ways, the workplace remains unchanged from the time when an organization presumed that when it hired a man it also had a right to the services of his wife, who would take care of the man's home, his children, his elderly parents and indeed all the personal requirements of the man himself! In short, for the organization to run smoothly, a man needed a wife. What happened when the wife was the one who joined the organization?

In her autobiography, *Living History*, Hillary Rodham Clinton points out how when she stated her desire to be a trial lawyer she was told that this was an impossibility because she did not have a wife. And 'without a wife to take care of all my personal needs, I would never be able to manage the demands of everyday life like making sure I had clean socks for court' (Clinton, 2003: 89).

Therefore, though so much has changed, the unchanging nature of the workplace creates a real dichotomy between women's potential and their performance. At the country's premier academic institutes, women apply in large numbers. And the admission lists show feminine names, often at the very top. In a country that has terrible crimes against women, such as female infanticide and dowry deaths, it is also true that some women face virtually no discrimination in their growing years. In many middle-class homes, both daughters and sons are given the same education and are encouraged to compete and excel in what appears to be an equal world. At both school and college levels, girls often do better academically than boys. And in an environment in which merit is the main criterion for employment, it is not surprising that girls go out and get high-powered jobs in virtually every field. The dual-career family is, therefore, now a contemporary reality.

Indeed, in some ways, it was and is actually easier for a woman to make it to the top in India than it is in the West.

How world-enlarging it was when we used the law to make newspapers stop advertising all the good jobs 'Help Wanted Male,' and the saleswomen, clerk, waitress, and cleaner jobs 'Help Wanted Female' (Friedan, 1963: 6).

While a sizeable number of Indian women worked as secretaries and waitresses, this was not a battle the middle-class woman had to fight. The role women played in the nationalist struggle, the emergence in the public consciousness of women like Sarojini Naidu, Lakshmi Sehgal and Vijaylakshmi Pandit, at par with the leaders of the freedom movement, gave at least some sections of Indian women an unqualified advantage. Upper-middle-class women were never seen as secretaries, for instance, and there is little resistance to accepting women as doctors, engineers, scientists, journalists, creative directors or even managing directors. However, in a way, even as women in our country were accepted in the workplace no allowance was made for the other roles they played. There are few organizations that have any childcare facilities for the children of their executives, or offer any flexibility with regard to working conditions. In an environment where caring for children and the elderly and taking care of the home is seen as primarily the woman's responsibility, we are yet to reconcile how these are to be managed, if women are to exercise their right to employment in the same way as men can and do.

The availability of special facilities for 'carers' either in the way of child care facilities, or in the form of special privileges for nursing mothers, or a parent who seeks some sort of flexibility to manage responsibilities at home, seems to be an indication of the bias towards women. Human resources (HR) managers of many companies believe that they would be criticized if they put nursing mothers on the night shift, for instance. And yet, if this is not done, they fear that the organization effectively becomes unfair to men.

Somehow, we are yet to acknowledge that the care of children and the elderly, or even the infirm and the sick is a woman's responsibility only because so far she has undertaken to fulfil it. Apart from the biological task of carrying a baby in her womb and then perhaps for breast-feeding an infant for some months thereafter, there is little a woman does as a 'carer' or nurturer which a man could not do equally well.

But so far, women have internalized a patriarchal society's definition of their role and responsibilities, even as they have gone on to seek their place at the workplace. So, on the one hand, we have organizations aggressively hiring women and on the other, we see women giving up their jobs to take care of their other responsibilities. They do so not because they wish to do so but because they feel that they have no choice. Just to report at work the regulation five or six days a week, can challenge all a young couple's resources. And since the woman still does take primary responsibility for the home, it is she who really bears the brunt of the sometimes terrible conflict that is generated by the dual responsibility between the commitments at the workplace and the demands of the home. The response of corporate India to the woman employee is almost schizophrenic. It mirrors the woman's own confused response to what she sees as her 'role', and her duty.

When one takes a closer look at the lives of working professionals and their equations with their children, their spouses and their parents-in-law, one can see that ancient stereotypes are trying to reconcile with modern realities. So even as women enter the workplace, they are not willing to break the barriers that impede their progress to the top.

In a survey of 500 working women in metropolitan cities, M. Krishna Raj comments, 'Indian working women share the general reluctance observed in earlier studies to take commensurate risks for the prospect of advancement.'

Of course, choices are always made in a context. So perhaps it is not fair to say that women are reluctant to take risks for the sake of advancement, they may simply not see an alternative In all these studies, 'the blame is laid squarely on the door of the employed women. There is no hint, let alone analysis of the structured condition that is responsible for this response . . . A woman cannot repudiate commitment to the family, nor would the family accept her repudiation'(M. Krishna Raj, quoted in Chanana 1996: 105).

Sociological research supports anecdotal accounts that a working woman has to constantly balance how much she can afford to give to her job, against what she and others feel she must give to her home and family. A woman must deliberate over and take a decision about things as minor as providing clean socks for her husband and more major ones such as whether to send a child to a boarding school or not, or whether to accept a promotion if it should involve relocating.

I found the household revolved around my needs . . . this was a new experience for me. In my earlier homes my needs had always been considered last. The man of the house, whatever his job, was treated in a special manner . . . On the other hand, I as a working woman was treated differently. The servants thought nothing of disturbing me for every domestic enquiry and problem. The children felt they could walk into my office at home and complain about some triviality even if I was in the middle of a judgement (Leila Seth [2003: 334] on her stint as chief justice of Shimla, where she lived alone).

It is, of course, undeniable that women themselves also accept and perpetuate this state of affairs. Most of the women interviewed, for instance, seem to be trying to be super-achievers in every sphere. They do not want to ask for concessions at the workplace; they want to do as much or more than full-time mothers when it comes to childcare.

> Men rarely helped with the housework. In our sample, men helped to wash the clothes or look after the children in only 3 per cent of the families. Moreover, it was not just the men but also the women who perpetuated gender-role stereotypes: 'It does not look nice if men work in the house'. Another woman pointed out, 'Men doing housework seems very odd, I will not ask my husband to help.' At that time, it was impossible for some women to even visualize that men should do the housework: 'I cannot see my husband working in the house when I am well. I would rather die' (Vijay Rukmini Rao and Sahba Husain, 1986: 175).

Though I did not find such extreme reactions, many women reported with some pride that 'in the house I behave like a housewife'. Listening to women, even middle-class women showed that there was a great deal of diversity in individual experiences. Most women believe that their position as working women has definitely helped their status within the family, and in society at large. However, others would talk of 'friends' who actually had to hand over their pay packets to their husbands and indeed behave in a fairly subservient position within the house. Research on the subject only re-affirms this.

> Urban middle class women have broken out of the status trap unlike the high status rural women. They have jobs that give them a regular income and social esteem (Srinivas, quoted in Chanana, 1996: 15).

This does not have universal acceptance. Neera Desai contests this view. She believes that the entry into and withdrawal from the labour market of white-collar workers is not their own decision but is determined by their socio-economic position and familial obligations. 'The familial role continues to get pre-eminence over the work role in spite of changes in her social role due to increased education and employment' (Srinivas, quoted in Chanana 1996: 15). While economic independence does not empower all women equally, it does give many more options than they would otherwise have had.

Everyone Needs a Wife!

Even women who marry into families that are supportive of their needs and ambitions view their rights and responsibilities differently from men. It is not surprising then, that marriage affects the career prospects of men and women very differently. While married men tend to be more successful at the workplace than unmarried men, the reverse is true with regard to women. Studies of successful professionals frequently show that high-achieving men are married whereas high-achieving women tend to be unmarried (see Herman and Gyllstrom, 1977; Houseknecht et al., 1987) suggesting that occupational attainment may be more difficult for a woman if she is married than if she is unmarried

Few men would acknowledge this and indeed not many might even be aware that this could be so, but a good wife can be a powerful career resource. Research in the West has actually identified four major contributions:

Direct substitution of the work of a paid employee, indirect support including entertaining, consultation and advice giving, and emotional support, which keeps the husband motivated and interested in his work. Kanter (1977) found evidence of all four types of contributions in her study of wives of corporate managers.

Predictably then, a supportive stay-at-home husband is also seen to be most useful in promoting the career of a working woman. In a survey of fifty working women on *Fortune* magazine's 'Most Powerful Women in Business' (2003), more than one-third had husbands at home either full-time or part-time. The conclusion that was drawn was that 'All workers need wives!'

It is interesting that even in Sweden, which has perhaps the most extensive welfare policy initiatives in the world for childcare, we are far from having an equal playing field with regard to a woman's ability to work and also have a family life. So though social policy reforms such as expansion of daycare facilities for children, parental leaves and measures such as family allowances, which have evolved into family insurance, have seen the percentage of women in the workforce rise from 54 per cent to 80 per cent and reach the figure of 85 per cent in 1989, the percentage of women in senior positions remains low (Kristindottir).

Over the years, though the pace has been slow, there has been an attitudinal change in Swedish society. 'A recent wave of resistance is occurring among Swedish women. The cries and frustration caused by slow progress towards equality has led, for instance, to the idea of a Women's party' (ibid.)

In my research too, I found a definite change of attitude and priorities amongst some of the younger career women who thought in terms of a career rather than just a job and were clearly giving their career the highest priority in their lives. Of course, the experience of some of the older women I spoke to did suggest that many working mothers who start giving their careers top priority redefine their priorities when their children reach the age of about eight. For at this time, many children appear to become resentful, or seem to develop health or behavioural problems.

For these interviews I spoke to women from many different communities who were located in the metropolitan cities. However, their caste or community did not make much difference to their situation. It is class, as defined not just by income but also a certain level of education and lifestyle that seemed to have much more of an impact in determining attitudes. Less was expected from women from more affluent families, not only because they were more likely to have domestic help, but also because their husbands were more likely to help with housework and the children, and there were fewer expectations from the parents-in-law that the daughter-in-law would come back from work to enter the kitchen. Women who carried home smaller pay packets did this unquestioningly.

Most Women Take a Positive View of Their Situation

But at this point of time, whatever course of action women opt for, they will have to make an extraordinary effort to make it work. Most women acknowledge that they do more at home than their husbands do, they are usually the ones to make the sacrifices on the career front as well, and yet, most are not really unhappy with their lot. As Nirmala Ravindran, a journalist from Bangalore who is single, states with some exasperation, 'All my married friends are in very unequal relationships but they will insist that they are in very equal partnerships.'

Indeed, almost all the single women interviewed believed that the contemporary Indian male was still very insecure about his status and held outdated notions of gendered roles. Most married women were far more generous in their assessment of their husbands. 'In our home, housework is shared', 'my husband is even more thrilled about my success than I am', 'I know friends who have your typical Indian husband, but it's not like that in our home', were fairly common responses. Less typically, some women confided that it was still a very unequal world and so assessments were to be viewed in the context of our times. Indeed, it becomes clear that it is a male-dominated world and so this reaction would be true anywhere in the world.

In a Swedish study, Wahl sees it as typical for women in male-dominated occupations to be positive about their situation. 'To stress the individual advantages for women in a male-dominated environment was much more common.' It was common for these women to describe career by descriptions of general life goals . . . to get all the pieces together in the life situation was seen as a prime goal. Promotion was rejected if it was impossible to combine with family life, for instance, the women often underlined the importance of adapting career to caring for children, not vice versa'(Wahl, quoted in Kristindottir). Perhaps this is what makes so many women adjust their hours of work to fit into their children's schedules, take on responsibility for the housework and yet feel that they are living life on their own terms.

If one wants to analyse the impact of work on family life in dual-career families, one comes across a host of very interesting contradictions. Research shows, for instance, that married women tend to be happier than unmarried women. But marriage tends to put a cap on their progress at the workplace. However, for entirely predictable reasons, married men tend to do better than single men; their wives actually play an important role in helping them achieve their potential. Men with wives in senior managerial positions earn less than men with wives in less important jobs, presumably because they have to balance their own demands at the workplace with perhaps conflicting demands of their wives' careers.

What is interesting is that not just in India, but even in the developed world, women seem to accept the many inequities they face in trying to balance work and family life, as compared to men. 'We have seen that even women in careered occupations put their family and their husband's careers first and their own careers second' (Kristindottir). According to research in Europe, and as confirmed by my own research, married women in dual-career families do not see themselves as victims, but have an alternate view of life. In fact, in most cases, these women see themselves as very successful, realizing exactly how well they have managed to balance the conflicting demands of the home and workplace so that they could have both.

In my study for the Dorabji Tata Trust in 2002, I did find evidence of a new breed of young women who put far greater stress on their careers. Perhaps when more such women enter the workplace, both the family and the workplace may finally see faster and more fundamental changes.

If one takes a long-term view, one could argue that in the future things should be easier for women. As jobs move from the manufacturing sector to the services sector, and as the nature of employment shifts from careers where one works one's way through a layered hierarchy to a more contractual approach where knowledge will be valued over both length of service or 'face time' (time spent at the office), working from home and also taking leave for varying lengths of time will no longer be of great import. In the meantime, however, we can see that change will come only when it is forced upon society. Recent demographic surveys in Europe show that birth rates in many countries are dipping quite swiftly as a new generation of women choose not to become mothers. The lead story 'The Great Baby Shortage' by Richard Girling in the *London Sunday Times* (Girling, 2004), points out the serious implications for those countries. With the population growing most rapidly in the over-eighties age group, and most slowly in the under-sixteen age group, in the future there will not be enough young people to pay the taxes that sustain pensions and other expenses that societies incur. People may have to work till the age of seventy-five and governments may have to relax controls on immigration. Countries where birth rates are falling below replacement level can find possible solutions to this problem in following the French example where larger families receive tax incentives. Another suggestion is for the introduction of a more flexible work week, so that work and family life can be better balanced.

In our own country, a falling birth rate may seem to be a very attractive proposition at this point of time. Indeed, Europe's problem may also offer us an opportunity in terms of easier immigration in the future, and yet, there is a lesson to be learned from that experience which we would be foolish to ignore. Birth rates are falling not just in the Western world but also in the highly developed far eastern countries such as Japan and Singapore. We need to address the predicament of this generation of men and women with both urgency and imagination.

Since combining work and family life proves to be so problematic many working women choose to remain single. What are the challenges they face? Is it difficult being a woman in a male-dominated workplace? Is it easier for single women to cope with long working hours? Do they face problems that married women do not?

The Effect of Work on the Family Life of Single Working Professionals

If looking after a husband and children are the factors that disadvantage women at the workplace, is life for single women free from conflict? What is the experience of single working women?

> Oh, yes, it's easier because though you retain responsibility for your parents, you don't have the responsibility of children. You have to put a lot into bringing up children (fifty-year-old Kamla Sinha, a single woman, working in a senior position with the government in Delhi).

Other single women agree that life is easier for them in some respects. 'I have only to bother about keeping me happy', says a Mumbai-based hotel executive. 'I'm not answerable to a husband and children', says a thirty-plus Kolkata-based ad professional.

However, many single women take on responsibility for family members, mostly elderly parents. The ad professional took care of her mother who died of cancer. Kamla took responsibility for her father who died not long ago. She also took four months off to be with her sister who lost a young child in tragic circumstances.

Most of the single women I spoke to did not feel that the organizations they worked for were less sympathetic to them because they were not married, and accepted that adult offspring, even if they were single, had to deal with family responsibilities. They were grateful that their needs as single people had been recognized and addressed by the organizations they worked for.

Interestingly, all the single working women interviewed believed that it was legitimate for working mothers to get special consideration at the workplace.

The Single Working Woman and the Work Environment

Is it awkward for single women to be in a work environment where most people are married and men outnumber women manifold? This is not seen to be a problem. Organizations deal with women employees in different ways. Some organizations have a benevolent, paternal attitude; this is often the case with public sector units and other government companies. However, as this is perhaps only a reflection of a bias that a woman deals with in her personal life also, she does not resent it as much as she might have done.

Kamla, for instance, is quite happy saying that in her organization, the environment is protective of women rather than exploitative. Could this have an adverse impact on her career? Kamla acknowledges that this is likely. For instance, she believes that it could be more difficult for a woman to find a mentor in male-dominated organizations because for a man and woman to meet after office hours is often misunderstood in our society. Kamla has a male mentor and when they were both located in Mumbai they often met at each other's homes. Kamla shares a very cordial relationship with her mentor's wife. Kamla has now moved to Delhi and when her mentor came to Delhi on tour, Kamla asked him over to dinner. He declined. 'Let's wait till she [his wife] comes on a trip', he said. Kamla believes this kind of feeling not only hinders women from advancing in their careers in the same way that men can, but also could lead to problems in their family life.

In fields such as advertising, journalism, or the hospitality industry, which have a high proportion of women, this was not an issue. Women in professions with a higher female ratio do not find themselves disadvantaged and believe a single woman is quite comfortable in today's environment. So though there is a fair amount of media reportage on how single women find it difficult to eat at restaurants alone, or even go to movies by themselves, the women I spoke to did not seem to face any difficulty in doing so. One woman remarked that while the streets were undoubtedly unsafe for unaccompanied women at night, if you had your own transport, living alone in a hotel, or frequenting a restaurant was not a problem at all. Indeed, as some hotel chains now have separate rooms for women guests with special facilities, the single woman often feels not just safe, but pampered too!

The Impact of Long Working Hours on the Childfree Woman

Women without children were once called childless; the politically-correct term is now childfree, but whatever the terminology, what is life like for such women? Are long working hours an issue for women who do not have to contend with a child's needs? How do they see their situation?

I would say the long working hours were perhaps 70 per cent of the reason why I got divorced. I kept long hours, my husband had long hours, and we slowly grew apart. Now in a new relationship, I make it a point to rush home as soon as I can (Maya Joshi, forty, a Bangalore-based manager of a call centre).

Most women believe that long working hours adversely affect a marital relationship. In more traditional families, women still see a wife's role in a fairly stereotypical way. Time was when men worked and came home after a 'long, hard day', to a wife who had changed into a fresh sari to welcome her husband home. Today, even as the woman is sharing the long, hard day at the workplace, some are actually regretful of their fatigue.

'*Hum to ghar ate ate, murjha jate hain*, (we are exhausted by the time we return home) *admi ko bhi accha lage agar wife fresh hoti* (the husband would like it if the wife was fresh)'. This is an extreme viewpoint and most working women are not likely to view the situation in quite this way, but at some level, women do find that the dual-career situation often gives rise to unanticipated tensions, as they discover with the passage of time that the suave men they have married turn out to have very retrograde mindsets.

As a journalist I often returned by 11 p.m. My husband would have switched off the lights and got into bed by the time I returned home. I used to feel very guilty about it. But later I was angered by his attitude because he also refused to let me keep a domestic help in the house, or to allow me to buy a gadget like the microwave. So, after I returned I could choose between eating cold food, or heating it up myself (Bratati, thirty, a Kolkata-based journalist).

Even women with supportive husbands said that long working hours were a major stress point. 'My husband doesn't expect me to take care of his needs, but he does wish I would learn to switch off', says a sales executive who is married to a man who is 'definitely not an MCP'. But since it is still a very unfair world, when it is the wife who works longer hours, the prognosis for the marriage is far worse than when it is the other way around.

Married women without children also experience the feeling of being pulled in different directions with regard to housekeeping responsibilities and career demands. Women who wish to have high standards on both fronts are the ones who face the most stress.

Those who need to socialize for the sake of their careers and are married to men whose jobs require heavy social commitment face even greater conflict. This is especially so since a husband's absence from a wife's social function may be acceptable, but the reverse is not the case! A wife who is unable or unwilling to accompany her husband to functions, or play hostess to functions he is hosting is still likely to face flak. She is definitely not in the running for the 'best wife' award as far as her husband's organization is concerned!

DINKS

The double-income-no-kids (DINK) syndrome is sometimes a decision that is consciously taken. Some people so enjoy their independence and the increased purchasing power the DINK status gives them, they do not want to become parents. Others simply do not enjoy children and therefore have no wish to become parents, but many couples are just unable to work a baby into their schedules. As the present demands all the person's time and energy, there may be nothing left for what is important but not immediate. This may well be the biggest fallout of a punishing work schedule.

I may never get around to having children and that is something I may always regret' (Kiran Uttam Ghosh, thirty-six, fashion designer).

Why Some People Choose to Work Long Hours

Sometimes the job demands long hours. At other times, people wish to work long hours to establish their commitment and gain points in an increasingly competitive workplace. But often, those who are seen at the workplace after office hours are there for quite a different reason. They are there because it is here that they socialize as they have few friends or interests outside the workplace.

My workplace is my second 'sansar', it's my family, I feel very possessive about my work and also my long working hours. I like being around the people at work. My work is very people-centric. I talk continuously. I socialize. My work style is such, I work for a couple of hours, then go down for a smoke, take a break, then come back for an hour or two (Bratati, the journalist, who is now divorced).

Such behaviour sets off a vicious cycle. The more time a women spends at the workplace, the more diminished her personal relationships will become, making it likely that she will be even less keen to leave the office.

However, such behaviour is still not the norm. As of now, most women do feel that long working hours are a major problem and many admitted to opting for less important jobs because these were more compatible with their need to look after the home. But one can see a new breed of women for whom this is not a major issue. These younger women are much more akin to men in the way that they measure the gains likely to accrue from the workplace against the effort and commitment demanded.

The Working Mother

'The hand that rocks the cradle rules the world', went the old cliché. It is undeniable of course. Bringing up a child gives every individual a chance at immortality, a chance to influence a new generation, a chance, if you wish, of leaving your own imprint on the world for all time to come. A child also ties up his or her parents in the most elemental way of all through its helplessness and need. Since, traditionally, it was the mother who had primary responsibility of the child; it is she who feels most responsible for it no matter what her position, pay, or perks at the workplace may be.

Being a full-time housewife and mother is, however, not an attractive or perhaps even a viable option for the educated, middle-class woman. As stated earlier, the increasing demands of the workplace have whittled down the importance of family as also community life, and the increasing fragility of marriage as an institution makes a full-time housewife's dependence on her husband's goodwill and good health a gamble few women would choose to take if they can avoid it. So meet the working mother. She is trying to be Superwoman. And Superman could definitely learn a trick or two from her when it comes to managing conflicting pulls and counter pulls.

The Working Mother is an Expert Juggler

Even women who come from supportive families have to be extremely adroit in juggling their many responsibilities. In a way, it is interesting that when you enter the offices of these women they appear to be indistinguishable from other employees. But when you take a look behind the scenes it is clear that while for the duration of the work day they are your regular office workers, that is where the similarity ends. When many of these women go home, they inhabit quite a different world.

> When the baby was born, my cousins helped look after her. Then my husband's cousins helped out. My mother came and stayed for four or five months. I coped like this till the baby was one-and-a half-year-old. After that, I kept a maid to look after the child. Whenever I had a problem with the maid, or if she left, I would go to my mother's home in Rajamundhry (a thirty-seven-hour journey by train) and

drop my child there. I would come and collect my child when I was able to organize a new maid. I sometimes made these journeys more than once in the course of one week. We (my husband and I) had a terrible time. This may be one reason why we did not have another child (thirty-five-year-old Lepakshi, who works with a public sector company).

Lepakshi's story highlights how a woman who lives in a nuclear family attempts to manage her dual roles as career woman and mother. First, like so many other women, she called upon every female relative available to help. When that help ran out, she was forced to travel half way across the country to her mother to ask her to help out. The problems are still there, but less acute as the child is now able to manage better on her own.

Was there perhaps an easier, better way to handle the situation. Would Lepakshi have been better off if she had perhaps left her child with her parents or parents-in-law, so that she could grow up in a secure environment? Sheetal's story shows how that may work out.

We are probably missing out on the best part of her growing years, I think we should have chosen to be together. No matter what the difficulties would have been, we should have chosen to be together. Somehow we would have managed (forty-year-old Sheetal, who works with a corporate office).

Sheetal's husband is posted abroad and since Sheetal is in a transferable job, the couple decided that the child was better off with her grandparents. However, it is an arrangement where the child misses her parents. 'She used to ask me, "Why do you have to work?" Now, she is older, she asks, "Why can't you work here?"' And, of course, it is an arrangement where the parents miss their child.

So perhaps the answer could have been for Sheetal to rely on her own resources. Was there no neighbourhood crèche she could have made use of? The next narrative is of a woman who did just that.

When your child is at a crèche, you have to take out a lot of time to drop and pick up your child from there. I had to leave home at about 8.30 a.m. and my daughter was often sleeping when I left her at the crèche. If you forget to pack something with your child in the morning, if say the lunch box is forgotten, the crèche will not help out. Then, the crèche is pretty inflexible about when you must pick up the child in the evening. So when you're working late at the office your stomach becomes a tight knot wondering whether you will be able to make it on time (Surekha, thirty-eight, an artist who works with a publishing house in Mumbai).

Clearly, we need many more crèches in India and a lot of improvement in the way in which they are managed before they become an attractive option for a working mother.

If finances are not a constraint would the best arrangement then be for couples to hire good domestic help and have the child looked after at home?

It was my neighbour's blind mother who made me realize there was a problem. She told me, 'the baby is not making

the sounds he used to. He has become completely quiet'
(Mita Saran, a forty-year-old Delhi-based executive and
mother of a nine-month-old baby).

Mita had hired two full-time maids, one whose only
job was to take care of the child. In addition, she had
asked the neighbours to keep an eye on the child, while
she herself would go home at lunchtime to check on the
child. Alerted by the neighbour, Mita began to make
unscheduled visits to the house and on one such visit
she found the maid beating the child quite harshly.
Shaken by the experience, Mita sought a transfer to
the city where her parents-in-law lived so that her
mother-in-law could look after the child while she
worked with an easy mind.

As we see from the stories of these women, almost no
course of action seems to be really satisfactory while
the workplace itself does not change. Lepakshi tried to
manage with the help of any relative who was willing
to pitch in and often had to travel across the country to
her mother's home so that her child could be taken care
of. Sheetal left her child with her parents in far away
Bhopal. It is a 'solution' that pains her and her husband
as also the young child. Surekha, the artist, leaves her
child in a crèche, which she finds far from satisfactory.
Mita turned down opportunities for advancement in
order to balance the demands of the workplace and the
requirements of home. Her experience reflects the
experience of many working women before her who
found, that 'Keeping a low profile in one's own career
enables the woman to be in both the worlds of work
and the family' (Chanana, 1996). The situation seems

to have changed little since Kala Rani and Krishna Raj (in Chanana 1996:105-6) and Ross in her study (1961) of businesswomen found that 'women tend to avoid taking up top-level business positions as their positions conflict with a women's role as a wife, mother and manager of the household' (see Chanana, 1996).

For many women the primary challenge seems to be to stay the course. Sometimes there is a financial need, which makes the wife's income essential to maintain the family's current standard of living. Or there may be a psychological need to work. Not every woman has the patience to spend day after day closeted with a small child. Some women who are used to an office go into depression when they have to stay at home. Then, many women are fortunate to have family support. Others chance upon reliable domestic help. Some children adapt to a working mother better than others do. But for the most part, in dual-career families, where the wife also works in a demanding corporate job, it is clear that behind the seemingly smooth facade of an office where the employees report at the dot of time, work all hours, travel over weekends and generally behave as if the only thing in their lives was the workplace, there must be a far harsher reality. What organizations really have are two employees who must be extremely tense and distracted for much of their time as they juggle timings and commitments to balance work and family life. Since the woman bears the primary responsibility for the family in our current social set-up, there must undoubtedly be a negative impact on her life, but there must also be an impact on the lives of the men and also the children who are part of the family.

Not only is there little time to attend to household and other chores, there is also less time for social functions and community activities. In extreme cases, this work-overload results in health problems for the entire family.

> There was just no time for anybody. My husband and I both wanted to be there for the child, so we would take leave separately, the result was that we would get very little time together. As I became more senior, I was not even able to take her calls at office, as I would always be at meetings. My daughter developed migraines and asthma, I put on weight, began losing hair, developed a thyroid problem. My husband and I had to constantly juggle our travel schedules. One day I decided it was just not worth it (Neera, a thirty-eight-year-old senior executive who recently quit her job to be a full-time mother to her ten-year-old daughter).

Neera, an alumnus of a premier management institute, is a pioneer of sorts, as she was the first woman to join her organization, a major agro-based MNC. Neera rose rapidly up the corporate ladder and soon was drawing substantial pay and perks. But Neera believes corporate India is still very unenlightened when it comes to work–family balance.

Corporate India Insensitive to an Individual's Personal Needs

Neera recalls with some bitterness how casual companies can be about an individual's other commitments. 'You were asked to go to Bangalore, then suddenly, the MD wants to continue the discussion and he's going on to Mumbai, so you're expected to go on to Mumbai too. You would be called in on a Saturday or Sunday without any warning. They'll call you on the mobile just as you're sitting down to a meal. There is just no respect for anything else a person may have to do.'

The Different Ways in which a Working Mother and a Working Father Handle their Responsibilities

Neera goes on to describe how differently working men and working women behave when they are at home.

> It's like this, when I came home, I used to get busy trying to get a grip on what's going on in the house, I would check the child's homework. My husband would settle down with the financial papers, or read a book to keep abreast with the latest trends in management. Not that he wouldn't lend a hand if there was no help or there was a crisis, but men and women, we do see our responsibilities differently. Even now. It's just the way it is.

Perhaps this accounts for the very different way in which marriage affects the career prospects of men and women. And may explain the study quoted earlier which cites how the homemaker wives of senior corporate managers help their careers.

In a retrospective study, Stewart found that those women who had children were less persistent in their career pursuits (for Stewart see Cooper and Payne, 1988). There is also evidence that a wife's post-marital educational gains show little relation to subsequent occupational attainment (Sharda and Nangle, 1982, quoted in Cooper and Payne, 1988).

For women like Neera, the choices are as difficult today as they have been in the past, and for them to expect to reach the positions they would otherwise be qualified for will demand unusual drive and dedication.

Not surprisingly, in families where the husband's income is substantial enough to make a second salary not absolutely imperative for survival, the couple chooses to opt out of the many complications that follow a dual-career family.

Is it the Tape Recorder Inside One's Head or is it Biology?

The Need to be the Primary Person in One's Child's Life

> I can't be there for my children when they are having their meals. It makes so much difference to a child's health if his mother is there. But for the children of us working women, the ayah becomes the mother (Caroline Denseappa, a middle-level police officer, happily married and a mother of two).

Though she may be a woman in uniform, at some level Caroline is a deeply traditional mother. She yearns to do all the things her own mother did for her. 'We working mothers wish to take care of things, working fathers don't wish to', she says. There are many women like Caroline. It bothers them that even though the child is well looked after it is not they who are being able to do the looking after.

Some mothers are more pragmatic. They appreciate that nobody can have it all, and accept the fact that somebody else may be the primary person in their child's life as a necessary trade off for being a career woman. But most working mothers resent the lack of concern the organization has for a woman's need to fulfil her maternal responsibilities, even as she discharges her duty at the office. They believe male colleagues rate women officers who tend to leave the workplace as soon as office timings are over as lacking in commitment, not factoring in the pull mothers feel towards their children, nor the need of the child for the mother.

How Children React to a Working Mother

More than mothers-in-law, more than husbands, it is young children who resent a young mother's preoccupation with her job.

> My younger son, who is twelve will sometimes scream, all the other children have mothers who help with school work, who bake cakes, you are a hopeless mother (Mita, forty-three, mother of two boys).

Some children learn fairly early that they can exploit the guilt the working mother experiences as she struggles to fulfil her often conflicting responsibilities.

> My seven-year-old will ring my office at 2.30 in the afternoon and say, if you come back now, I will study. But I won't study if you come back late in the evening. I worry that because of the guilt we experience because we have to

leave my daughter alone for so long we indulge her. If she opens her mouth to ask for a toy, we buy it for her (Surekha, an artist with a publication house).

Other children do not indulge in emotional blackmail. But they manage to make the mother feel even worse as they try to fashion solutions to complex problems in their own childish way.

'You also get married!' my daughter tells me. She sees that her aunt stays at home because she has a husband who earns for her and feels that I have to work because she has no father. But with my experience of matrimony, I don't think I would give up my job even if I did re-marry (Archana, a divorced woman and mother of an eight-year-old daughter who lives in a joint family).

Archana's daughter will probably gain a greater understanding of her circumstances as she grows older. At the moment, however, her attempts to explore ways in which life could become easier both for her and also for her mother cause her mother much distress. When children grow up, they see things with a fresh perspective. They are now better able to appreciate the contribution of the working mother to the home and family. If the mother is a success in her own field, the children feel a sense of pride. Mita says that recently she has overheard her son boasting that his mother was a general manager! Not only do some children take a proprietorial pride in her achievements, many also say that as they grow up they find a mother's achievements inspirational.

Adult children are supremely grateful that a working mother has interests of her own, her own social circle and is likely to be more independent and therefore less likely to need their help. Young women, and even young men, who have to navigate the difficulties of managing work and family life on their own, often see their mother with new respect. They then begin to focus not on what their mother could not do for them, but rather on all that she did do.

The problem is that neither the child nor the mother is aware that is likely to happen in the future. So the years between nine to thirteen or sometimes even nineteen can be very trying for both the mother and the child. Research on the subject in the West suggests that the children of full-time mothers actually do the worst academically, even worse than the children of working mothers (children of mothers who work part-time do the best) (Germaine Greer, 1999: 200-1). However, the stereotype of the advantaged child who has a full-time mother, as compared to the disadvantaged child of the working mother remain deeply etched in public consciousness. In an article in the *Economic Times* titled 'Educating Rajesh and Richard', for instance, Chidanand Rajghatta says, 'Typically Indian kids seem to go home to a mother, a homemaker, who is waiting for them when they return for them when they return from school. There's food and attention, intimacy and affection, scrutiny and oversight [sic]. After the kids are done with play or the little distraction they are allowed, mothers supervise their assignments; it's a strict, disciplined regimen.

'I have no empirical evidence [he states], but in many cases, American kids seem to go home to an empty . . . house. They help themselves to food in the fridge and get down to watching TV or playing their video games. Both parents may be out working and return much later in the evening.'

One problem is that because of societal pressures, on the one hand, and the mother's own instincts, on the other, many women themselves believe that their children are disadvantaged compared to the children of full-time mothers. 'The children of working mothers are not monitored as closely. I think my nephew is better behaved than my daughter is', says one working mother whose sister-in-law is a full-time housewife. Point out that she must surely know many children of stay-at-home mothers who are ill-mannered and this working mother smiles wryly, acknowledging that it is her own anxiety that sees a direct co-relation between the working status of the mother and the way a child behaves, ignoring any number of other factors which may also affect the child.

What Really Stresses Out Working Mothers?

The family has changed. The old gender equations, values, relationships, lifestyles are forever altered. The workplace has also changed. There is a difference in the employee–employer relationship, in the types of jobs available and the attitude to a career. And yet, some things remain unchanged. All over the world, the attitude of the family to a working woman who has children under school-going age, and the working mother's own conflict are the same. The stress factors, too, remain the same.

In an article in the *New York Times* News Service, carried in the *Telegraph*, 16 December 2004, Lisa Belkin takes a look at the changes that have occurred since Deborah S. Kliger's thesis on 'The Effects of Employment of Married Women on Husband and Wife Roles: A Study in Cultural Change' looked at women in the workplace, fifty years ago. Only 25 per cent of women worked then, which was a ten per cent increase from the 15 per cent that worked in the 1940s.

It is significant that this study is still relevant half a century down the line. 'It's striking that Dr Kliger had to work so hard to find subjects' the report says, elaborating how 'At first she hoped to find her subjects by contacting one, maybe two large employers in the New York area and asking to talk to women working there who had young children'. When that did not work, Dr Kliger asked sixty different companies for just a few names apiece. Only thirty-two were able to provide even one. My experience in locating professional women with children was similar. Ringing up leading firms in the professional fields such as law, chartered accountancy, or even regular marketing or manufacturing companies saw a real dearth of working women with young children. In general, amongst more affluent families where the second income was not essential, women often left their jobs when the children were young, returning to work, in the same area, or in any field where they found a suitable opportunity, when the children were older. Some women who worked when the children were very small found the going tougher when the children turned around eight and were better able to compare their situation with that of friends and cousins who had full-time mothers and therefore did not enjoy the compromises they had to make. Or, perhaps, these children just needed more attention than a working mother could give them.

Dr Kliger mentions the guilt working mothers experience with regard to their children and also details the depression and lack of self-esteem which full-time housewives experience. Four of the women in the study were actually advised by their doctors to resume work to treat depression and 'general nervous condition'. The situation remains unchanged, half a century later, as is brought out in the chapter on housewives.

Leaving an Infant at Home to Go to Work

It is interesting, really, how universal the stress factors are. Some of them, doubtless, are the result of both nature and nurture. The cry of an infant is, for instance, profoundly difficult to ignore. How much easier it is to blank out other extraneous sounds, the sound of traffic, for instance, or the sometimes very raucous cawing of crows, even higher decibel industrial sounds do not cause the stress a baby weighing less than 3 kg can cause! So, leaving an infant to go to work profoundly stresses out mothers. The baby's helplessness and vulnerability, the belief that no one else can or will do for the baby what the mother would do, are profoundly disturbing for most mothers. And what makes it worse, is, if the working hours and commute time is such that a mother has to leave for work when the child has not yet awoken, and return from work when the child has fallen off to sleep.

Tucking in a young child seems to be important to both mothers and their children. Kolkata's Sabarni Das, a senior journalist with Sananda magazine, describes the experience of putting her eight-and-half-year-old daughter to sleep, as amongst the more pleasurable experiences of the day. Sabarni is aware that her daughter is perhaps getting a little old for this, 'it's a bad habit, but she wants me to do it, and I love to do it', she says.

Since, at the present time, a working mother has exactly the same demands on her time as any other working professional, it makes a simple thing like taking a client out to dinner, or staying late for a meeting, a guilt-ridden exercise for a mother. Women say somewhat resentfully, 'If a man works late, it's a very positive macho thing to be doing, but if a woman has to do this, it's as if she's trying to emasculate her husband'.

Most mothers also regret not being home when a child returns from school. For it is at that moment that the child is keen to talk about whatever happened at school that day. The small triumphs and failures are all forgotten by the end of the day. One mother who had to stay home unexpectedly one day was surprised to see her six-year-old son effortlessly cycling round the block. 'When did you learn to cycle?' the mother asked her child. It turned out that it was a quite a while ago. So, along with pride at her son's achievement this mother had to contend with the regret that this was one more feat he had not been able to share with her when it happened.

Travelling

> The mother of all guilt is the guilt of a mother. I used to kill myself, taking early morning flights and returning as fast as I could. And yet, when my daughter was a teenager, she confided that when she was a little girl, she used to miss me so much, she used to smell my clothes. You can't imagine what that innocent little disclosure did to me! (Sheema Rizvi, Mumbai-based media person).

All executives sometimes get delayed while travelling. Work deadlines get stretched. Trains and planes get re-scheduled. This causes unbelievable stress for dual-career families, and since mothers still own primary responsibility for the child, especially for the mother. 'My husband and I used to make sure that we timed our tours so that one of us was always home for our daughter. But this once, after my husband left on his tour, my flight home was cancelled and I was stuck in Chennai while our daughter was all alone at home in Kolkata. I talked to her on the mobile for almost the whole night trying to reassure her. It helped me decide that quitting was absolutely the right thing to do' says Neera.

Mothers of young daughters are more likely to leave their jobs because of stress created by work-related travel, but even working mothers who have sons feel considerable pressure. Mita Saran is now a general manager in her organization. Her husband is a partner in an American company and is constantly on the move. 'If he's in Chennai on Tuesday, he's quite likely to be in Chicago on Thursday. If it's Bangalore on Saturday, it's likely to be Bangkok on Sunday.' That is the downside to what is otherwise a really enviable job as the family has the comfort of two chauffeur-driven cars, holidays abroad and every luxury money can buy. So how does this equation affect Mita? 'Quite frankly, I do everything to avoid travelling. A course other people would pull strings to go on, I'll put off, hoping I don't have to go. I realize I will have to pay the price with regard to future advancement, but it really freaks me out leaving the boys who are now in their early teens alone in the house. You know the other parents are probably sitting and going over the children's studies, but even if they are in the midst of their exams, your kids could be watching TV. And that's the good scenario. I don't even want to think about other things. Yes, we do have full-time domestic help, but I have always found them totally unreliable.'

Working mothers often do everything possible to cut down on work-related travel; they try to accomplish whatever they can without leaving base, for the sake of the children. Many even turn down professional courses that would involve long stints away from home. Does this affect their careers? This is quite likely. For apart from losing out on the training, and the fillip a stint away from routine work tends to offer, their disinclination to travel means that they meet colleagues at other centres less often, a definite disadvantage in today's world where networking is so important. They are also less able to see, physically, the changes that have happened in other cities and other offices.

However, technology may come to the help of the contemporary working woman. As we move towards a world where teleconferencing becomes more common, this will probably be less of an issue in the years ahead.

The Pressure to Have their Children Excel at Academics

In a society where academic achievement is prized not only for itself, but also as a means to both success and security, parents are obsessive about their children's performance at school and college.

Many of the working women interviewed expressed concern over their child's academic performance and experienced guilt if the child's performance at school was below potential. If the child was doing better than the child of a full-time mother was, this was stated with some relief. Do children of full-time housewives do better than children of working mothers? I have mentioned a British study earlier in this chapter but there is little research on the subject in our own country and it was hard to tell on the basis of the experience of the women I spoke to. Speaking to teachers at schools, I was informed that some children of working mothers were exemplary students, others showed slightly higher instances of behavioral problems. The children of some working mothers did very well. The children of other working mothers did not. The same was true for the children of housewives. Some children are motivated by the fact that both their parents are high achievers and are more likely to listen to a mother who they admire for being a person in her own right. Others cope less well with the reduced attention a working mother can provide and do not perform to potential. Some working mothers, especially those with some degree of flexibility, actually spend more time with their child's schoolwork than many full-time mothers do. Ad professional Deepa Kakkar, who worked flexihours, was actively involved with her daughter's curricular and extra-curricular activities. Her daughter has always done very well. On the other hand, Neera's daughter's grades have shot up since she left her job.

But there is absolutely no doubt that working mothers experience great stress and guilt if their children do not excel at academics. Neera voices the feelings of many other working mothers when she says that, 'It reached a stage where I began to blame myself for all her insecurities.' In Neera's case, being home for her child has resulted in a dramatic improvement in her child's personality and performance at school.

Mita Saran believes that as working mothers get less time with their children, and since the anxiety over their academic performance is so overwhelming, the mother–child interactions become very one-dimensional, 'leading to bad vibes'. In fact, after talking to scores of housewives, it is clear that with older children, say from the age of fourteen or so, the situation is not very different in the homes of full-time housewives and mothers. The acute pressure in urban India to get cutting-edge grades means that children, all children, attend a string of tuition classes. The time they get at home with their parents tends to be limited and overly focussed on test results. However, since the working mother tends to feel greater guilt and responsibility for all her children's inadequacies, she experiences greater stress about this.

Often, the only way in which the working mother feels vindicated is if her children do better than the children of relatives and peers who have stay-at-home mothers. Mumbai's Sheema Rizvi, for instance, states with some satisfaction that her children have performed better academically than their cousins who have a full-time mother. And indeed, many working mothers do have children who emerge as toppers.

The Demands the School Makes on Parents

It is obviously essential for there to be some interface between the school, where a child spends a substantial part of the day, and the home. So you have parent–teacher meetings and parent–teacher committees. You have sports day, school concerts, science exhibitions and debating competitions. All these require parental attendance. Indeed, for most parents they are the highlights of their children's school-going years, and certificates gained at these events are prized and provide cherished memories and mementos. The problem arises when parents are stuck in work environments where absence from an important meeting due to a child's school function can be tolerated only once in a while.

In addition, many activities require items to be procured from very specific locations with very little flexibility with regard to timing. 'Teacher says we have to get rust coloured hand-made paper just like this sample from Commercial Street, or purple satin from Chandni Chowk, or this book for the project from the school-approved shop on Park Street.' Or a six-year-old has to get a sprouted lentil planted in a pot, or a craft project which is likely to require parental help, something the working mother may not be able to provide at short notice because of her commitments at the workplace. This often draws a very negative reaction from the teacher and sets off deep feelings of resentment in a child.

What Women Who Have Greater Control Over Their Timings Have in Common

Expectedly, many women who choose to not work under the many constraints of full-time employment work on their own. Life for them is sometimes as hectic as it is for those in full-time jobs, but being in greater control over their timings seems to make an important difference. Let us share the experiences of these women before we come to that finding.

Every year, my timings change to accommodate my son's schedule. Till he was three years old, I worked from 11 in the morning to 4 in the afternoon. I left him for five hours and he used to sleep for three out of those five hours. I used to leave him with his grandparents, if his grandparents were not there I would take a break. Even so, resuming work was not easy. I was crying the first day that I left him. I was consumed with feelings of guilt (Ratna Bhargav, a thirty-eight-year-old mother of a five-year-old boy).

Mumbai-based Ratna was in a senior position with JWT Associates before she quit to set up her own design studio. Leaving an enviable job, and working on her own, enabled Ratna to manage work and family life, but it was still something that called for adjustments. Ratna gives full credit to her mother-in-law, who helped her deal with the conflict she faced as the working mother of a young child. 'She told me that "you must not lose touch with your work. If you lose touch, you will lose confidence, and then it may become difficult to work in the future". I am very selfish about the time I spend with my son. When he was smaller, I wanted to be there when he woke up from his afternoon nap. Now that he goes to school, I pick him up from school myself. I've done everything for him from the day he was born; I've loved every moment of it.'

Is there a downside to such a tailor-made arrangement? Yes. Loneliness is something someone who works from the home has to guard against. 'In the last three days, the only people I have talked to are my husband and my child', Ratna says. It is something many working women would echo. Also, those who work on their own have to ensure that they remain current and do not lose out on new developments in their field. 'In an organization, you are constantly being sent for training courses, when you are on your own you have to consciously update and upgrade your knowledge and skills.' Being in touch with former colleagues and being aware of new literature on the subject, attending conferences and seminars when possible are all ways to ensure one remains in the loop.

I make calls in connection with my work, after dropping off my daughter to school at 9 a.m. These must be concluded by 11.30 a.m. when I have to pick my daughter up from school. From 2.30 p.m. to about 6 p.m. I work at my cybercafe. I am able to devote time to my daughter from 6 p.m. to 7.30 p.m. I have to be home every evening at dinner time as my eighty-two-year-old father-in-law only eats chapattis made by me (thirty-three-year-old Suchismita, who lives with her husband and three-year-old daughter in a joint family with her parents-in-law, who are both old and in poor health).

Suchismita, who was a star performer with Compaq and Modi Xerox found herself unable to work to the rigid demands of a full-time job as she has elderly parents who need care. She has set up a cybercafe and also sells computers.

In Kolkata, thirty-five-year-old Seema Sanon, an architect and the proprietor of her own company, is deliberately keeping her operations small as she wants to be there for her children. Seema's eldest daughter, aged ten, is mentally challenged and she also has an eight-year-old son and a three-year-old daughter. Seema, whose specialty is commercial interiors, enjoys the creativity and the interaction with people her job entails. She believes she is only able to work because she is her own boss, 'I can't see it work anywhere else', she says. Seema gives priority to her children. Once when her younger daughter complained, 'why can't you come and pick me up from school, like the other mothers', she did so. Though, 'for me it was very difficult, because I'm constantly with clients and on sites'. Seema says the demands of her children, especially their childish squabbles, sometimes stress her out.

Seema finds time for exercise and her special hobby of painting between 11 p.m. and 1 a.m. at night! But she believes she has the ideal job.

Women, who had been pharmacists, chartered accountants, placement consultants, teachers, journalists or caterers and were unwilling or unable to continue in full-time jobs after they became mothers, have worked in-between and around their children's timings to somehow manage to handle both. Many women say that they turn down opportunities for growth, as they believe that that could jeopardize their hard-earned equilibrium between work and family life. There is little regret. Most women in such arrangements have friends who are married and who have had to give up their careers and become completely housebound, so they believe they are really well off to be able to have both, even if the career is on the slow track for the moment.

As we can see, working from home is not easy. Women who work from home often work harder than those women who are in regular jobs do. And yes, they feel stress too because they are taking on responsibility both in the home and in the workplace. As expected, the very highly structured career paths of professions such as medicine which require intense career building in the early stages, present a special barrier to women with children.

Younger Women Less Likely to Sacrifice Career for Family

My daughter doesn't say her first word when I am not there (Dipali, a thirty-three-year-old executive who is climbing rapidly up the corporate ladder).

Dipali is reluctant to sacrifice professional growth to cater to the demands of the family. She also seems to be extremely comfortable both with the demands of her job as well as with job-related travelling. Dipali does not feel any pangs about missing out on her three-year-old daughter's milestones. She likes to believe that this just has not happened. Her father, she says, worries that both she and her husband are neglecting their child, but Dipali pushes such thoughts away. She seems to be more consumed by job-related irritants and problems than concerns about her child. In the future, will the fact that Dipali worries less about her daughter mean that the child will not face the problems that the other ambitious and highly successful executives have had to contend with? Time will tell. However, the fact that a new generation of women will think like men do today and be willing to make no concessions on the home front to balance the demands of the family, means that the need to find solutions to balance home and family has become even more urgent.

What is the Best Time of the Day for a Working Woman?

Driving to work, listening to music, anticipating the workday ahead, that's the best part of my day (Ratna Bhargav, self-employed mother who works flexitime).

Most women who work flexihours find the time when they are working, whether it is from 9-12 in the morning, or 2.30-6 in the evening, the best part of their day. Almost all the women in full-time jobs, on the other hand, consider the mornings when they have to rush off to work as a period of stress-filled madness and look forward to the evenings when they are home again as the best part of their day.

Women who have sacrificed promising careers to take better care of their children, find that even with ambitions having been curtailed, just being in touch with professional pursuits provides a welcome break from the often exhausting demands of the home and family. 'When you get to the office, the tensions of home seem to recede. Similarly, when you return home, the stress of the workplace diminishes. Having two different types of stress actually provides perspective and makes each easier to handle', was something many women said.

If you notice, the women who work for themselves actually may be working harder as they take on responsibility for more of the activities in the home as well as the responsibilities of the workplace, but having more control over their timings, eliminates the stress and makes them feel in charge.

Indeed, women like Mumbai's Deepa Kakkar who stuck to their organizations and reached very senior positions because they were able to work flexihours for at least part of their careers say they never looked at other jobs, because their needs were accommodated by their employers. From an organization's point of view, there is certainly a point to be made for those in fields that need to understand the concerns of the ordinary person to lead a more representative life themselves. 'I think I was not only more relaxed, I think I became a better human being because I was able to be there for my child when I thought she wanted me to be there for her. I also think I was a better ad person because I lived a more normal life. I had a better idea of the consumer', is how Deepa Kakkar describes it.

From the woman's point of view, however, working flexitime or taking time off to attend to family responsibilities is likely to result in a loss of both seniority and emoluments. 'In career terms, the qualified individual can develop a linear career either in a profession or an organisation. Alternatively, the qualified individual can remain at a practitioner level. Many qualified women develop occupational careers, which might include extended periods at practitioner levels, perhaps during part time employment' (Crompton and Sanderson, 1990). Crompton and Sanderson note that 'It is in respect of linear promotion that women are at a disadvantage compared with men. Men predominate at the higher levels of organisations and professions, and organisational hierarchies are not sympathetic to women' (Crompton and Sanderson, 1990:71).

A More Complete Existence: Flexible Timings

Every single woman interviewed wished to have flexible timings. Failing that they wanted to have a job that gave over ideally by 4 p.m. so that there would still be time for a walk, or some physical activity, some time with the family. Even amongst the high fliers there was a sense that they wanted the job to be a part of and not the sum total of their lives.

It was interesting, that while women who worked for themselves actually handled more than those in full-time jobs did, they were happier in most respects. Most such women said that they had the ideal job. Some women did say that they wished they could have continued in regular jobs with some flexibility. One woman mentioned that organizations should try to work out some method by which they could take leave of absence to look after children and then re-join without having to lose out on seniority and perks.

From the experiences of the women I interviewed, it appears that women in jobs within the creative field, such as designers, copywriters and feature writers who work for magazines may be in a better position to get the flexibility they seek. It is also these women who find it easier to get back into the job market when they are ready and less likely to lose out on seniority, pay or perks than women in other fields are. For one, hierarchies seem to be less visible in creative fields, so re-entering the workforce, may not be as problematic if one has talent. For another, these women may actually be able to leverage real life experience or a different kind of exposure positively in their jobs.

How a Career Affects a Working Woman's Marriage

Most women felt that their careers had a very salutary effect on their marriages. They felt their husbands were proud and supportive of their careers. They felt that having experience of a workplace enabled them to better understand their husband's problem and made them more equal partners. Most of the women interviewed said their husbands enjoyed talking to them about their careers and about problems at work, which they were able to better empathize with, as they were themselves employed. Women in secure careers also felt that their jobs acted as a safety net and reduced pressure on their husbands. However, women with demanding careers did report that their husbands were sometimes irritated by the demands of their careers on the family.

Most women also said that husbands were not threatened by the success of their wives. They claimed that their husbands would not mind being in a less well-paying or less high-profile job than their wives.

While some women I spoke to were actually in better-paying or more high-profile jobs, and it was clear that this was not a source of conflict, one could sense that, in some cases, it was a sensitive subject. One woman was reluctant to even mention what her husband's occupation was. The women who were doing better than their husbands in the workplace did say, however, that they were sensitive not to rub it in ever and never to mention it during marital spats. One divorcee believed her ex-husband had been jealous of her success and that this was one of the reasons her marriage had broken up.

When it comes to the wife's job, it is apparently easier for men to adjust to a wife's better-paying job, than to a more high-profile one as the salary 'was private', but a high-profile job was in a way a public acknowledgement of the wife's evident success.

The Effect of a Job on Women's Self-development

Every single woman interviewed believed that her working status was essential to her sense of self worth. Not one wished to be a full-time housewife out of choice. Even the women who had to face what seemed to be monumental problems would not like to be full-time housewives. Most women believed that the economic independence a job gave them, plus exposure to the outside world, made them more self-confident and allowed them options that their mothers did not have. Even though many said that young children resented their responsibilities and commitment to work, they also believed that the children respected them more because they were working women.

Overwhelmingly, working women believe that housewives face as great stress as they do. And even amongst the women who are really under pressure balancing their multiple responsibilities, there was a clear feeling that they were better off than their mothers had been because of greater power, vis-à-vis the husband, than their mothers had had, and more options. There was a feeling that their mothers, having devoted themselves to others, had not had an opportunity to develop themselves.

Help with Childcare and Household Responsibilities

Is the husband supportive? Does the woman still have to take on responsibility for the household? Does the husband share household chores and childcare responsibility to any substantial extent? A vast majority of the women I spoke to said that their husbands were supportive and took on equal responsibility. A few went so far as to say that their husbands actually took on as much or more than they did. Andrea CostaBir, editor of *Savvy* magazine says that 'when my child is unwell, my husband treats her with naturopathic medicines and will stay up all night if necessary. I would just give her an analgesic and go to sleep.' Andrea says her child is more attached to her father than she is to Andrea herself. Another mother says, 'Husbands experience as much stress as wives do when it comes to childcare. When my husband was in Singapore, and my daughter in Mumbai fractured her arm, my husband flew down immediately.'

However, even as the contemporary husband tries to get more involved with household chores, it is clear that women continue to shoulder the major responsibility for both childcare and housework. Some of the women appear to be reluctant to give up control of the kitchen and maintain that they do not allow their husbands to help because they like chores done in a particular way. In other households, financial constraints offer no alternative. The artist, Surekha, goes home after a day's work and a two-hour commute to help her mother-in-law with the cooking, because that is what the household finances require. Occasionally, the pressure for some chore, generally one that demands physical presence at a fixed time, to make chapattis, or to serve the evening meal personally, is a fairly obvious ruse to control the woman and tie her down to the house.

But very often, the reason why women are doing so very much more is the skewed way they themselves see their situation.

My husband and I share the housework equally (Smita, a clerk in a Delhi office).

So what does Smita do? She makes the morning tea, breakfast, packs lunch and makes dinner. She also does the dusting. What does her husband do? He helps with some of the ironing. If you ask her how she considers such a distribution of household chores fair, Smita says that she does not allow her husband to help more because friends or relatives often come to visit and 'they may not understand, they may think I think too much of myself ', Smita explains, 'I am the only working lady of my family'.

Most women have so internalized the idea that as women they are primarily responsible for hearth and home, that though they may be tired by the dual responsibility, they are not resentful of it. Indeed, it could also be said, that they are often responsible for it.

Women took on responsibility for the home, and whenever necessary, they also did the work physically. Paid help and household gadgets made some chores fairly manageable.

Child care, however, was seen as a major problem. Almost all the women I spoke to were uncomfortable leaving their children with domestic help, and if a mother or mother-in-law was willing to come and supervise, then this was a source of relief.

Women Ambivalent on the Role of the Joint Family as a Source of Support

Opinion was fairly evenly divided on the merits of the joint family as a support system. While some felt it was a great support system, others said that the joint family itself was responsible for engendering the maximum stress in their lives. However, even women who had problems with the joint family, conceded that it had helped them cope with providing childcare.

Mita Saran, the Delhi-based executive, asked for a transfer to her parents-in law's home in Bihar so that her mother-in-law could look after her children. 'I couldn't have managed if they hadn't pitched in when they did', she admits. Andrea Costa Bir, the Mumbai-based journalist, also says that she can work with a relatively peaceful mind because her retired father-in-law is at home to keep an eye on the children. 'He has had a stroke, so I do not expect him to do very much but at least he can keep an eye on the maids.'

But some women believe that the parents-in-law subtly turn their grandchildren against their working mother by making unfavourable comparisons to other daughters-in-law who are full-time homemakers. This may occur more often in tradition-bound joint families, where the working woman has broken the mould so to speak. 'I value the safety net the joint family provides in the sense that someone is always "there" for the children, but the subtle disapproval of my commitment to work, increases my stress. Sometimes I think the joint family is the source of my greatest tension', was a common refrain one heard in this context.

Many Women Believe the Role of the Housewife has been Downgraded

> A man who is doing well would like a high-profile wife. He would be embarrassed by someone who is a 'mere housewife'.
> (Salmoli Mukerji, thirty-three, PR manager, Kolkata)

The role of the housewife has now been downgraded. Most working women are emphatic that this is so, but it appears that even children are reluctant to admit that their mother is a housewife. One woman says that her child who had to write about his mother, who was a housewife, in a school essay, wrote that she was in 'the house business'.

If there is one message that came out strong and clear, it was this: there were no good old days as far as women are concerned and no woman would prefer to stay at home. Only one woman said that she thought her mother had had a better life than she herself had had, and that was because she felt that her mother lead a more unselfish life than she herself leads. Otherwise, today's working woman is clear that there is only one way she wishes to go. And that is forward!

The Impact of One's Spouse Being Located in a Different City Due to Job Compulsions

Even as they move ahead, working women hold onto very traditional notions of their roles. They see themselves as professional women. And they see themselves as wives. And trying to figure out how much of themselves to give to each role is problematic. Sheetal, the senior Mumbai-based executive, is regretful of the decision that her family took to live apart. And though in this case, the problems were aggravated because there was a small child involved it is a difficult situation, even if the couple is childless.

> I found it very stressful. My husband used to insist that we spoke on the telephone every day. But we really missed each other. I think one also tends to pick up habits that annoy the other partner. We had to re-adjust to each other when we began to live together as a couple again (Kiran, the Kolkata-based fashion designer, whose husband spent a tenure in Kochi).

In this case, the separation was not of the couple's volition. When his company transferred her husband, Kiran could not really pack up her carefully built up business and move, especially as her husband was likely to be transferred back to Kolkata.

At other times, women choose to move base and live apart for the sake of their career progression. Interestingly, this does not alter the effect of living apart for either husband or wife. Rajeswari Srinivasan chose a challenging assignment that required her to relocate to Delhi away from her Orissa-based husband. It is a move she does not regret; however she does admit that there was a downside.

> It can get lonely. There is no one to have shared conversations with, no one to share the silence. But the real minus is that after a time you begin to think solo, only care about what makes you happy, and then it needs adjustment to function as a couple again

Some jobs are more demanding of time and energy than others are, so the partner in the less high-pressure job was likely to feel greater pangs of loneliness. Over time, this led to feelings of resentment or sometimes indifference, which stemmed from a tuning out . . . both pose an equal threat to the marriage. 'My husband has now become very self-sufficient', was stated as a definite negative by countless women who had to live apart. Even ambitious career women who have chosen to live in a different city in the interest of career progression admit that though they are happy about developments on the career front, at the end of the day it is lonesome coming back to an empty house. 'I have no one to talk to, no one to share with. We miss each other emotionally and physically'.

From the experience of the women I interviewed, being located apart had a detrimental effect on the marital relationship. Most were willing to sacrifice their career ambitions for the sake of the family. Many admitted that this was a major problem they faced in a dual-career family and some had taken a job lower down the ladder to be located at the same place as the husband, something that did hamper their career progression. 'Yes, moving (or sometimes not moving) has had a negative impact on my career but one has to choose and prioritize, and since having a happy marriage is my priority, I can't make a big song and dance about what I have had to sacrifice to do this. If you look at the big picture, I have a good job and a fulfilling career. Those are the positives I focus on.'

How many husbands would do this for their wives? Not very many. Even today, a husband gets high marks on the marital mark sheet for 'allowing his wife to live separately for the sake of her career'.

Do Women Experience Any Kind of Sexual Harassment at the Workplace?

In the mid-1970s, when women at the workplace were much less commonplace than they now appear to be, the prospect of a woman doing night shift at a newspaper, for instance, was deeply disturbing, for the establishment and for the woman's parents, even if the woman herself was not overly concerned by it. Though. middle-class India may shy away from openly discussing the fall-out of the impact of having a solitary woman in an office otherwise peopled with men, gender is an issue for many people. While many organizations are concerned about sexual harassment at the workplace, I wanted to also be guided by the individual responses of the women interviewed. Did these women consider this an issue?

The women I spoke to did not feel that this was a major problem. They saw it more as an irritant. As the situations the women mention are, in fact, fairly offensive, one can conclude that women in India experience some degree of harassment outside the workplace as well and so do not take exception to the rather tasteless comments that they may encounter at the workplace. It is clear that being at work does not increase the harassment they face.

Caroline, the policewoman, says that it is irritating to find men talking about women in a crude way, especially men's obsessions with 'big boobs'! She says that it can be difficult for women in junior positions who are attractive, 'though of course there are advantages too', she concedes.

One woman executive who works for a large Indian company says that though the organization itself is clean, there are individuals who cross the line. On one occasion, a senior male colleague reached out to take a cellphone from her breast pocket even though he had a cellphone of his own. Another will announce 'I enjoyed sleeping with you' if he happens to be on an adjoining berth in the train!

Senior officers harping on the fact that she is a woman when they talk about her progress up the corporate ladder also irritate many women executives who are concerned that they are seen as quota candidates who are being given preferential treatment because they are women. 'Someone will say, "you know you will be the first woman on the board". I don't want them to remember that I am a woman!'

The Effect of Work on the Marital Relationship

With so many factors affecting a marital relationship, the working status of a spouse is probably not of pivotal importance. But today's working woman does feel that when the wife has a career she is more fulfilled. She can pursue her own dreams and fulfil her own ambitions instead of expecting her husband to do it all through his performance and his rewards.

Being in the workplace herself also helps her to understand the stresses her husband may be going through. 'The workplace is a jungle, if you've been there, you know what your husband goes through!' is one common response. A working wife, then, can understand the issues her husband has to grapple with, the tensions, the problems with inflexible deadlines, difficult bosses, unpredictable developments in the world outside which may render even the most sincere promise to be back on time, schedule a holiday or visit an elderly relative, void. A working wife then has the advantage of knowing the territory and understanding it. On the other hand, if her job is demanding in its own right, a working wife is less likely to be attuned to the needs of her husband, and research in the West shows that she is less helpful in helping him climb up the corporate ladder.

In some marriages, the wife's career opens up a whole new world for her husband. It provides exposure to events, people, ideas he may never have got to learn about on his own. These may be stimulating and fun, or they may be really useful in a variety of ways. Andrea, the journalist, feels that her husband enjoys accompanying her to various events and this becomes entertainment for both. Salmoli, the PR professional felt her contacts were sometimes helpful for her husband who is in an allied field.

But, of course, a wife who has her own contacts and her own sphere of influence may be a little threatening for some men.

I think my husband liked the fact that I was a journalist in the public sphere. He enjoyed the fact that I was recognized.

I think it made him feel good that he was a new-age man with an independent wife. But he also expected me to provide the same level of comfort that his mother had provided him. That was not possible. And I think he could not handle the fact that I was earning more than him. He began to become increasingly jealous not only of my success on the career front but also in other spheres. When friends would come over, I used to enjoy trying out new recipes, but when our guests praised what I had made he would say, 'she doesn't normally cook, she only does it for praise'. After that he forbade me from cooking for parties. He would make me do all the cutting and chopping and cook himself (Bratati Banerjee, a Kolkata-based journalist).

There are other women who believe that society is deeply hypocritical when it comes to working women. 'I think we have to acknowledge the forked tongue approach of men. My husband appears to be a super-progressive man in our community. He enjoys that. Some of the "glamour" of my job rubs off on him, and he likes that too. But the truth is that he wants the remote to be with him. He wants to "control" things. He isn't a bad guy, and he does help out in the house when he's needed, it's not a 50 per cent thing but then I don't expect that. We are the in-between generation.'

Indeed, it appears that even as most women are angered by society's double standards that they have to live with every day, there is also an acceptance by both partners that though we do not as yet have gender equality, we are getting closer to that every day. Now, as earlier, it is actually the women who say that their husbands help substantially, while their mates acknowledge that their wives do more than they do. As one husband put it, 'I would differentiate between the actual doing of tasks (which I do), and taking responsibility for running the household, which my wife does.'

Are Things at the Workplace Getting Better or Worse?

Opinion on this question is divided. The factors that women considered were, the new desire of organizations to be more gender sensitive and the introduction of new technology such as email, the mobile phone and facilities like video-conferencing which make physical location less important, on the one hand, and the downsizing of manpower that has taken place in the recent past whereby everybody is expected to work harder, on the other. These conflicting movements had the potential for altering the workplace to make it more or less family-friendly.

Just over half the women interviewed felt that all in all things were probably getting worse. Employers were getting more demanding and there was less tolerance for problems at the home or 'excuses' of any kind. Some of the more highly qualified women interviewed said that organizations would have to change as sought-after employees would seek better balance in their lives.

Working women face dual responsibilities. They wish to be at par with the best at the workplace and they wish to fulfil responsibilities at home as well as a full-time housewife would. Problems arise after women become mothers. For though organizations today wish to be 'gender neutral' and often go out of their way to recruit women and would like them to reach senior positions, most organizations remain so unchanged from the time when the employee had a wife at home to take care of the household and childcare responsibilities, few women are able to achieve a satisfactory work–family balance.

Working women often compare how well they fulfil their responsibilities as mothers compared to full-time mothers. The academic performance of the children is seen as a crucial test in this regard. Inflexible work conditions and the unpredictable way in which work spills over into private time are major irritants. Women enjoy the economic independence the job gives them and the socialization and stimulation of the workplace and believe these factors have a salutary effect on their personalities. Married women believe that their relationship with their spouses is better because their working status helps them understand the stresses of working life.

'Today's woman has no tolerance; she is unwilling and unable to adjust. Working women will walk out of marriage at the drop of a hat'. That is an extreme view, but that does not mean that it is not expressed. It is also totally inaccurate. Most working women still do far more housework than their husbands do and they shoulder far greater family responsibility. But it is changing. And it is changing quite dramatically. The impact of this change on the marriages of the future is yet to be seen. Perhaps men will take on greater responsibility at home to adapt to the changing woman, or the workplace will change to enable couples to better balance commitments at home with career responsibilities. If this does not happen, we are likely to see women either choosing not to marry, or to walk out of marriages that do not allow them to realize their ambitions as career women.

5

Today's Working Fathers: Bonding with the Family or in Bondage at Work?

The decision to have a child is to have a piece of your heart walk outside of your body (Actor Shah Rukh Khan on what being a father means to him on the chat show, 'Koffee with Karan', November 2004).

What is Fatherhood All About?

Motherhood is a cliché. The word mother has been voted the most beautiful word in a survey of 40,000 people conducted in 102 countries of the world. (The survey was conducted by the British Council in 2004 and was reported in the British Council's in-house journal *Connecting*, February 2005, p. 2.) The word father, on the other hand, does not find a place in the list of the seventy most beautiful words. Fatherhood is still relatively unexplored as a concept. And this is the case not just in India but perhaps everywhere in the world. 'The culture, especially in the United States, Australia and Western Europe, gives lip service to egalitarian gender values. However, the preponderance of work-family research indicates that actual behaviour is much more aligned with traditional gender roles' (Coltrane, 2000; Larossa 1988 quoted in *Studying 'Working Fathers': Comparing Fathers' and Mothers' Work–Family Conflict, Fit and Adaptive Strategies in a Global High-tech Company*). Understandably, then, most work-family research has focussed on mothers' challenges on balancing their work and family lives. 'There is no commonly used male counterpart to the "working mother" which is an anomaly in our language . . .' (Hill et al, 2003).

In an article on fatherhood that I had done for a leading newspaper in 1985, I had confided that, 'Trying to define what a father is turned out to be a surprisingly difficult task. Every father I spoke to had to pause and think deeply before he could state what his role was. And children who responded to the question "Do you know what a mother's role is" without stopping for breath, were stumped when they were asked what they thought a father's role in the family (apart from the obvious one of being the breadwinner). Mothers were predictably more sure what they thought a father should be'(the *Hindustan Times* Sunday Magazine, 6 January 1985, p. 5).

Then, as now, one saw that 'Even in families where the mother holds a full time job, it is she who is almost wholly responsible for bringing up the children' (ibid). 'The concept of fatherhood is hazy. A father sires the child who bears his name, inherits genetic similarities, and if he's lucky, some property. Till a child comes of age, a father supports him financially, so much is clear. But is that all? How do fathers of today view their role? Has it changed with the times? And what about the increasing number of fathers who work a ten-hour day, how do they cope with fatherhood?' (ibid).

Two decades later, there is little I would phrase differently. I had begun that article with a quote from my two-and-a-half-year-old son, Anurag, 'A Papa's job is to say, "lovely" when Mama cooks something. And when there is a party and Mama says "Oh! There's no soda", a Papa's job is to go to the market and get soda.' It was his impression of what a father was. It surprised me at the time. For one, I thought the reflection on my culinary skills implicit in that statement unjustified! But equally, I thought of my husband as a far more hands-on father than that. Obviously, to his children his role was seen as far more peripheral. Today, I know that the average mother does so much more for her children than even a caring father is likely to be doing, it is not surprising that children form the impressions they do. Has anything changed? Yes, indeed. The contemporary father judges himself by a far more exacting yardstick than fathers did earlier.

Having written on the family for over twenty years, I see a real difference in the way fathers rate their contribution to both home and family. In the early 1980s, fathers who gave one bottle feed in the day, or changed nappies, saw themselves as exemplary fathers. By the 1990s, fathers were far more aware of what the real score was. So even though most of the women perceived their husbands as sharing the household responsibilities pretty evenly, the husbands themselves saw the distribution more as 70: 30 in favour of their wives. As one father told me when I probed a little deeper 'I see a difference in the mere doing of a task and actually taking responsibility for it. My wife takes responsibility for the child, I will take him to the doctor, or make a feed, depending on what is required.' This consciousness could be seen in any number of answers that I got when doing interviews for this chapter. Interestingly, this is also recognized as a characteristic common to fathers in other parts of the world. Kelley Holland, associate editor of *Business Week* (USA), says in the 21 September 1998 issue that though fathers are now helping at home more than their fathers did, men are very task oriented when it comes to childrearing and mothers are still the preferred parent for emotional support. She exhorts men to take a more holistic approach to childcare

In a way, it is ironic that just as the contemporary father is wanting to get involved with his children and to help with the housework, we seem to be entering a phase where the job is increasingly demanding more and more of the employee's time, and perhaps all of his energy. In a world where people are working more intensively than ever before, many working mothers end up giving priority to their role as mothers and become only mothers. Though they may not themselves realize it, many working fathers cease to be very active as fathers and effectively become only workers. This is not a development that anyone is particularly pleased about. While in the UK on a Chevening Press Fellowship to study the family, I saw that the newspapers were full of concern that fathers were perhaps not spending more than fifteen minutes a day with their children. The concern clearly was that 'Fathers must be more than walking wallets', as one scribe put it. Surveys of young men showed that, in fact, they wanted to be far more involved as dads than their own fathers had been with them. My own interviews with international MBA students at INSEAD, France, in the summer of 1999, showed that young men from countries like Germany were actually looking forward to a four-day week. In-depth interviews with young Indian men in the twenty to twenty-five-year age group for the chapter on young singles also clearly demonstrated that the parenting role was one that was of crucial importance to today's young male.

Historical and Religious Viewpoint

And yet, it is dangerous to assume, as we sometimes do, that in earlier times fathers were uncaring and unconcerned about their children and that the contemporary father plays a more important role in the child's life than he did in the past. If one takes a historical perspective (to the extent it is possible to do so with a subject as complex as fatherhood), it appears that a marginalization of fatherhood took place in twentieth-century Europe and the US. Earlier, to quote Jung, 'Behind the father stands the archetype of the father, and in this pre-existent archetype lies the secret of the father's power . . . The personal father inevitably embodies the archetype, which is what endows this figure with its fascinating power.' The archetypal father is Brahma, Vishnu, Mahesh, creator, preserver and destroyer, but also 'Our father who art in heaven', in the Lord's prayer. In every scripture the deep love of the father for his child is clearly manifest. In the Ramayana, King Dasrath banishes Rama to the forest in accordance with his pledge to Queen Kekeyi to demonstrate the importance of being true to one's word. The incident was remarkable because of the pain a father was expected to have felt in so doing. Similarly, in the Old Testament, Abraham is asked to sacrifice his son as the love of a father for his child was considered the greatest love of all. For Shia Muslims also, the martyrdom of Hussain, the beloved grandson of Mohammed, whom he often affectionately called son (as he had no surviving son), is ritually mourned every year. Though canny advertisers may have cottoned on to the immense potential of the sensitive, caring father quite recently, paternal love is as old as time.

In India, the bond between father and son was seen as a natural and powerful force, amongst all types of families. Letters between the young J.R.D. Tata and his father show a fatherly anxiety and a filial concern that are heartwarming. In a letter written by the young J.R.D. (who is obviously less than comfortable in English) to his father in 1944, he expresses regret for having sent off what must have obviously been a rather matter of fact letter, 'I am so disappointed as you had written in the letter which we received this morning about not to have written a word of tenderness but I

hope that you are fine to forgive me. My poor papa I
see how you must be sad and disappointed'(Tata, 2004:
4). The love between father and offspring is palpable.
And the same could be said of the relationship between
Jawaharlal Nehru and his daughter, Indira, and B.K.
Birla and his father, G.D. Birla. In the case of Mahatma
Gandhi, he actually turned celibate because of the
remorse he experienced on learning that he was with
his wife when his father lay dying!

The Modern Perspective

Work–life conflict is generally seen as a woman's issue.
Traditionally, the workplace was the man's sphere the
home and hearth was the woman's. Since society was
based on a male breadwinner, female homemaker model,
men could work as intensively as required. Long
working hours, night shifts, tours, transfers, none of
these was a cause for concern as it was assumed that
the male employee had a wife to take care of everything
on the home front. Not all men and certainly not all
wives may have enjoyed one or all of these
developments, but while there was a woman at home
to take care of these eventualities, they were not issues
that concerned the organization.

Of course, it is also true that there was a fair degree
of balance between home and work till the 1980s and
the work pressures as far as the middle class was
concerned were such that most families could have a
fairly fulfilling social life. Indeed, quite often, the
organization the man worked for was largely
instrumental in providing facilities for recreation for

the employee and his family. The workday ended at about 5.30 p.m. leaving more than enough time for socialization with colleagues and other friends. Since club facilities were provided to many employees, activities like swimming and tennis were popular. Less affluent working men would probably spend time with the family on more mundane but perhaps equally satisfying activities like going to the market or the cinema.

The Change in Work–Life Balance

With liberalization, even as salaries have risen dramatically, working conditions have become tougher. One now has to deal with the cut-throat competition posed by a free market. We are now in competition with countries like the US where men work the longest hours in the developed world, a phenomenon which is sometimes described with the catchphrase that has been picked up by a television channel: 24/7! New fields such as call centres require employees to work to time zones in the UK and US. In addition, in an increasingly insecure work environment, all employees, but especially male employees, are clocking in even longer hours to show commitment in the most obvious way of all. It is a development that has grave consequences for family life. Housewives who are alone for most of the day experience feelings of loneliness and depression. Working women are even more stressed by this, as it means they have to shoulder a disproportionate share of the responsibility in looking after the home and the children. But, of course, it is hardest on the children themselves, as they have to deal with the phenomenon of the invisible father! What is just beginning to be recognized, however, is that many men would like to be more involved with their families and are unhappy about being so caught up in their jobs that they cannot be there to participate in and influence decisions regarding their children.

If we are adopting Western work practices, then research on the subject in the US should be of interest. The Radcliffe Public Policy Centre Study (3 May 2004, press release, www.radcliffe.edu/news/pr/000503-ppc_harris.html) finds the new generation of young men focusing on family first. 82 per cent of young men aged twenty-nine to thirty put family time at the top of their list, keeping pace with 82 per cent of the women in these age groups. Paula Rayman, director of the Radcliffe Public Policy Centre and principal investigator of the study saw young men beginning to replicate women's sensibilities instead of women in the workforce trying to be more like men. The study also found 72 per cent willing to give up pay for more time with their families and sought a more active role in bringing up their children. The study also pointed out that most workers perceive that their loyalty towards employers is not reciprocated. My interviews of Indian working fathers showed an identical response. In addition, the new possibilities for advancement, the fact that it is possible for some men to be able to finance a truly luxurious lifestyle for themselves and their families, puts those who cannot under pressure.

Male Pain is the other side of male power. Not all men, contrary to the rhetoric of masculinity, can be at the top of the pyramid. The contrast between rhetoric and reality is very painful for men whose race, class, health, or even height does not allow them to wield power, exercise authority, or just cut a figure imposing enough to qualify as a 'real man.' Even successful men pay a high price for their control and authority. The competitive, hierarchical environment men are encouraged to operate in, cut them off from intimacy and penalize them for letting down their guard. The myth that male power is all individually achieved, not socially structured, means masculinity can be lost if not constantly proven in daily behaviour (Coontz, 1997: 22).

Being a provider is still seen as an important attribute of masculinity and is perhaps integral to conventional notions of what a good father is. The growing job insecurity of our times clearly has important repercussions on the family, even if the wife's income is sufficient for the family's needs. Indeed, though there are certainly signs that things are changing, in a study of senior women managers of companies in the *Fortune 500* list, for instance, a third of the married women had stay-at-home husbands, a reversal of gender roles that is still a deeply disturbing phenomenon for most couples.

Most working men are married and are fathers. The proportion of working women who are single, and even when married are childless, is far higher. Research suggests that provided adequate support is available, a multiplicity of roles is associated with greater satisfaction. Women who are married, working and are mothers, are therefore likely to be happier than women who are unmarried or women who are childless, or women who are not working. For men, marriage and fatherhood bring even greater benefits than marriage and motherhood bring to women.

And yet, contemporary fathers often experience very great stress in adjusting to changing realities. A study on fatherhood in the UK shows that commonality exists between conditions there and the situation of the middle-class family in India.

> Contemporary families are adjusting to more women working, households with two earners, long working hours and the possibility of the father facing long periods of unemployment or early retirement. The need to understand how families negotiate such issues provided the impetus for this study.
>
> Fathers and mothers had different attitudes to paid work. Fathers tended to stress the financial rewards and feel compelled to work out of a sense of duty or responsibility. Mothers did see money as important but saw their earnings as 'contributing' rather than 'providing', reflecting a pervasive assumption that the father's earnings were the mainstay of the family budget. Women were also much more likely than men to see paid work as a choice and to link it to questions of personal freedom or self-development (personal interview of Dr Charlie Lewis whose comments were on the basis of a study in progress).

Such attitudes infuriate feminists, especially when, as stated in the UK study, 'In one family, the mother was described as contributing to the family income in a way which concealed the fact that she earned considerably more than her partner.' But I found very similar attitudes amongst the families I spoke to where the couples were over thirty-five years of age. Amongst younger couples, attitudes appear to be less based on tradition and more on logic, but the outcome of such attitudes are still to be tested by time.

Indian Father Connected to Family and Children

Research in the West tells us that compared to the father in the US, the Indian father is much more deeply connected to his family and to his children. Indian children turn to the father as much or perhaps even more than to the mother for help with academics at senior levels, as also for guidance with regard to career choices. In a study of 100 families in north India (70 per cent of the families were Hindu, 30 per cent were Sikh), the researchers found that the men 'felt less engaged, more content and in control of their time while at home'. At home, 'they clearly reported being quite connected to their adolescent children . . . a lot of the children including daughters, reported having lengthy conversations with their dads about all sorts of topics including politics, philosophy, social lives and the future'(study by Reed Larson and Suman Verma, quoted in Barlow, 2001). Dads in the US, on the other hand, according to Larson are generally absorbed in their working lives and their job-related emotions often dictate their moods and those of their families. Adolescents in the US tend to spend less time with family and daughters rarely engage in personal conversation with dads.

In the UK, ' Most parents and children, but fathers in particular, viewed providing an income for the family as the central aspect of fathering.' Where other aspects were mentioned these were viewed as additions to, rather than replacements for, this role.

'A significant number of both fathers and teenage children felt this "provider role" was intensified by living in a consumer culture.' It was clear that many fathers themselves had a strong 'investment' in their role as provider. This role acted as a channel for feelings of emotional attachment to their family and gave a sense of purpose to work, which might otherwise seem quite meaningless. While many 'bread-winning' respondents expressed the view that fathering 'should be about more than providing, this was nevertheless perceived, almost without exception, as the fundamental basis of fathering, regardless of whether fathers were actually able to fulfil this role' (personal interview of Dr Charlie Lewis).

Fathers' reluctance to give up their 'traditional' position may be further underpinned by the attraction of the relative simplicity of this role compared with the tensions, confusions and stresses of trying to become an 'involved' father. The conflicting pressures on fathers of 'providing' and 'being involved' were clear in some accounts, suggesting that some might experience a 'double burden'. One mother summed up her husband's struggle to sustain different aspects of his paternal identity by drawing a parallel with the figure of the 'supermum' media stereotype who expertly juggles multiple roles. Dads these days, she said, are expected to be 'superdads'.

Studies in the West show that despite the rise of the dual-career family, the roles of the mother and father continue to be complementary. Mothers take care of the more mundane duties of parenting while fathers go in for more 'exciting' and less usual activities. Out-of-work fathers, who have the time and the opportunity to provide more active parenting are less likely to be able to provide it. The loss of self-esteem that occurs when a man loses his job, appears to negatively affect his ability to be a good parent.

For this chapter I interviewed working men from many parts of India, but I have changed some names and identifying details to protect identity. All the working men interviewed were married and were fathers. This was in line with reality. While many working women are single and most middle-class women drop out of the work force when they have young children, the same is not true for men. Also, though unceasing demands on their time and energy does affect a man's marital relationship to some extent, it is actually his role as father which is really affected by the excessive demands of the workplace.

Many men were excessively concerned about the impact of the inputs they were giving for this chapter, on their careers and on their family life. Very vocal in casual conversations, they were extremely anxious when being interviewed. 'If I lose my job, you'll have to find me another job', was something more than one man said in 'jest'.

Did Dad Have it Better?

There is awareness of the role conflict the modern working mother undergoes, but it is interesting that even women who appear to live incredibly tough lives are emphatic that they are better off than their mothers were. But my interviews with working men indicate that the contemporary working father is much more ambivalent about whether he is better off than his father. He faces much greater pressure to succeed at the workplace. He also has to fulfil new and sometimes complicated notions of what a father must be.

> Was life better for my father? You bet it was. As a senior army officer, he commanded respect wherever he went. Was he a hands-on father? Of course not. How could he be? He was away at the front a lot of the time. But in those days he was not expected to do very much in the home. Things are much, much more difficult now (Ved Rajkumar, a thirty-year-old army officer in a dual-career family).

At other times, men who remember a father who gave them a comforting sense of security in their own childhood, are troubled that they cannot do as much for their children.

> The father is like an umbrella, he protects his children, and I still remember how my father who was in ONGC was always there for me right up to the point that I was fourteen or fifteen. I used to go to him with all sorts of questions and all sorts of problems. He wasn't always able to sort out my problems, but it meant a lot to me that he was there for me. I think just the presence of the parents is very important for children (Forty-year-old Joydeep Banerjee, a dentist,

who believes that a father's role in a child's upbringing is crucial).

At other times, one can see that men experience a real nostalgia for the past, for a simpler time where life was slower, and it appears to them, from the viewpoint of their frenetic schedules, better.

In Burnpur you were cut off from the world, the telephones didn't work, so you could devote yourself to the family. My father used to come home for lunch, play tennis in the evenings, have Saturday and Sunday off. Today with the mobile phone and the Internet you are connected to the world all the time, so it is impossible to switch off (Sandeep Merh, a successful entrepreneur whose father was a corporate executive).

Even though this entrepreneur is much better off than his father in material terms, he believes that his father had a better life.

Sons of self-made men do acknowledge that they had it easier in that they had the benefit of a superior education and of growing up in a world with many more opportunities than their fathers could have dreamed of. But there is a downside to living in the shadow of a man who beats the odds and becomes successful by his own efforts.

I have a base. It is he who set it up. He had to manage his work and look after his family with no help or guidance from any one. In that respect, it is easier. But then my father did not have to answer to anyone. Whatever he earned was his. In my case, it is completely different. Every paisa I earn goes into a common pool and my father has

total control over it. I cannot plan anything for the future, not my own future, nor my son's future. I cannot question any decision.
(Gautam, thirty-four, photographer, whose father came to Mumbai from a village in Uttar Pradesh).

It will be interesting to see whether, in the far future, the sons of these fathers will think that their lives are even more difficult, or whether they will find them easier.

Lack of Family Time

One parameter on which today's working fathers feel that they fall short is the amount of time they are able to devote to the family.

I see my daughter after such long absences that she can barely recognize me. I miss out on all the little things that make life with a young child so interesting. Her first word, her first step, her reaction the first time she saw a puppy. My wife sometimes videotapes her birthday parties, but it's sad having to watch your child grow up on film (Ved, an army officer, is posted in the Jammu and Kashmir area).

Ved is married to an ad professional who lives in Chennai. They have a four-year-old daughter. In the five years that the couple has been married they have only lived together for about nine months at one stretch. Ved gets sixty days annual leave, his wife gets much less, but they manage just enough time together to stay connected. In Ved's case, his long stint at a non-family station is the reason he has missed out on much of his daughter's childhood.

Right now, of course there is no way we could be together. At best, she could live in the accommodation provided for the families in Jammu, or some such place, but my problem is that when I get a family posting, how do we handle that? I can't possibly ask her to give up such a promising career just so that we could be together, but the alternative is a whole life apart (Ved).

Ved's story shows how some jobs are and will continue to pose challenges for work–family balance. While the armed forces are acknowledged as being very sensitive to the family requirements of their soldiers and officers, something Ved refers to when he talks about the superlative facilities and also special educational opportunities for the children of army personnel, the rigours of field postings, the stress and danger, and the enforced separations, are just some features of the job, which are likely to remain in the near future.

But even fathers who have never been located in a different city, admit that as far as being a father is concerned, they have played a role that is biological, more than parental.

'I often feel very concerned that I am not able to give quality time to my wife and child. My working hours are erratic, sometimes just as I am about to go home, some assignment comes up, and then there's no telling when it may finish. I am virtually a stranger to my children', says Gautam, the professional photographer.

There has always been a trade-off between what one gave and what one got in the professional sphere.

Multinational corporations were likely to pay better and give a more luxurious lifestyle but were associated with a more demanding work environment. Government and public sector companies were likely to offer more modest salaries, a less glamorous lifestyle, but greater security and better work–family balance. The new requirement for public sector companies to be globally competitive means that this is no longer the case. 'Yes, earlier, the workday ended at 6 p.m. or 6.30 p.m., but in today's more uncertain work environment, people are working much longer hours. And of course, even if there isn't work, people will hang on at the office just to score points', a public sector employee confided. It is ironic, however, that in some ways the most 'happening' professions, those of MNC consulting companies, are in some ways a throwback to a way of life that was prevalent before civilization altered living patterns in society. In many ways today's consultants have a way of life that is nomadic.

As a consultant, I think it is fair to say one is not 'based' anywhere. I travel wherever there is an assignment and stay for as long as required. This could be six days, six weeks, or six months. I am a visitor at home' (Satyam, thirty-three, consultant).

There's adrenaline-flowing excitement 24/7, an opportunity to be as familiar with the airport at Buenos Aires as at Beijing, and the unabashed attraction of making the biggest bucks in the business. But the downside is stark. There is constant stress and very little family time. Many men in such professions are deeply dissatisfied with the way their children are turning out. They see a lack of commitment to academics, often find them lacking in family feeling and somewhat 'disrespectful to elders'. Paternal involvement is only one factor that contributes to a child's upbringing. Changing social mores, a globalized world, the Internet and TV, are obviously other factors that influence values and behaviour. But today's father is conscious that he is able to give much less of himself than he would like to and therefore experiences a sense of responsibility for what he perceives as negative behaviour patterns in his children. When it comes to family time, however, few men seemed to have control over the amount of time they are able to spend with their family.

Being the boss, having control over one's job and over one's schedule is associated with a reduction of stress. But it is not a panacea.

Because I have my own business, the pressure is much greater, so many people are dependent on me, so many salaries have to be paid every month and of course I can't deny the fact that the realization that it's my money at stake, does make a difference (Sandeep Merh, the entrepreneur, formerly with the merchant navy).

Work–family balance is obviously something not many working fathers can claim to have. But some men do get it right. Joydeep is a self-employed dentist who has his own practice and works from 10 a.m. to 2 p.m. and then again from 5 p.m. to 8 p.m. His wife works from 10 a.m. to 1 p.m. Balancing work and family is 'very easy' for this family. 'I get time with my family before we go to work and the children go to school in the morning and then again after they return from school at lunchtime. Indeed, in the near future, Joydeep intends to change his chamber timings. By working from 10 a.m. to 5 p.m. and eliminating the evening shift, he hopes to be able to spend even more time with his children. Another man who experiences no work–life conflict at all is Ashish, a physical educator. As a physical educator, Ashish works from 8.15 a.m. to 3.15 p.m. 'I get to spend quality time with my parents and my wife. I socialize a great deal with my old friends; we love to have get togethers, which are great fun. In fact, I also get to spend a lot of time with my sisters and my wife's family.' Ashish and his wife share the household responsibilities, 'I do the groceries and other such work, my wife takes care of the cooking and cleaning, it makes life easy and smooth.'

Do they enjoy their work? Ashish does, and looks forward to starting his own fitness centre one day. Joydeep, the dentist, finds his work monotonous, but feels that it is an acceptable trade-off for a more congenial family life.

The Stay-at-Home-Father

In the UK, the US and even in Japan, we are just beginning to see the stay-at-home father, or house-husband. It is one way that couples with young children can balance work and family life. Sometimes, the wife earns more than the husband and therefore if the family has to choose one job, they choose the one that offers better compensation. Or, the wife's job may offer better medical benefits, which may be required to take care of elderly relatives or a child with special needs. Or it could be that the couple decides that psychologically, the man is better geared to be the full-time parent than the woman is. Or it could for reasons that range from logistics, to the perception that the woman's job is somehow better suited to the family's needs.

> It's been very, very hard. Looking after the home and two young children is just about the toughest thing any man or woman for that matter can be asked to do, but since my wife had a stable job as a chartered accountant and I had decided to launch my own firm with an associate, a move that did not quite pan out, I concentrated on being a full-time father. I can tell you, as most mothers must, that it's hard but rewarding (Naveen Kumar, a thirty-six-year-old stay-at-home father of a five-year-old daughter and a three-year-old son).

Naveen confesses that he has had to battle demons full-time mothers are familiar with, a loss of self-esteem, a sensitivity to possible barbs from the earning spouse, a feeling of loneliness, of feeling 'blue' for no good reason. 'In my case, my divorced mother has re-married and is busy with her new family, and my mother-in-law has a very demanding job, so it was the best solution. We men have to let go of our hang-ups. Being the stay-at-home housebound parent is difficult, whether you are male or female is really irrelevant.'

Naveen is the only stay-at-home father I met. Does he signal the beginning of a trend? If worldwide norms are an indicator, the answer is yes.

Housewife or Working Wife?

You are working long hours in a demanding environment. You are stressed and feel over-extended. So what would you prefer to have? A stay-at-home wife, or a working wife?

It is interesting that increasingly, as far as the middle class is concerned, a stay-at-home wife is seen as something of an anachronism. So the desired scenario definitely includes a wife who has her own career. But even if the working father would like his wife to be a working mother it is often not possible.

Dev is a forty-nine-year-old executive who works for a large manufacturing company. Dev is on the fast track. His wife, Diya, who was a colleague at the Indian Institute of Technology (IIT) continued to work after marriage, but had deliberately put her career second so that she could also look after their son who is now twelve. Work–family balance was difficult but manageable till Dev's move to Dubai a year ago.

We had a full-time maid to look after our son and since Diya only accepted assignments that were not too demanding we coped. Of course one made tremendous compromises, the maid's standards of hygiene left much to be desired, so we had to turn a blind eye to many things. Also, though we gave him 'quality time' when we were home, I did feel he was growing up a little spoilt. My mother had much more exacting standards on housekeeping and child-rearing than Diya could manage with her work schedule, so there was a little friction on that score but it was okay. I knew the sacrifices she was making on the job front to appreciate what she did do for our son and for me. However, our problems really started after we moved to Dubai. Diya cannot work here so our child has a full-time mother (Dev).

Foreign postings are sought-after in today's work environment, but an overseas assignment often makes it impossible for a spouse to work. At other times, family commitments pose problem for which the only solution appears to be for the woman to give up her job.

My father is seventy years old, my mother is sixty-two, and their health has to be monitored. My two-and-a-half-year-old daughter needs attention too, and then of course there are all the problems connected with running a house; problems with maidservants, plumbers, etc. I wish we had better support systems so that it could have been possible for my wife to work. I can't deny that it does bother my wife from time to time. She says, 'I am becoming totally dependent on you'. It hurts her. It hurts me too. But right now, it is perhaps the best option (thirty-three-year-old Nilanjan Dey, a principal correspondent with a leading publication).

Nilanjan has been working for ten years. He got married six years ago. Nilanjan's wife, who was a working woman earlier, has given up her job because since her husband's working hours are from about 10.30 a.m. to about 8.30 - 9 p.m., someone has to be at home for his elderly parents and their young child.

In line with research all over the world, working fathers do prefer a mother to be home when a young child comes home from playschool or even from school. Many said, 'I think it's very important for children to have a mother's attention, I think children whose mothers are not home when they return from school feel some "pain"', or 'servants can never give a child the attention a mother can.' However, today's father is fully conscious that such a situation even if it is good for the child, is not fair on the mother. The contemporary dad is also aware of his own responsibility as a father. 'I think as a father I should be a role model for my children, inculcate a value system that will stay with them all through their lives.' And he's anxious to do more hands-on parenting, which includes some degree of housekeeping. 'I drop my daughter to school, do the shopping about half the time. I also help with the child. I enjoy telling her a bedtime story', says Nilanjan, the journalist.

If the circumstances allow it, most men are more comfortable with a working wife. 'I think it is much better to have a working wife. You not only have a dual income but both partners have a sense of independence. The responsibilities of a man who is married to a full-time housewife are awesome. The entire responsibility of the family is his. He not only has to provide for all the wife's financial requirements, but also to take care of her emotional needs', was a typical response.

Men who keep long hours and have to do a great deal of work-related travel undergo the most stress when they think of what this does to their wives.

For the middle-class working man then, the options are fairly stark. If you have a wife who works outside the home, you have to deal with constant brinkmanship to fulfill your responsibilities in the home, especially if you have young children and elderly parents to care for. On the other hand, the comfort of having a full-time homemaker in the house is offset by the knowledge that you are not able to provide her with the companionship she must obviously crave, being alone in the house for most of the day. The lack of a second income also puts an intolerable strain on the sole working member of the family. This is of increasing importance in an environment where job security can no longer be taken for granted. David's story captures exactly what 'being Atlas' did to one man when circumstances changed.

The Impact of VRS on an Employee

> One day, my boss sent for me. I was told that the bank was re-structuring. The requirement now was for younger men with a different set of skills . . . To cut a long story short, I was advised to go in for VRS (forty-six-year-old David Menezes, a senior executive in a well-established foreign bank).

David lived in a well-appointed flat in Ballygunje Circular Road, Kolkata. David's eighteen-year-old son and sixteen-year-old daughter were looking forward to college education in the US. His wife taught in a prestigious school, which offered a very modest salary but a good work environment. Life for the Menezes family was good. They had corporate membership to two of the city's élite clubs, an annual holiday abroad, chauffeur-driven company cars, all the perks one associates with a blue chip company. David never realized his dependence on these company perquisites till they were abruptly removed. It was only then that David discovered that 'there is often little V in the VRS'.

Though the compensation package he was given has been helpful, the loss of his job has led to a real and very sharp drop in their living standards. His children have had to realign their aspirations to the new and changed reality, as have David and his wife.

Today, there is greater awareness of the psychological impact of measures such as VRS on the employee. David was one of the early victims and was totally unaware of how to deal with this development. He did not know how to break the news to his wife. In the beginning he thought he would first find another assignment and then inform her about the loss of his previous job and the acquisition of another. Unfortunately, the new assignment did not materialize. So after pretending that he was working for close to a month, one day David just did not get ready in the morning. Pamela asked him what the matter was. 'Nothing', he told her, 'I lost my job a month ago'. Pamela was devastated.

'The first mistake I made was not sharing the news with her immediately. The second was pretending that I had *chosen* to opt for VRS when in reality I had little choice in the matter.' Pamela felt anguished that David chose to take such an important decision concerning the family without consulting her. Their marriage has suffered and now David is drinking more than he should and often experiences frustration at being housebound. The household has seen frequent changes of domestic help as David acknowledges, he ' drive[s] them up the wall'.

Menezes sees almost nothing of his former colleagues. 'I don't want to see the ********!', David says, but it has led to his leading a fairly solitary existence, which for someone who once used to be the life of every get together, must be difficult. 'For men whose identity is very closely associated with their jobs, losing a job may make them feel degendered, they start interfering in household affairs. It is a sign of their frustration', explains psychoanalyst Rotraut Roychowdhury.

How the Loss of Job Security Affects Some Men

When experts talk of the stress of being the sole breadwinner, Nilanjan would provide a suitable example. 'Hatred is a strong emotion, and when you experience it at the workplace, it is hard to deal with', Nilanjan says. 'Hatred?' I ask him, 'don't you mean frustration, or perhaps resentment?' But Nilanjan is quite clear that hatred is the word he wishes to use. 'An average working man has to report to somebody who can destroy his career and his peace of mind. Your boss can take credit for your success, he can take advantage of you and finish you. In my last place of work, the owners sold the paper. For them it was a simple business deal. Though we were all retained, we didn't know this for about a month. We received no communication from the management. When you are responsible for so many people and then realize exactly how powerless you are, it's something you cannot forget easily', says Nilanjan. He felt the stress far more acutely because he was the sole breadwinner of the family.

Men Experience Nostalgia for the Past

Women, whether housewives or working women, are emphatic that there were no 'good old days'. They are aware that they face many problems balancing work and family life, but they believe that by any reckoning, things are better for today's woman. They have greater independence, greater respect, more options. Life is, unquestionably, better than it was in the past. But for the contemporary working father things are not as clear-cut. There is a great deal of nostalgia for the past

Some men regret the passing of a gentler era, where one could take one's job for granted. 'Increased competitiveness has turned colleagues from companions to rivals. It means, at some level, it is no longer possible to have friends at the office.' Many mourn the decline of the importance of the extended family in today's more aggressive, work-oriented world

'In the old days, one felt so connected to uncles and aunts, not like today's families which are so limited. Holidays meant going to the family home. Every one had to adjust, to make do, to do without, but it was fun. No one is willing to compromise on anything—from what they want to eat, to bigger things. What's the point in being together in such an atmosphere?' asks one father.

Another says 'growing Westernization and greater individualism has led to a decline in traditional Indian values, we no longer have the warmth and closeness that once existed in families, and this does bother me.'

But today's male does admit that 'since this has been accompanied by greater freedom for women, I think it is an acceptable trade-off. Today, women are educated and they want to have their own goals and their own lives, and I think this is a very good thing'.

The Widening Economic Divide

The best thing about today's world is the opportunity it offers those who have grit, guts, and good sense to improve their lot. Rags to riches is a distinct possibility. Unfortunately, this also poses new problems. When Ved joined the army and was able to join his father's regiment, it was a dream come true for him. Today, Ved is beginning to wonder if his dream was flawed. 'There is a distinct incompatibility between the demands of my job, which is in many ways ideal for me, and the requirements of my wife's career. As I see it there's no real solution.' Then there is another problem. It is something Ved is reluctant to talk about. He does not wish to appear to be jealous. Ved is, in fact, quite content with the terms and conditions of his job. It is just that he realizes that in relative terms he no longer measures up in the way that he once thought he did. Ved's wife is doing well at her job and, in fact, earning far more than he is. Ved's sister, who is a consultant, is also earning more than double his salary. Though the relationship with both remains good, Ved confesses, 'When they talk about their investments, about holidays abroad, fancy cars, I feel I live on another planet. As time goes on, will the bond we feel be able to stand up to the very different lifestyles we now have. I used to be really proud of our institutions like the regimental mess, the sprawling houses of senior officers, the facilities for things like horse-riding the family can enjoy, the special MBA institutes for army children. I thought I had a lot to offer, but it all looks very meagre compared to what others are now able to afford. I am torn between the widening divide between my world, and the world of those who are closest to me.'

In many middle-class families, the choice of career has led to such economic disparity between brothers that it causes problems. Lifestyles have become different, so have viewpoints.

Old Certainties No Longer Work in a New and Fast Changing World

If relationships within the family have become more difficult, so has marriage, that hoary old institution that survived the millennia so effortlessly. Time was when a 'suitable girl' belonged to the right caste and came from a good family. This is no longer enough. Today, much more important than the caste and family is the fit between the man's lifestyle and the lifestyle the girl is accustomed to.

> Beena would have been happy married to a professor in Madhya Pradesh where she grew up. Going to the latest Bollywood film, getting dressed for the neighbourhood wedding, these things would have made her happy. She's absolutely miserable with the life we have and I have to say, that she makes me quite miserable a lot of the time (Rishi, a fifty-three-year-old senior executive in a Mumbai-based MNC).

Rishi was educated in the US at time when a foreign degree was not quite so commonplace. Rishi has done very well professionally. He joined his company at a fairly senior position and rose to the top rung in record time. He was given enviable postings in London and New York, and then less glamorous places in Latin America and Africa. Rishi and his wife Beena have two daughters, aged twenty-seven and twenty-two. Both married early and are now living in the US.

Rishi and Beena had an arranged marriage. All his years in the US had made Rishi very family oriented.

I just wanted a girl who was intelligent and loving and would fit in with my family. Arranged marriages seemed to have worked in our family, so without thinking about it too much I agreed to one. It was a mistake. Beena, who comes from a small town was never able to adjust to my rather more Westernized work environment. She grew up in a society where to have a drink at a party, or to dance socially was evidence of a depraved lifestyle. So she has spent much of her life at her maike, her parents' place. Even that would have been all right, if she didn't get so upset if I ever want to spend time with my family. We stay together because I don't believe in divorce. I think it has a really terrible impact on the children. Like this I've missed out on a normal happy marriage, but it's not too bad most of the time. In our own fashion we do love each other. But yes, I've made some huge sacrifices in my life. Of course I realize she has made very big sacrifices herself. This is something people who see things from the outside don't realize. In Beena's hometown, there were other things to keep the women occupied, participating in marriages, getting involved with the preparations for religious festivals . . . A big city, however, is hard on women like her. Since she has never held a job, she has spent most of her life in idleness. She is always pushing me to reach ever-greater heights. So though she doesn't enjoy their company, she will go to any lengths when entertaining professional colleagues, and of course the red carpet is always out for her natal family whom she tries to impress with the perks of my job. I do whatever is required of me. But I can't help feeling bitter that no member of my family has ever been made welcome in our house.

Psychoanalyst Rotraut Roychowdury says such cases are far from uncommon. When a girl from a more traditional family marries and has to adapt to a lifestyle where she feels inadequate, she may react by trying to tie her husband more closely to her by keeping him away from his family. And many women who are full-time housewives live their lives vicariously through their husbands. Their identity is as 'so and so's wife'. So they can only progress through their husbands' rise up the ladder. The only solution in such cases is for the husband to try and make the wife more independent early in the marriage. If she becomes more self-confident, then she may become more relaxed.

Working hours are not an issue in Rishi's house, and though some of the problems are probably due to a personality clash, there is also something else happening here. Rishi and his wife are victims of a society in transition. The old certainties of a good basis for an arranged marriage are even more suspect now. Being compatible is much more of a challenge than it was earlier. Earlier one married the man, and if one married into the same caste and class, the family was likely to provide a greater zone of comfort than may now be the case. Today, the man's job and the job-related lifestyle are likely to be powerful determinants of how easy the 'fit' in the marriage is going to be.

Those Who Are Climbing Up the Ladder are Happier About the Changes

See, a lot depends on your expectations. When I was growing up, my father, who was a primary school teacher, had to support seven people on his teacher's salary, so we often had only one meal in the day. In comparison, my circumstances are much better. My wife feels she has much more freedom than her mother and mother-in-law did. Our lifestyle is simple, we don't need curtains and carpets and all those fancy things. We have essential furniture and useful gadgets like a mixer and washing machine. We have a TV and that's enough for us. In this house, the food for the whole day is cooked in one pressure cooker, so the load on the housekeeper is minimal. Our sons are doing well, so I am not under too much tension regarding their future. Sometimes, I feel exhausted and since there are so many people living under one roof, naturally there are some disagreements from time to time, but no major problems (T. Ramesh, thirty-eight, a sales representative for a small private company).

Ramesh and his wife live in a Chennai suburb about two hours away from his office. A sixty-eight-year-old widowed aunt and her forty-year-old unmarried daughter live with the couple and their two sons aged twelve and ten. Ramesh commutes to his office by local train and bus. His wife, who is a teacher in a small private school in another part of the city, does the same. Ramesh's aunt looks after the house. She is helped by her daughter who gives music tuition to girls in the neighbourhood.

Ramesh spends about fifteen days in the month travelling. And his working hours are long and erratic, but when you talk to Ramesh he mentions few problems. Ramesh's views reflect how one's viewpoint is also influenced by whether one is going up or down the economic ladder.

In contemporary middle-class India, work–family issues affect men in many different ways. There is obvious conflict when trying to balance the requirements of the wife's career in a dual-career family. Ved, the army officer, is hardly able to get any time with his family because the non-family stations of his career and the locational needs of his wife's career make it virtually impossible for them to be together. Dubai-based Dev's wife is with him after having given up her job to do so. Dev feels her sacrifice has changed her and he feels some degree of guilt and sadness that they had to choose this option. Rishi has a full-time housewife and mother as his spouse and is perhaps the most miserable of all as he has had to deal with fulfilling his wife ambitions through his own career progression. He also has to make allowances for the problems her inability to adjust to a new environment have made on their marriage.

In this chapter, we see how while women take the responsibilities on the home front as unalterable, and make adjustments at the workplace, men do the reverse. They accept the demands of the job as inviolable and make adjustments at home. Thus, Dev, the executive, will go to Dubai whatever the impact of the move on his wife and children, and Gautam, the photographer, will accept assignments at whatever hour they come, expecting the family to adapt and adjust to the requirements of the job.

Though women's attitudes to work have changed, and increasingly young women today believe that they can only marry when they are established in their careers, the attitude of men to their careers has remained unchanged, or has changed only a little. So, though men married to working wives did say that this gives them greater flexibility, to change jobs, or to strike out on their own, it is still not easy finding a husband who is supported by his wife. Most men liked the idea of having working wives, but few were really willing to make major sacrifices to help facilitate their wives' careers.

The phenomenon of elderly parents living with their children is just becoming discernible. Men wish to do their bit for their parents. But after talking to men who lived in joint families, or men who had parents living with them, it became apparent that in many ways as great sensitivity was called for at home as at the workplace. Fathers who have to uproot themselves and live with adult sons have to adjust and adapt to a lifestyle which may be very different from what they believe is a healthy, or even moral, way to live.

It is also difficult for adult sons who are now given training in cultural mores across the globe, depending on their job requirements to accommodate the wishes of elderly parents beyond a point. This sometimes causes stress, which is difficult for both to handle.

Elderly parents, who compare the amount of time and attention they gave in their own time to what they may be receiving, will, of course, find the comparisons odious.

What often aggravates the problem is that earlier families were larger and responsibilities were shared by many more offspring. With only one or two adult children, the burden each shoulders is obviously greater. The lack of a family home and the fact that there may be only one son to look after the parent may also require the parent to relocate to a foreign country as there is no other home for the aged parent. This calls for tremendous adjustment on both sides. India is just beginning to see the emergence of old-age homes to deal with this and similar eventualities, but there is still a huge stigma that attaches to a family that chooses this option.

Also, such homes are expensive and only viable for those who are well off financially. Those who are dependent on modest pensions, or even more alarmingly, on VRS payouts, are likely to be very sharply hit as they try to make both ends meet.

Indeed, men wish to be able to fulfil their responsibilities to both their parents and their children and to have more family time. They would like time for work and time for leisure, but somehow seemed to feel powerless to influence the work environment in any significant way.

6

Young Singles: Living the Good Life or No Time for a Life?

A New Sense of Possibility

If you wish to see where the Indian family is today as also where it is headed, it is imperative to talk to young people. What are their hopes and dreams, their fears and problems? What do they want from life? How do they see their circumstances? How much has changed from a generation ago? And what remains constant?

This chapter is based on over fifty very in-depth interviews, some of which were face-to-face while others were over email. I talked to scores of young people aged between twenty and thirty living in metropolitan cities all over the country. They provide an engaging snapshot of young India today. I spoke to lawyers, designers, HR executives and journalists. I spoke to chartered accountants and research assistants, and I also spoke to a very large proportion of management students from the premier management institutes of the country. The sample in this chapter belongs to the middle class just as does the sample segment in all the other chapters. But there is a difference. In many ways, a majority of the young singles I spoke to are in a position to make choices with regard to how they wish to lead their lives. So, though many come from families that are far from affluent, they are privileged because they have competed and gained entry into institutions that give them a decided edge over their peers. It is interesting therefore to see what is important to these young people. Do they value getting ahead in the rat race above all? How important is work–family balance to them? Indeed, what *is* important to them?

These young singles are poised on the crest of a new wave of possibilities and will perhaps anticipate attitudes and aspirations that will become more widespread in the years to come. With their permission, I have used the actual names in the vast majority of interviews in this chapter. This generation has come of age as India moved from the shadows of its socialist past into the bright strobe lights of consumerism. With grandparents who had grown up in the days of the heady nationalism of the Gandhian era, and parents who had lived with the chronic shortages of the 1950s, 1960s and 1970s, this 'MTV generation' is keenly aware that their aspirations need only be limited by their vision. It is a generation that is growing up with access to opportunities their parents' generation could never have dreamed of. Their ambitions are not circumscribed by state or national boundaries, but span the world. In every field of endeavour there is an Indian success story.

Indeed, as I found to my pleasant surprise during my stint at Cambridge, because of the very high academic standards set by Indian students in the last few decades, Indians today are expected to excel! On a balmy summer evening, at a well-attended formal hall, the president of Wolfson College was exulting at the victory the Wolfson cricket team had scored over a rival college. What made the victory particularly sweet was that the rival team was full of South Asians (read Indians)! My academic supervisor too, believed that it was the Indian family that somehow had the mantra for success!

This is also a generation that has grown up when multiculturalism is in fashion and thus may never experience in interactions with the outside world the rank racism that previous generations may have encountered. The Indian diaspora and the large NRI populations in the UK and the US have actually had an influence on mainstream preferences in those countries. That tikka masala is Britain's favourite food, displacing fish and chips, has been widely reported in India, making a new generation far more self-assured about its preference for Indian food. We now hear that even British toddlers prefer curry and rice to pizzas or pasta! Bollywood icons like Amitabh Bachchan and Aishwarya Rai now rub shoulders with Pierce Brosnan at Madame Tussauds. Indian names, from Salman Rushdie to Rupa Bajwa, are now fixtures on international prizewinner lists and Indian entrepreneurs, techies and executives now head international organizations, making a young Indian feel integrated in the world in a way that was never possible before. This then, is a generation that need never have felt that somehow it was second best.

Many young people made fortunes on the dotcom boom. This encouraged entrepreneurial activities by these young people in areas that their parents would not have considered possible. Twenty-four-year-old Saket Agarwal launched Aqua Java, which specializes in serving eighty varieties of coffee, in fairly conservative Kolkata, in 1999. Five years later, Aqua Java has four outlets in the city and another is to open in Siliguri shortly. Kolkata itself has since seen the launch of a cha (tea) bar at the Oxford Bookstore and Gallery, a Barista's, a Café Coffee Day. The city now has a reputation for being a great place to launch eateries. A twenty-four-year-old had anticipated the trend and also had the courage to give concrete shape to a dream! His success story and the success stories of others like him have encouraged a whole generation to have faith in their own genius, to become entrepreneurs, or to launch into areas which now generate as much income as conventional fields such as engineering and medicine did earlier. The outsourcing of jobs from the US and UK to call centres means that anyone who is a graduate and fluent in English can start working on a salary of Rs 15,000 a month. That is enough money to really live it up. It is also money that can be saved and used to fund further education, yet another way to better one's chances. There are other fields to be explored: being a deejay, or a veejay, a TV anchor, a quiz show host, or a model co-ordinator. Why not when you may earn in an evening what your father would have earned in a week or perhaps a month!

The Rise of a More Materialistic, Consumerist Lifestyle

The liberalization of the economy and the consumer boom of the 1990s have not only created new job opportunities, they have also whetted an appetite for many of the gadgets and gizmos that are advertised in the press and on TV 24/7. The mind boggles to think of how, till not so long ago, there was a waiting list for an Ambassador, a Fiat, and even the humble scooter. In the 1980s, when the Maruti 800 appeared on Delhi's streets, it was a much sought after vehicle and attracted a premium of about Rs 40,000 to Rs 50,000 on its price of Rs 40,000! Today's status-conscious youth would rather travel in a taxi than in that particular model of car!

As Pavan Varma says in *The Great Indian Middle Class*, ' on one aspect the MNCs were dead right: they knew that even if the middle class had limited money, there was little limitation to its wants' (Varma, 1998: 181). Peer pressure, the constant beaming of ads selling every thing from cosmetics to clothes to condominiums has made 'wants' into 'needs'.

In a survey of 4,000 women conducted by Grey Global in five metros, in the nineteen to twenty-four age group, there is the entirely unsurprising finding that 85 per cent of the women interviewed consider creature comforts, including a big car, as pre-requisites for happiness. (Vinita Faridi, *Hindustan Times*, City, 1 December 2003, Kolkata).

That young men have an identical viewpoint on this issue was clearly apparent in the hundreds of conversations with young people and the over fifty in-depth interviews I did for this chapter. This is one area where young singles in India are fairly close in attitude to young singles in the West

Has the New Materialism Led to a Greater Selfishness Amongst the Young?

'Young people today can only think of their own pleasures, their own career objectives, where do they have the time to think of the family?' said more than one old-timer when discussing the younger generation. The young themselves think that they are far more selfish and self-absorbed. A student of IIM, Lucknow, puts a profit and loss spin to it by saying, 'Today's young are more career oriented. For a middle-class family bringing up a child has become a loss in investment, as demands have increased but when the time comes for the child to pay back by looking after the older generation, he leaves in a hurry'. One young man attributes the change in attitude to the cut-throat competition, which calls for a killer instinct to survive. Twenty-three-year-old Sameer Lal from Rudrapur is of the opinion that 'this generation is more comfortable with the fact that people are selfish, always have been, they don't take the trouble of hiding their selfishness under a mask.'

But as we analyse the answers young singles have given on a whole range of questions, this rather negative assessment does not appear to be accurate.

Living on Credit

Today's young are more driven by material benefits than perhaps ever before and they are comfortable going into debt in a way earlier generations never could be. The Bharatiya Janata Party (BJP) government's attempts to reduce the fees at the premier management institutes in 2004 brought to the fore a fact that not everyone was aware of, that a large number of students go through management institutes on credit. Indeed, after they graduate, they and others like them are likely to buy a car, a house and every gadget they feel the need for on credit. To use a phrase of our times, there has been a paradigm shift in attitude.

What this Generation of Young Singles has in Common with their Peers in the West

> Indeed what is most interesting about youth at the start of a new millennium is that youth experience is as varied now as it has ever been in history and yet, paradoxically, young people continue to be bonded by common experiences and concerns (Williamson, 1997: 3).

There are stereotypes about young people abroad just as there are stereotypes about young people in India. In this context it is useful to compare attitudes between the two, to see where attitudes are the same and where they differ.

In the book, *Geeks and Geezers*, recently published by the Harvard Business School Press, the authors list out a series of attributes that are common to geezers, people who came of age between 1945–54, and geeks, people who came of age between 1991–2000, to arrive at some conclusions about how attitudes have changed.

Geezer's Concerns
Making a living
Earning a good salary
Starting and supporting a family
Stability and security
Working hard and getting rewarded by the system
Listening to your elders
Paying dues to the organization

Geek's Concerns
Making history
Achieving personal wealth
Launching a career
Change and impermanence
Working hard so you can write your own rules
Wondering if your elders got it wrong
Deciding where loyalty should lie
Achieving work/life balance
(Bennis and Thomas, 2002: 84).

Attitudes Amongst Indian Young Singles

It is interesting that in most areas the geeks' attitudes would be fairly similar to the attitudes of our own young singles. However, unlike the geeks in the West who wonder if their elders got it wrong, young singles in India are acutely aware that their parents' generation just grew up in an era where there were far fewer opportunities and that their parents worked extremely hard to provide the younger generation with the head start they needed to get ahead in life.

A major cultural difference between East and West is that in India, most young men and women who are located in the same city as their parents, are likely to be living with their parents. Even the joint family still has substantial support. The Grey Survey of young women mentioned earlier states that 62 per cent of young women would like to live in a joint family because they believe that the presence of grandparents would have a healthy influence on their children. The young singles I talked to, both male and female, were unequivocal about the very great importance they attached to their family. But just to underline how the gap in attitudes between the West and East is narrowing, parents in the US are now reported to be more open to having their adult offspring live with them. A classic study of the parents of boomer high school graduates in the 1960s and early 1970s showed they were much more flexible than the researchers anticipated, changing their views along with their children. If that was true, then how much more so with 'baby boomers'. After all, they share with their children much higher educational levels. Revealingly, too, they are much happier about sharing their home with grown-up children than were their parents. (Jennings and Neimi, 1981: 309-10).

(The study by Jennings and Ncimi reveals a sharp fall between 1973 and 1989 in Americans aged thirty-five–forty-five answering that sharing a home with children is a bad idea.)

Attitudes to the Family

Despite the rising divorce rate and despite the fact that one can no longer take family support for granted as one might have been able to in the past, the Indian family is still very strong. Most young people have a very good equation with their families. And it is still the family one turns to in both good times as well as bad. There are, of course, countless young people who do have problems with the family. A real concern is the burden today's young carry of being forced to bring to fruition their parents' dreams and of fulfilling their families' often unrealistic expectations. Every year the media reports suicides caused because of an inability to measure up to societal and parental pressure. A tragic reminder of the terrible price some young people pay for not being able to take flight and soar in the way that they wish to, and in the way their peers may be doing.

Cultural dissonance is another problem many young people have to contend with. If you have been brought up in a conservative Indian home, there are a hundred things you have to adjust to in the life you now live because you have achieved success in examinations that open doors to a new, exciting but sometimes confusing world. You may handle these changes with more self-confidence than any previous generation of Indians may have done, but still they are changes that call for behavioural and lifestyle changes, which always take their toll.

I have worked with organizations that deal with the problems of young people who are coping with stress and competition, but this chapter is not about them.

Here, I deal with success stories. I talk to people who are perceived to have succeeded, to see what their experience and viewpoint has been. What are their priorities, what are their dreams? If they do have a nightmare, what is it? These are the people employers wish to attract, to hire. And provided they deliver, these are the people they will wish to retain. These young people then are in a position to influence the way in which the workplace is changing and the way it may do so in the future. Thus, though they may never have thought of it, these young singles, and others like them, may determine whether we have more, or less, work–family balance in the future.

Family First

'I can dream really big dreams, because my parents believe in me, my brother and sister will help me in practical ways, little things like keeping an eye out for the right opportunity, collecting forms, or just seeing that my clothes are in order. When I fail, the one thing I can count on is my family's support.' Too good to be true? Perhaps. Except that one heard it repeatedly. The emotional scenes one witnesses on the popular reality show, Indian Idol, when the wannabes go for a quick trip home, may just be more than media-generated hype. The family inspires respect and love. And even young people just embarking on a career who would, one imagines, be bedazzled by the promise of a very bright future, seem not to lose track of this. A real feeling of bonding and an innate pragmatism makes the family an unbeatable support system.

A twenty-two-year-old trainee executive, Sumit Tibrewal, puts taking care of parents and the larger family first on a list of five priorities which include career, satisfactory relationship, marriage and a balanced and interesting life as other options. Many others such as twenty-five-year-old Akash of the Management Development Institute (MDI), Gurgaon, put it second on their list. Twenty-six-year-old journalist Monjima Sinha says the family provides 'support in every sense, both emotionally and materially'. She adds with candour, 'If I lived alone, I couldn't live in the kind of luxury I live in right now.' Twenty-four-year-old executive, Pallavi Murty, describes her family as 'the backbone of my life. They provide help, relaxation. They make tremendous adjustments to cope with my timings.'

The Family also Reflects the Value System of a Patriarchal Society

The family provides the support, which allows some young people to achieve goals that they could never have reached on their own. This is of course most apparent in the case of child prodigies. Where would a Vijay Amritraj be without the help of his mother, Maggie?

But sometimes it is the family which through its regressive attitudes may actually hold an offspring back. Indeed, it is interesting how men and women interpret the very same question differently. When commenting upon the role of the family, many women remarked on how it needed to be sensitive to the contemporary woman's need for greater control over her own life.

Twenty-year-old Sukanya Sanyal of the National Institute of Design, Ahmedabad, says that 'the family plays a very important part—it needs to be encouraging of her work otherwise she may feel guilty in pursuing her ambition'. Twenty-six-year-old Shilpa Bakde of IIM, Calcutta, describes the role of the family as 'Huge. If the family supports her and stops pressuring her and putting all her male interactions under the microscope then a woman can really move forward'.

The Saas–Bahu Conflict

Do in-laws have to be out-laws? Can the divide between one's own parents and the parents of one's spouse be bridged? This generation is willing to give it a shot.

Shradha Shah, a chartered accountant aspirant, is offended by the question, 'How willing are you to take responsibility for your parents and parents-in-law if the situation should so demand?' 'There is no question of willingness to take responsibility of parents. In-laws is a bad term', she says, 'parents are parents are parents no matter what, we owe our life to them. It would be our privilege to have them with us.' However, for some, the duty to one's parents will be balanced with an equally strong desire for privacy and perhaps for independence. One young man wished to take care of parents and parents-in-law, but did not want to live in the same house as them. He hoped to be able to afford another flat for them, with suitable arrangements for elder care!

Parents Heroes for Young People in the West

It is a widespread belief in India that respect for the older generation is an Indian attribute and that young people in the West have very little time for the older generation. However, as the authors of *Geezers and Geeks*, a book which compares the attitudes amongst old-timers and youngsters in the West found, in contrast to the older generation, which looked up to legendary world figures as their idols, young people in the US today actually look upon their parents as heroes.

Heroes among Geezers and Geeks

Geezers
Franklin D. Roosevelt
Gandhi
Abraham Lincoln

Geeks
My parents
Friends or co-workers
My grandfather
(Benison and Thomas, 2002: 80, Table 3.2).

One reason for the lack of heroes from public life is undoubtedly the intense media coverage of public personalities today. 'The pervasiveness of information (whether it is accurate or not) renders heroes temporary and makes the idolization of individuals a risky business. Perhaps to compensate for the lack of public figures worthy of their sort of regard, geeks chose people closer to home, people of less monumental accomplishments, but people whose accomplishments were tangible (perhaps even verifiable?) and who thus deserved their respect' (ibid: 80).

In my conversations with young singles, the fact that they had seen their parents struggle through difficult times to give their children better opportunities made them very keen to pay back. Across a whole range of questions, the desire to take care of parents and parents-in-law came across quite strongly.

It was also interesting that while older people were pleasantly surprised about the high priority young singles gave to their parents, younger people were amazed that anyone should be surprised by this. Indeed, my twenty-two-year-old son cautioned me not to present this as a 'finding' or I would irrevocably damage the credibility of the book. 'People have always cared for their parents', he said, 'why should it be surprising that this is still the case. Wanting to earn a six figure salary or a top of the line car is hardly in conflict with looking after your parents.'

In Fran Siemensma's report on MBA students in India and Australia, which draws upon a wealth of research on the subject, the conclusions drawn were that 'students placed primary importance on family and their responsibilities as sons and daughters. Many sought to balance personal and parental wishes, such as the expectation that an older son would provide financial, housing and emotional support to parents' (Siemensma 1999).

Attitude to the Larger Family

While conducting interviews for the chapter on the joint family, I met a matriarch who told me that 'for this generation the family means parents, spouse and children; they do not count any one else as family'. This has been characterized in the West as the beanpole family that has closer interaction with parents and siblings and less with other members of the family. To some extent that observation is correct. Except for a few young people who had a wider perspective on the family, the family was indeed circumscribed to this very small circle. Many of the young people interviewed had grown up in nuclear families in an environment where priority had been given to getting the right academic qualifications. They had missed out on the long holidays at the family home, the attendance at family weddings and at chattis, annaprasans and funerals that had shaped the sensibilities of an earlier generation. Those who grew up in joint families had experienced some of the bonding with family members an earlier generation of Indians took for granted.

However, what was interesting is that while this generation feels a degree of protectiveness with regard to its parents, they seem to feel that children can get by on a very tough regimen.

Twenty-five-year-old Aviral Bansal, a research assistant from Ahmedabad, speaks for many of his ilk when he says, 'I think everybody should lead a tough life as it is going to be still tougher in future. So I would like my family [wife and kids] to have a tough life. Parents are excluded. They have had their share [of trouble] so I would like to make things easier for them.'

The Attitude to Work: Impatient for Success

Today's professionally-qualified young singles have high aspirations. They see themselves going into top-end jobs and reaching senior positions at a young age. They are self-confident and demanding about the kind of jobs which they wish to take on. Jobs that offer professional challenge as also high rewards are perhaps the only jobs that fit the bill. It is a world that even as it has expanded in some ways, has shrunk in other ways. Travelling from Chennai to California is now easier than ever before. Being global jet-setters and global job-trotters are dreams that can now be realized. There is a huge employment opportunity for young Indians in the outside world. The demographic profile of developed nations (with the exception of the US), shows a negative growth rate, and these societies are ageing with the over-eighties being the fastest-growing segment in countries like the UK. If they wish to continue with the social security systems they now have, they will need to import people from countries like India. We have already seen this happen with low-end jobs in the software industries, and to a lesser extent with nurses and doctors from India working for the UK's National Health Service for instance, but there is every likelihood of this trend continuing and creating a vast opportunity for Indian executives, Indian teachers and so on.

Many seek to balance their overwhelming need to earn big bucks and acquire the many trappings of today's consumerist culture, the condominium, the flashy car, the home theatre, etc., with a young person's natural desire for adventure. They do this by reversing the sequence that an earlier generation would have followed. So, when they are young, what most seems to excite them is work. They look forward to being able to retire by the age of forty. This is when they see themselves with time for things they would really enjoy. Aviral Bansal dreams of climbing Mount Everest, twenty-four-year-old Anand Dalmia of IIM, Lucknow, would like to go around the world, play golf, learn to play a musical instrument and read and write more. Twenty-five-year-old Akash from MDI, Gurgaon, sees himself partying, going to pubs, pursuing an interest in rifle shooting apart from wanting to pursue psychology and palmistry!

Women predictably are far more rooted to reality. They wish to get a head start in their career, because they are aware that there may be a slowing of tempo to accommodate marriage and children. Somehow they want to do their best by both.

Chastening Effect of the Economic Slowdown

This is a generation that saw the dotcom boom that made millionaires of young people very like themselves. And they also saw the anguish and uncertainty that accompanied the economic downturn that followed. They saw the brightest and the best go to the US with the promise of mega-dollar salaries with some having to return having 'earned' an air ticket and sometimes a mobile phone! They saw 'right-sizing' that saw some being mercilessly axed, even as others zoomed ahead in ways that were not always clearly understood.

MBA graduates in earlier studies (*IIM B Management Review*, April 2004, p. 24) have appeared to be callous. One participant criticized most MBA students for their impersonal acceptance of 'downsizing', which she described as the 'euphemistic' language of management which disguised workforce losses. She believed that there was a possibility that students were unable to empathize with a situation that they hoped never to experience. (*IIM B Management Review*, Volume 16, Number 1, March 2004). In my research, young people were sensitized to the harsh downswing of the high-flying job and were only too aware that it could happen to anyone, that it could happen to them.

Bitterness of those Who Cannot Join the Party

Rejected job seeker stabs woman in office
A youth on Thursday stabbed a receptionist on Larsen and Toubro's staircase with a pair of scissors because she didn't provide him with the job he was looking for.
   Kanchan Dutta (22) often went to the L&T office at Park Street to look for a job, but Jhulan Dey (39) would turn him back every time saying there was no vacancy. He finally took his revenge . . . lying in wait with his scissors, he stabbed her in the stomach (*Hindustan Times*, Kolkata Live).

Elsewhere, before the test for a grade four job in the railways, aspirants from Bihar were savagely attacked in the neighbouring state of Assam as they believed that they would lose out on jobs if the visitors were allowed to take the exam. This set off a chain of communal violence till the matter was resolved. The knowledge that some young people will be earning salaries upwards of Rs 50,000 a month, while others may not be in a position to earn more than Rs 6,000 a month, or indeed may have to remain jobless, sets off deep feelings of frustration and resentment amongst those who are unable to participate in the new prosperity. In a meritocracy, the opportunity to soar, to sink, or to swim, is open to all. Sometimes, siblings and close friends go on to reach very different levels of material success. The pressure this creates is considerable.

Some Choose an Alternative Lifestyle

Some young people from institutes such as the National Institute of Design, Ahmedabad, and indeed, sometimes even MBAs who one would expect to be the very epitome of the yuppie, or young upwardly mobile professional, go on to repudiate success in the conventional sense of the word and wish to do socially relevant work which gives rewards which cannot be measured in material terms. Vinayak Lohani, an alumnus from IIM, Calcutta, has an engineering degree from IIT, Khargapur, and worked for a year in Infosys, before turning his back on the corporate world. Vinayak now runs an organization called Parivar, which is a residential school for socially-disadvantaged children (Bose, 2004: 104). Vinayak first found his background to be more of a hindrance than help, the report tells us, but now has the support of senior alumni and Parivar is growing satisfactorily.

The Younger Generation Prefers Security

The large personnel cuts made by corporate houses, which were earlier seen as safe havens, and even by rock solid institutions such as the State Bank of India, made a subtle but sure difference to the mindset of the young urban middle class. There was, in their mind, no safe haven any more. If security was desired it had to be self-created, one could no longer expect an organization to provide it. So young singles are in a hurry to acquire a house and security. They are also looking at loans to get themselves cars and everything else an earlier generation of salaried wage earners would have expected the organization they worked for to provide them with by and by. But in my conversations with young singles, while most young people would like performance to be recognized and rewarded, they actually prefer the idea of a long-term career and security rather than high-risk-high-reward job-hopping career progression, which is currently in favour with corporate houses.

In answer to the question 'Do you personally like the American culture of hire and fire with high rewards and swift terminations or do you prefer the more conservative relationship-building work culture that we adopted from the British', the overwhelming majority plumped for the latter. All the women did. And so did more than half of the men and almost all the men studying at the IIMs. Akshay believes that ' unless one develops the feeling of oneness and loyalty for an organization, one cannot perform to potential'. Anand feels that trust, belonging and peace of mind are all going to flow from the British model. Abhishek feels 'European work practices are better because they are more humane'. Nidhi Bagaria is of the view that ' a healthy relationship between the employer and employee is very important in an organization. This gives the employee a better environment to work where they try to put in extra effort indirectly benefiting the organization. The American culture is tough and may be suitable there but not in India.' One student from IIM, Bangalore, makes the point that the British way 'is more conducive to working women. I don't have to worry that if I tell my boss that I have problems at home he will view me as a liability for then I will have problems in my career too!' Another IIM colleague, Shilpa Yadav, says, 'I don't like the hire and fire culture as it leads to a lot of anxiety and instability'. Nag Ya Lamanchili is for the conservative relationship-building culture. 'But it's important to have a good employee–company fit. There should be some element of security in the job.'

Aviral Bansal, the research assistant from Ahmedabad, however, is strongly for the American work culture. 'If by relationship building culture you mean to say a culture where you are getting paid not because of the results you produce, but because you have a nice PR with your boss, I definitely would not like that kind of culture. Imagine a person sticking to a 1950 Ambassador in 2003 because he has built a 'RELATIONSHIP' with the car, it's stupid.' Another chartered accountant prefers the American culture 'because it gives a fair chance to anybody who has the talent and is willing to make it big in life.'

Some want a mix. Sivaramakrishnan B. from IIM, Calcutta, says, 'I would like something in the middle. Surely fire, if someone has no inclination to work, otherwise keep him. Performance must be rated and one may be penalized if required, but one should not be fired.' An IT professional wants a balance between the two, 'rewards must match performance and there must be no compromise on this, but swift terminations should be avoided'. NID student Sukanya Sanyal would like to work in an organization with high risks and high rewards now and change to a more conservative company later!

In an attempt to truly gauge how attitudes to work and family life have changed there was a question, which stated: 'Earlier a man rose up the ladder slowly and reached his peak when he was in his fifties and his responsibilities to his children were reduced. Today there is a trend for promising people to be pushed into very senior positions at a young age when they are likely to have the greatest demands made on their time from their children. What do you feel about this?'

A twenty-three-year-old woman management student expresses the dilemma of many others like her when she says, 'I have no idea how I'm going to cope with this but I certainly don't want to compromise with my career.' Another believes 'I think one has to make a clear distinction between work and family life and allot a specific amount of time for both and should not let one thing encroach upon the other [in terms of time and emotions]'. Twenty-four-year-old B. Com student

Nidhi Bagaria is of the view that 'children should not be neglected, particularly when they are too small to understand. One parent has to take the responsibility of bringing up the child. And if both parents aspire to senior positions then they should plan out their future before thinking of having children.' Many women students say that they believe that ' being a part of the rat race for the sake of a position and keeping the children deprived of your time can only get you money and status which is no good if the peace of the home is lost'. Twenty six-year-old management student Shilpa Bakde believes peer pressure is responsible for this to some extent. 'Unfortunately that's what most of us want. We are fed with the image of VP at thirty, partner at thirty-five. All my friends talk about retiring with a huge bank balance at forty. But I don't want to miss my child's birthday party or my anniversary dinner, so I hope there is a way to balance both.' And as far as the young can see, the resolution will come with a change of attitude at the workplace. As Sivaramakrishnan B. says, 'Due to excessive stress burn-outs, organizations have started improving their work–life balance so I guess it can be managed'.

Even though they are yet to become parents, some young people are aware of what may be going on in our society. A student from IIT, Delhi, makes the point that parents sometimes feel that that they are doing everything for their children [by working long hours to achieve early financial independence] but they tend to forget that they are sacrificing the child's present for the future'.

Attitude to Children in Dual-Career Homes

Surveys in UK and the US have consistently shown that men would like mothers of young children to either be full-time mothers or work part-time. A British Social Attitudes survey shows that while 80 per cent of men feel that women should work full-time after they get married and before they have children, only 5 per cent of men would like women with children under five years of age to work full-time (British Social Attitudes Survey, Twelfth Report).

However, such a response was not found amongst the young men I interviewed. The vast majority do not envisage their wives sacrificing their careers or even giving up promotions or postings to fulfil childcare responsibilities. Many wistfully imagine that somehow, when the time comes, solutions will be found. Indeed, many young singles feel that children actually develop independence and useful competencies growing up in dual-career families. They hope that the natural disadvantage children of dual-career families suffer, may be rectified with both parents giving quality time. Boarding schools or (being looked after by) grandparents are seen as other possible solutions. Practical solutions include measures like parents setting aside weekends for the children. A student from ICFAI (Institute of Chartered Financial Analysts of India), Hyderabad, exhorts those who find the situation problematic not to have children. Kanishka Sinha, who is working for a Mumbai-based MNC is amongst the few who believes that this is not an issue. 'Children will suffer only if the parents are incapable of making them feel wanted and if this is the case, they will suffer even if the parents were not working'. A twenty-four-year-old working for a leading consulting firm with its headquarters in the US believes that a change in emphasis from 'face time' to a greater focus on output, or results, in organizations, especially the corporate sector, would be helpful.

A Career Break for Motherhood?

'I would ideally not like a break. My mother managed to bring me up without staying at home, I think I can do it too', says one daughter who was brought up by a single working mother. In an age of equality, many young women look for parity here as in other aspects of life. 'I don't think I'll take a break, but if that is required than I would expect my spouse to take a break too.'

However, motherhood still does command a premium and some women, a small minority of those interviewed, do plan to take a break from their career when the children are small. Twenty-three year old Shradha says, 'The child will be my top priority. I intend to take a break from my career the day I become a mom.' Shweta Bagaria, a twenty-four-year-old chartered accountant says, 'A break from a full-time career is desirable at that stage. Something on a part-time basis can be an option.' Human resources executive Divya Kashyap sees herself doing something part-time 'like open my own consultancy/teach/work for an NGO'. She is forthright that 'money is important as one is used to being financially independent'. Nidhi too is emphatic that 'I will take a very short break from my career for four–five years so that I can give them time and make them comfortable with the idea of my working later.'

So when one looks at the big picture, it is clear that though childcare is a major concern for young singles, it is no longer acceptable to slot it as a woman's issue. Except for one young man who wanted to marry a housewife so that she could take care of their children, all the young men saw it as a joint responsibility for which both partners had to make equal compromises on the job front. A few women were prepared to let their career take a backseat for a short while but they were clear that being financially independent is an imperative, so solutions are obviously required. There is a great deal of ambivalence of how fast track progression is to be balanced with childcare responsibilities in the future.

One young man asks rhetorically, 'Why can't a thirty-two-year-old CEO go to office with his toddler? Why can't he have daycare facility at his company where employees can leave their children with peace of mind?' He goes on to say that ' I am sure that the companies in India will provide daycare facilities for [the children of] their male staff as well.'

Do Young Singles Experience Stress from the Pressure to Excel?

Most of the young singles interviewed were in situations where they were constantly in competition with their peers. They seemed to take this in their stride and indeed to thrive on the gruelling demands that were made on them. Most young people are fairly resigned to the fact that those who had jobs which paid them top of the line salaries were not going to have time for personal pursuits or even for the family. Choices are made in a context, and since this is the only lifestyle this generation has seen, it does not quarrel with the lack of balance between work and family life at this stage of life. They see conflict only when they marry and have children or perhaps when elderly parents may need special attention. Since, in many ways, these young people were actually living out the middle-class dream, parents too accepted their predicament without demur.

When these young singles experience another lifestyle with better work–life balance, they are quickly converted to the benefits of this. Karthik Karunanithi went to do an MBA in Australia. When he saw that they had a five-day week and working hours from 9 a.m. to 5 p.m., he applied for permanent residency! Twenty-nine-year-old Ashish Sinha, a banker is also considering a job in the UK because 'of the more decent working hours and the weekends off!'

Ambivalence

They want work–family balance, but seem unclear as to how they intend to achieve it. While many say that they will be willing to refuse promotions and postings for the sake of the family, and few would like to live in a separate city from the spouse once they are married, they also envision themselves either at the top of the tree, or in a position to retire by the age of forty or fifty!

With regard to childcare and elder care, one senses ambivalence. Some say they will take their children to the workplace, others have the attitude that solutions can and will be found. Generally, there seemed to be a greater concern for parents than children. Happily, many also included parents-in-law in this category. With today's greater need for space and freedom, some wanted to look after their parents but were uncertain whether they wanted them to live with them.

Of course it must be said that when questioned on working hours for instance, many young people acknowledge that gains on one front would probably mean sacrifices on another front. It is just that when questioned about how they intend to cope with factors like childcare or elder care in a dual-career family for instance, the answers seem to portray unbridled optimism rather than a more pragmatic realism.

In a way, this is a little paradoxical. For if this generation is more hungry for the visible signs of success, if driving the right make and model of car is important, which it appears to be, then this is not accompanied by a more realistic appraisal of sacrifices on the home front. Will these young people sacrifice rewards at the workplace for more time at home, or will the workplace itself change to allow better work–family balance remains to be seen.

Being Located in a Separate City from One's Spouse

While it is entirely possible that attitudes may change once these young people get into real-life job situations, right now, being located in a separate city from the spouse except for a very short time frame gets an unqualified 'NO' from all but one interviewee. 'How can one stay apart from one's better half?', and 'I don't think that I would be ready for such a situation. I'd see it as a big negative as I believe that companionship is the basis for marriage and I would not sacrifice it'. 'Long distance relationships rarely work' is what the young clearly believe. Sivaramakrishnan B. qualifies it a bit. 'Early in my career for short stints it would be okay, once we have kids it would be a pain.' Kanishka Sinha would find it acceptable if it were possible to meet 'a day in the week or a few days at a stretch in the month'. But for some the idea is completely unacceptable. 'Would not do it, the institution of marriage itself would fall apart if such a thing happens.'

Amongst the women, Sukanya is clear that she would not compromise on the career front. 'I wouldn't make that sacrifice because I will be unhappy and it is pointless to stay with my husband if I am living with regrets, it will give rise to other problems. Maybe distance will make the heart grow fonder', she says. Shradha, on the other hand, believes that 'it depends on the time for which the job is taken. If it is on a temporary basis I do not mind living separately, but if it's for a considerable length of time, I would not mind giving up my job to be with him.' Paramita too says, 'I would consider giving up my job as I would love to be together and can sacrifice for that. I would not expect a similar sacrifice from my husband as men do have their ego.' Shweta is of the opinion that the choice is not between whether it is the husband's job or the wife's job, but on the basis of the pay, the status and relocation possibilities of each.

Those who have greater experience doubt that the issue is as clear-cut as this. Leena Chatterjee, Professor of Behavioral Science at IIM, Calcutta, believes that a wife's refusal to leave her job and be with her husband often cause problems as it is seen as an indication of the reduced importance the working woman is giving her husband or the marriage. 'It is translated as "how much do you love me?", she says.

Attitude to Marriage, Sex and the Family

How have the attitudes of young people changed with regard to sex, marriage and the family? Well, the figures tell their own story. The divorce rates across the country have risen. Surveys taken by a diverse range of organizations from condom manufacturers to marketing research agencies show clearly that there has been a quantum change in social mores.

> Indians are having more sex, and with more partners, the KamaSutra annual survey has found.
> Fifty three percent of 13,000 individuals polled admitted to having pre-marital sex, half of them before turning 21. Boyfriend/girlfriend emerged as the number one partner (79 per cent), with 26 per cent saying they ended up marrying their partners.
> Almost 60 per cent agreed that incidence of pre-marital sex had increased. Over a third of the married and more than half of the unmarried respondents said that they have had pre-marital sex.

The survey that covered Mumbai, Delhi, Bangalore, Calcutta, Pune, Chennai, Hyderabad, Ahmedabad, Lucknow and Chandigarh found that since last year, the population having sex more than once a week has increased to 57 per cent from 48 per cent last year (Soondas, 2004: 6).

However, when I meet my children's friends and my friends' children, there does not seem to be much difference in attitudes or social behaviour in the last two decades. And the interviews of the young singles I have taken show a fairly traditional behaviour pattern. Just about half of the young people interviewed believe they will go in for arranged marriages and in conversations it transpires that in some ways many of these marriages will take place not very differently from the way marriages were negotiated two decades ago. Internet sites such as shadi.com and Indian matrimony.com may now have taken over the role family, friends or the matrimonial column in the newspaper played earlier.

For most of these young people, who come from middle-class backgrounds, life offers limited opportunities for social interaction. The preoccupation with qualifying examinations right from school level to professional courses and the long working hours, which in India often extend over weekends as well, means that there is little scope or opportunity for socializing. While it is entirely true that many young people do manage to achieve success without completely sacrificing their personal lives, only three of the respondents mentioned being in serious relationships and a very large number indicated that this is something that was still on the back burner.

Is sex on campus more commonplace now? While the research clearly points to this being so, the young people I spoke to gave out a very mixed message. While some agreed that living together without marriage was completely acceptable now, from conversations with others it appeared that very little had changed with regard to the sexual habits of young people. One possible explanation for the mixed message was that while the behaviour pattern of the more Westernized middle class may have not changed very much, today's merit-based professional institutes also see representation from far more conservative communities and the change in behaviour for these people may indeed be quite dramatic. A girl from a Marwari community for instance, who may earlier have been married by the age of twenty, may today be staying in a hostel with both men and women and later travelling with male colleagues on tours both before and after she is married!

Many Young People See Themselves Having Arranged Marriages

Roughly half the people interviewed see themselves as having arranged marriages. While it may be more acceptable to go out with the prospective partner a couple of times, and to be in touch through SMS, email and phone without any pressure for marriage, many young people would be exchanging photographs and having marriages in ways that were prevalent a quarter of a century ago. Is there much stress on this account? Only in those cases where a compatible partner was proving to be elusive.

In an environment where young women are also equally committed to their careers, finding the right person in a job and a city that would make a marriage feasible certainly throws up a whole new range of challenges. For this class of professionally-qualified middle-class people, caste and class are no longer major issues. Most parents, even as they may themselves continue to look within their own community, would be willing to accept a young man or young woman their offspring found suitable whatever the caste or community. For one, regional differences are much less apparent now, so there is not usually much parental opposition on these grounds any more.

Are Marriages More Fragile Today?

Will these young people's marriages be less solid? Most young people think that this is indeed their reality. They believe that marriages are more fragile now. Expectations from a partner and from marriage are both extremely high. And though marriage is still seen quite clearly as a lifelong commitment, it is also apparent that most would rather end a bad marriage rather than go through life tied to a partner who is not compatible or in a marriage that is less than fulfilling. Twenty-six-year-old Kanishka believes that this generation will not have as much 'pent-up frustration, sadness, as people [had earlier] trapped in roles, marriages, jobs, arrangements due to societal pressure'. Therefore, for him, the break up of a marriage may actually spell less, and not more, frustration and unhappiness.

But when it comes to identifying the reasons why their marriages are likely to be unstable, the primacy of work, work–family conflict and the independence of the contemporary woman were seen as the prime causes. A student from IIM, Bangalore, feels that 'the transfer of workload from workplace to house' is a primary cause. While a young man working in an MNC believes that 'it is increasingly becoming difficult to separate professional and personal life, and tension and anxiety has disturbed family life. With both partners having their own careers and independent ways of thinking, disagreements are frequent. The emphasis has shifted from the relationship to the career.'

Some attribute the changes to the influence of Western mores through TV. 'The invasion of America in our lives through TV and films is making us more vocal about our problems and less willing to change ourselves for others.'

Kanishka, who has spent much of his youth in the UK, reveals his time abroad through his comment: 'Marriages are more fragile now', he says, 'because people have usually experimented with a relationship or two before marriage and they expect their spouses to have all the good points of their previous "exes" and none of their faults. And they also realize that there are more options out there. This is destabilizing. Having no options always leads to people accepting their situation more easily.' A stable marriage is not associated with much glamour in our country. In the

UK, however, since marriages are now becoming less common amongst young people, I encountered a very interesting response to marriage. When a young Welsh student heard that I had been married for twenty years, he exclaimed 'How exciting!', marvelling at how people must change and evolve in so many years, and how interesting it must be to be part of such a relationship. And what about him, I asked. ' Oh, my life is boring', he said, 'I have so many relationships and they are all the same. You tell the girl the same things about yourself, you hear the same things, you make the same moves. Everything is the same except the face!' That was a new take on relationships, and on marriage, for me. Of course, in India, the young at this point of time, are more concerned with the many less than satisfactory marriages they see all around them.

However, Kanishka is optimistic that after an initial period of adjustment, people will use the knowledge gained in earlier relationships to create better and more stable relationships.

The young women are equally clear that today's marriages can no longer be expected to provide the security they may have done in an earlier time. Twenty-five-year-old lawyer Saswati Poddar says, 'I am scared to get married and then be left [in the lurch]. I would like the security of my own job.'

However, most young women say that though it is undeniable that today's generation has less tolerance and also that there is a constant pull between work and family life, their need for financial independence is not linked to the quality of their marriage.

Most Men Want to Marry Working Women

Most of the young men interviewed said that they would prefer to marry working women.

A twenty-three-year-old, who is currently working with a prestigious multinational bank, believes that a working woman has a more practical and mature approach to life. His colleague is equally emphatic. 'Definitely a working woman because I believe an exchange of ideas is very important between couples and I think that could only happen if my wife was a working woman and had something interesting to share with, I don't think a housewife would be suitable for that.' A management student believes 'working women have more personality'. So it is apparent that young men in their early twenties find the idea of being able to relate to a housewife a little difficult.

Also, aware that they are going to be working fairly punishing hours themselves, these men are perhaps reluctant to come home to a wife who would perhaps expect her husband to provide her relief from the monotony of her life at home, and perhaps to take her out in the evening. A student at the IIM, Lucknow, says, 'I would like to marry a working woman. This is something I was against previously but now knowing what my working hours and work pressure are likely to be, I don't think my wife would be able to spend so much time at home [as a housewife would have to do].' A twenty-five-year-old research assistant at Mudra Institute of Communication, Ahmedabad, MICA, says that, 'it's really hard to think of a drawback of having a working wife'. And it is interesting that he believes that it would be more relaxing to come home to a wife who has been out busy with her own career and therefore, 'would get less time to create problems for me because she has been waiting for me, and expects me to feel guilty about the problems at home'. On the one hand, remarks such as this would bring cheer to some women in dual-career families who fear that men would prefer to come home to women who had been at home and were 'fresh', rather than those who were themselves exhausted after a long days work. On the other hand, however, it is a pointer to the urgency with which we need to make the workplace more accommodating to the needs of married women and women with children. For, clearly, not only this generation of young women, but also this generation of young men is aware of the stress that the full-time housewife and mother faces being confined to the home.

There is also awareness that being married to a working wife would relieve the man of the pressure of being the sole breadwinner in what are unquestionably uncertain times. A second income also provides some scope for experimentation. As one IIM, Calcutta student admits candidly, 'the cushion would allow me to try other things if I wished to'.

A very small minority expressed a desire to marry a housewife; one because he wanted a wife like his mother who took care of the home and the children, and the other because he felt in today's demanding work environment, trying to balance two careers would cause too much stress. He admitted that if every man thought like he did, the world would become very difficult for women.

Most men did not see themselves as house-husbands in the near future. However, one young single who envisages an early retirement saw it as a possibility, as did another, who intends to retire to write poetry at the age of forty. Only one man saw himself doing it for the sake of his wife or children.

Young Single Women

Why should there be a different questionnaire for young single women MBAs? Many men asked this question, not one woman did. The women were well aware that in their present unmarried state, their concerns were probably identical to those of their male peers; but they did foresee having to deal, in the very near future, with work–family issues that would affect their male peers to a much lesser extent.

Women Want to be Financially Independent before Getting Married

It appears that just as a young man could not and cannot contemplate marriage till he was 'settled', because a stable career was a pre-requisite for marriage for men, today, it is increasingly becoming so for women as well. Twenty-four-year-old hotel executive Monalee is clearly at a stage when career takes precedence, 'I would like to climb the corporate ladder in my field, even if it means moving to another city or another country'. Or as a young CA puts it, 'marriage according to me should happen at the time when you have attained financial independence'. A design student from the NID echoes this, 'Establishing myself in my chosen profession comes first, then marriage will follow'. A twenty-five-year-old advocate would also like to delay marriage till her career takes off. While another twenty-three-year-old is even more emphatic, 'Strict no, for the time being. Only after I realize my immediate goal can I think of getting married.'

Young Single Women Prefer Career to Marriage

Nirmala Ravindran is a Bangalore-based journalist. At the time of the interview, Nirmala was bureau chief with a magazine group, and at thirty this is, undeniably, success. Nirmala is forthright that she is enjoying her life too much to contemplate giving it up for marriage right now, or perhaps ever. Is there pressure from the family? 'Plenty of pressure', she admits candidly. 'I have a widowed mother who is rather melodramatic about the whole thing'. But with a supportive younger brother who understands her compulsions, Nirmala is sure that in the immediate future she intends to stay resolutely single. 'Not even Brad Pitt, who agrees to do the housework, would inspire me at this point. I'm having too much fun on my own. I don't want to take on even an ounce of additional responsibility', this feisty journalist confides.

In a way, Nirmala exemplifies many other daughters of full-time housewives who wish to fashion a different destiny for themselves. Nirmala is emphatic that for her it is not the fact that marriages today tend to be more fragile that is disenchanting. It is the sheer difference in the quality of life between a housewife and a working woman. When asked to choose between two very extreme scenarios of being a success at the workplace and single all her life, or being happily married and being housebound, Nirmala says, 'Without any question, never marrying. Even if I didn't enjoy professional success, I would choose it. Being housebound sounds like being in jail. If a woman doesn't work, what does she do while her husband works, supervise servants, change nappies. I can't see anyone being inspired by that. I'm very reluctant to face the monotony and drudgery that matrimony brings. I'm quite happy with the thought that I may never marry or have children. This feeling of unmarried girls being insecure is nonsense. Maybe I'll end up feeling like that at forty, but at least I've had some glorious years unlike anything my married friends can imagine. So I'm willing to risk old age and loneliness—maybe I'll even marry then. As long as I'm left alone now, in my best years.' Perhaps Nirmala's attitude is indicative of the mindset of the Indian woman of the future. It is certainly in line with trends in the developed world which show both a drop in marriage rates and an increase in the age at which women are marrying. In the UK, for instance, marriage rates have been falling by 3 to 4 per cent every year since the early 1980s. In the 1960s, the average age at which women first got married was 23.3. By 2000 it was 27.3. In Sweden it is over 30, reports Dr Sarah Hooper, director of Oxford University's

Institute of Ageing (Girling, 2004: 23). The situation in Asia is no different. 'The number of unmarried women in their 30s and 40s (in Asia) is skyrocketing', Gavin Jones, a professor at Singapore's Asia Research Institute, told a conference on marriage trends (an Associated Press Report, Singapore, 27 August 2004, published in the *Hindustan Times*, Kolkata, 28 August 2004, p.14). The report went on to say that women give priority to career and independence and that more are staying single and childless to pursue their careers.

Amongst the women I spoke to, most wanted both a happy marriage and a successful career. But if they had to choose between being a housewife all their lives and being successful career woman, most women would say no to being married and domesticity. This was expressed in one word, 'career', by some. More explicitly, management student Shilpa makes the candid confession that, 'I dread being a housewife'. The realization that marriages were now more fragile makes women reluctant to become dependent on a husband. They prefer to have the security of their own jobs. Other responses were, 'I would prefer a late marriage when I'm well settled' and 'I wouldn't like to take a break now and lose out on the rat race, but later I would like to take good care of my children.' Shilpa Bakde, twenty-six, is conscious of the dual pull of marriage and the workplace and so plans on getting married after at least a year on the job so that 'I don't feel the tug too early'. She goes on to say that 'in the first two years I just want money. But once I have children I want one of those organizations that offer flexible timings, distance working etc.' Young women are aware that they will have to constantly assess their situation, and see how they can best balance the many roles they wish to fulfil and to weigh what they are giving up and what they may expect to gain with every choice that they make.

One young woman expressed the view that 'there are many reasons why married people are worse off. The only way in which they are better off is that they have someone to share their woes with but even a boyfriend can do that.'

Amongst the women interviewed, it was interesting to note that young single women who were at MBA institutes, were more likely to say that work-family balance was more important than salary, while those young women who were in institutes that were less well known, or in jobs that were offered poorer prospects, were more likely to give greater weightage to a job which offered a higher salary. Perhaps the great differential in the emoluments the two categories of women were likely to receive may explain this difference. The non-MBAs may perhaps be looking at exactly the same amount of money that the MBAs would not mind settling for. However, as they may be in poorly-paid jobs at the moment, a good salary is a priority for them.

Amongst the many very detailed interviews I did for this chapter, some reflected an alternative, more traditional, sensibility—Divya Kashyap, an IIMT, Ghaziabad graduate and Mumbai-based HR executive would like to be there to provide 'quality time' to her child. About her ambition she says, 'I always wanted to balance career and family but was fairly career oriented'. However, when faced with the all or nothing option of being single and a success at the workplace, or a happily married housebound housewife, Divya chooses the happy marriage!

It is interesting that some of the young women like Divya, who, when faced with two less than perfect choices, chose the housebound one, are those who have very good career prospects. For in this group, we also have Shweta Bagaria and Shradha Shah, both chartered accountants with outstanding academic records, and of one other student from a reputed management institute.

Could it be that, being at an institute that establishes their abilities in the world of work, they are easier about seeking emotional happiness or fulfillment in the more untried world of family life? Monjima Sinha, a twenty-six-year-old journalist certainly gives credence to this view with her response to where marriage fits into the picture at this point of time with her answer: 'Not anywhere in the picture right now. Not till I have a job that is more stable and gives me more satisfaction.'

Interestingly, in Fran Siemensma's study of MBA students in India and Australia, Paraswati, an MBA from India says that she 'lived to work' because she was 'at the bottom and trying to break in . . . at work'.

Some respondents, like hotel executive Monalee Borah, or Nidhi Bagaria, refused to be boxed in by these extreme positions and say firmly, ' I would choose none. I have faith in myself and will have a successful career and a happy married life'. In many ways, this book has been driven by a desire to see just how they, and several others like them, manage to do this.

Women Want It All

Young people, who have in a sense proved themselves in today's society by competing and succeeding in what are considered to be the most challenging examinations in the country, wish to seek balance between professional success and personal happiness. In many ways, attitudes amongst the women interviewed in India in 2004, are not too dissimilar to those found amongst college-going women in the US in 1991.

An informal 1991 survey of female college students conducted at Cornell University revealed that many held high occupational aspirations coupled with a strong commitment to marriage and family life. These contemporary young women declared their ambition to be successful doctors, lawyers and executives by the time they are in their thirties and to marry and have as many as three children. Because of their (and their parents') substantial investment in their education, they are unwilling to sacrifice career for family. But it would appear that they are equally unwilling to sacrifice family for career.

This is beginning to be recognized in India as well, as the report in a leading financial daily points out.

India seems to have followed a similar pattern (as the US). There's no question of either/or any longer when talking of career and family when talking of career and family for a large majority of women in the country. The Indian woman wants to prove her worth all the time as Ms Neera Misra, Ficci governing body member and consultant to Ficci Ladies Organization told *FE* . . . Ms Misra goes on to state that 70 per cent of educated women would be combining family and career in the future.

How Women's Attitudes Differ

In Fran Siemensma's study on MBA students in India and Australia it is stated that some female students said that they were compensating for their mothers' thwarted ambitions. In my conversations, it also appeared as if some young women having seen the problems their mothers had faced with their life choices (whether they were the problems of the housewife or the working woman in a dual career home), wanted to see what it was like to be doing the actual opposite. A young woman whose mother graduated from IIT and works for a leading corporate house, says that she feels her mother never got the time to do simple things like watching a movie in the daytime, or teach underprivileged children, something she feels she would have liked to do, given the time.

Women whose mothers were full-time housewives, on the other hand, saw the many ways in which they were disadvantaged compared to those women who had full-time jobs and were therefore prepared to make considerable sacrifices to get and retain their jobs.

A Snapshot of Young India

So what is the picture that emerges as one pulls the film out of the camera? It is of a generation that is self-confident and optimistic and keen to have it all, success at the workplace and fulfillment at home. There is much greater gender equity than has been there in the past. A career is as much of a priority for young women as it has always been for young men. Most young men see childcare responsibilities as something that affects them equally. A minority of the women seem prepared to make career sacrifices for the sake of the marriage and the children. Others would like fulfillment as wives and mothers, but do not contemplate becoming housewives to do so. They cannot conceive having to contend with the drudgery and monotony that they imagine being a housewife would involve. They are clear that being financially independent is an imperative. Also, in an environment where marriages often do not survive, they believe being saddled with a child sans husband is an unenviable situation to be in. These young women are acutely conscious that being dependent on a husband is relying on the goodwill and good health of one man!

Most young people seem to feel a great feeling of responsibility for their parents and great affection for the family, which appeared to be a major source of emotional and material support. A majority of young people appear to be very focussed on their career aspirations at this point of time. Some actually believe that they will have time to enjoy life and nurture their other interests after they establish themselves by the age of forty. Sometimes it appeared that it was peer pressure rather than personal inclination that dictated some particularly high-flying aspirations. Contrary to popular belief, most young people seemed to put great store by job security and wished for an organization that believed in a long-term relationship with the employee. Only a minority liked a culture with high rewards and quick terminations. While they believed that pay should be linked to performance, some made the point that it was exceedingly difficult to assess the worth of individual contributions, and disliked the emerging trend of a very competitive work environment.

These young people are still on the threshold of their lives and careers, which may, in fact, turn out quite different from the way they are now envisaged. Many of them may actually act in ways that appear difficult to imagine at this point of time. However, it is still interesting to see what their hopes, fears and aspirations are as they embark on life's journey. It may help us understand whether attitudes on work–family balance at the workplace based on assumptions on what would help attract and retain young talent are accurate. It appears that assumptions today's employers make about what young people seek may not, in fact, be grounded in reality. Young people want it all—a lucrative, challenging career and time and space for personal pursuits and for the family. However, today's workplace has perhaps not factored in the second part of this wish list satisfactorily. A deeper understanding of what is desirable and possible in the way work is regulated and rewarded, will undoubtedly lead to better work–life balance.

7

Today's Workplace: Dream Come True or Living Nightmare?

How Work Defines the Individual

A man's job has always defined him. It decides position and power, both 'jaat' as also 'aukaat'. Doctor, engineer, lawyer, civil servant, consultant, banker, place you as firmly in the hierarchy as 'Pundit', 'Jauhari', 'Chamar', 'Batliwala', or, even more specifically, 'Sodabottle-openerwala' did, a generation ago!

> [A] man's work is the primary base for his life in society. [Through it he is] plugged into an occupational structure and a cultural, class and social matrix. Work is also of great psychological importance; it is a vehicle for the fulfillment or negation of central aspects of the self (Levinson, 1978).

A More Egalitarian Society

So what is new? Simply this, today the job and your position in your profession is often all people know about you. Till very recently, a man was also identified by his town or village and his lineage. Indeed, in villages and small towns, people are still introduced as being so-and-so's son, or belonging to a particular family. Much more than the job, it is this which earned a man his perch in the pecking order. It is still not unusual to find long lists of highly-placed relatives, ostensibly to show 'family background', on letters accompanying job application forms. Till the time of independence, candidates for prized jobs were actually picked because of their family background. 'In our days, a 60 per cent average was considered good for a seat in a medical college, or a first class liberal arts college' and 'If you had come out of a public school and were good at sports, you could just walk into a corporate job', you hear with more than a hint of nostalgia from those who belonged to the English-educated middle class, which happened also to be part of the country's fairly small élite. There were so few eligible to partake of the pie, it was perfectly possible to be genteel and also successful. Today, the best opportunities have only one criterion, the skills the candidate brings to the table. And gender is no longer destiny. A qualified young woman is as likely to get the 'day zero' (or most desirable job) as her male counterpart.

Merit-based selections have made our society much more open. The population explosion is one factor which has made competition so very fierce, but perhaps as big a factor is that people are no longer denied entry to any institution or any organization because of who they are, or who their parents or grandparents are or may have been. Do we today have a level playing field?

Perhaps not. It is undeniable that a large proportion of our people were stigmatized for generations through caste prejudice and so may find it considerably harder to get ahead than those who were born into more privileged families. But there are any number of success stories from those who come from very humble homes, to indicate that if an individual really does have intelligence, drive and ambition, whatever his circumstances, he can strive for and touch the stars.

The positive aspect of this is an opening up of opportunities to merit rather than to privilege. The negative aspect is that in a country where there is virtually no dignity of labour, there is huge pressure on middle-class parents to see that they do everything they can to see their offspring get ahead in the rat race. It is imperative that he or she gets into the very best school the parents can afford and avail of every tuition or coaching scheme possible to gain that vital edge. Entrance exams from the nursery level up involve much preparation that involves both parents and child. From the age of two to twenty-two, the overriding preoccupation is geared to getting the very best results at the very best institutions to finally attain the prize of the desired job!

The New Focus on Work

Thus the new pre-eminence of work over virtually everything else. Having spent all one's childhood and early youth in getting a job, it is obvious that retaining it would be of primal importance. In a globalized economy, workplaces all over the world face a new situation where, to remain competitive, the organization has to be faster, better, cheaper.

While much of Europe is protected by legislation stipulating the maximum number of hours organizations may allow people to work, in the US, and much of Asia, working hours are becoming longer and work itself is becoming more intensive. The average worker will spend more of his or her working hours at the workplace than anywhere else. The workplace then, is also your community, and increasingly your family.

Not all of this is new. Some organizations are acutely aware of the role they play in an individual's life. The armed forces, for instance, seek to compensate for the trying conditions soldiers and officers may face in dangerous and inhospitable environments by creating powerful support systems and an enviable infrastructure for the soldier and his family. The house of Tata also created a city for the employees at the steel plant they set up at Jamshedpur over a hundred years ago. In 1902, Jamsetji Tata said, 'Be sure to lay wide streets planted with shady trees. Be sure there is plenty of space for lawns and gardens. Reserve large areas for football, hockey and parks. Earmark areas for Hindu temples, Mohammedan mosques and Christian churches' (Lala, 1981: 14). Other steel cities that came up later also set up virtual townships with enviable infrastructure and a range of facilities for the employee and the employee's family. What is different now? Simply this, in the new IT campuses, everything—gym, canteen, swimming pool—is set up at the workplace. The office seeks to also become the home and the club. In this scenario what happens to the spouse, the children and elderly parents? What happens to relationships with the family and community?

The Companies Interviewed

In a country that is as populous as India, with its enormous pool of both skilled and unskilled manpower, working on this chapter required much thought. Most people work in the unorganized sector and are extremely vulnerable to exploitation of many kinds. On one level, obviously work–family balance is not going to be an issue for people who want a job, any job.

But increasingly, today, even in jobs that would be on the top of a young person's wish list, work–family balance is conspicuous by its absence. Very high salaries and an opportunity to reach senior positions at a very young age bedazzle young people who may not realize till it is too late the price they are paying in personal terms, in their ability to have a life and not just a job.

What Jobs do Young People Want?

If one identifies what are considered the most sought after educational institutes in the country and then checks out the career aspirations of the best performers there, it is possible to see that the corporate sector, especially MNCs or firms with a foreign connection in fields such as IT, finance, consulting, is the most favoured by today's young. Studying these firms is worthwhile because they have a powerful influence on the rest of Indian industry. They are also very sensitive to what they believe young people want.

Just as competition for the top jobs is fierce, so also is the competition for the best talent. So, on the one hand, you have students gearing up to give the employer what he wants, while on the other hand, companies wish to attract and retain talent, and seek to offer employees what they believe the best and brightest want. I thought it might be interesting to check what the situation was in companies that were seen as top draw. Do they offer family-friendly policies? Could they work as role models for others? Identifying these companies was not a problem. Ratings of how companies fare on a wide range of parameters are now done on a continual basis and these receive considerable media attention. However, getting a response on record was extremely difficult. One public sector company, which is credited with many women-friendly policies, withdrew permission to use the interview after emailing it. Finally, I spoke to senior people at PricewaterhouseCoopers, ITC Hotels, Tata Steel, Boston Consulting Group, Cognizant Technologies and HSBC. I believe they are representative of companies that would feature in an Indian best practices list. This is not to say that many other companies would not also find a place on the same list. This is a representative sample of what could be considered enlightened companies that operate in India. And the conditions and the mindset that prevail here may help us anticipate the direction Indian industry may take in the future.

The New Age of Uncertainty

'Ek biwi aur ek naukri ka zamana gaya', said one executive wryly summing up an era where one is no longer tied to either the same wife, or the same job all of one's life. Till not very long ago, an individual joined a company and then worked his way up till he finally retired at the age of fifty-eight or sixty. Today, to retire from the company you joined as a trainee would be considered unusual. Earlier, unless you were grossly incompetent, or dishonest, you were unlikely to lose your job. Today, an organization is constantly reassessing its core strengths and strategies, and re-evaluating which individuals would bring the experience and skills most likely to achieve those goals. An employee who no longer fits the bill would be asked to go without too much deliberation.

> The linear career path that once kept people working in the same job often in the same company, is not the standard route for today's workers . . . Employment security is no longer tied to an organization but to an individual's career management resilience skills (Moses, 1999).

In this new work environment, employees not only focus on the job assigned to them, but also measure how the organization, and the job they are doing, is adding value to their CVs. Since the rewards and reprisals for perceived performance or the lack of it, may be brutal and swift, individuals are constantly measuring how they are performing in comparison to their peers both within and outside the organization. This is the age of opportunity. And that is both promise and threat.

The Pressures this Creates

In a more leisurely work environment, there was time for work and for leisure. There was time for socializing with colleagues and with neighbours. There was interaction with the immediate family and with the extended family. Today, people work longer hours and they work more intensively. The plus is that if you are found to have promise you can rise faster and higher than was possible earlier. However, it does mean that every employee today faces unprecedented stress. The super achiever is constantly challenged to raise the bar, the average performer lives in fear of being axed, in a way he would not have had to a decade or so ago.

This is an environment where work consumes a very great deal of an employee's time and energy. People are now so focussed on work and spend so much time at the workplace, that bonding with colleagues often tends to be more than with members of one's family. Indeed, one's colleagues become the family. 'Is there work–life balance today?' 'Of course, yes', answers one HR executive. 'Organizations make it a point to celebrate employees' birthdays etc. at the office, and since people spend about fourteen hours a day at the workplace, what could be nicer than celebrating the special days of your life with those who are your nearest and dearest?' Yet, in an environment where your colleagues are closer to you than your neighbours at home, the loss of the job, can be traumatic. In one swift, brutal blow, you lose not only your job, but also your family and your friends.

When the Office Becomes the Home

It is trendy to have a gym, a canteen, a basketball court and a swimming pool at the office. Having an office that is fun, perhaps so much fun that the employee is quite happy putting in longer and longer hours, is now eminently fashionable. If employees are to spend most of their working hours at the workplace, then it makes sense for that workplace to be congenial. But having individuals become so tied to the office makes it that much more difficult for them to form relationships outside the workplace. Bonding with fellow employees is certainly one way of humanizing what would otherwise be a stressful work environment, but it does have disturbing implications in an era where jobs are more contractual than relationship-based, as was earlier the case.

If the only relationships individuals have are with their colleagues, how do they have family lives, and how do they cope when they lose their jobs, or have to move on?

The Workplace is not Homogeneous

Before considering what conditions are like in today's workplace, one must first point out that the workplace is not, of course, a monolith. Each industry has its unique ethos and offers those who work in it different perquisites and different problems. The IT sector has one set of pressures that may be very different from those that exist in the media. Bankers and those who work in financial institutions face greater stress at particular times of the year. The norms in heavy industry differ from those in the fast moving consumer goods (FMCG) companies; the hospitality industry has its own rewards and requirements, while the self-employed and those who work in the NGO sector have compensations and challenges of their own. Within each industry too, different job functions have different requirements. In the manufacturing sector, employees who work in the plant often have a shift system, those in marketing and sales would need to be more attuned to the time requirements of their customers. In journalism, people in desk jobs may work office hours; those in reporting have to work to sharp deadlines. The demands of newspaper journalism are different from those of magazine journalism. Television journalism is different from print journalism. In the IT sector, those who have client interface have different requirements from those who do not, and the timings would be different if the clients follow American time schedules. In the hospitality industry, those in operations have to respond to quite different circumstances from those who do not. In the medical profession, doctors and nurses have to face completely different pressures from those of pathologists.

The Workplace is More Competitive Now

'Compared to say ten years ago, the world is a far more competitive place today. This is so not only in terms of the demands on personal time, but also in terms of demands on the organization. The organization

is expected to be that much sharper, more nimble footed
. . . With that kind of paradigm shift, it's obvious that
the demands on an individual's time, the pressures on
him, have increased. I know lots of people who do fall
into a rut; they are working eighteen–nineteen hours a
day, but I think people have to be able to prioritize.
There's no way an individual can finish every single job
that has to be done. He must be able to recognize what
must be done today and what can be deferred till
tomorrow', says Ramnath Krishnan, executive director,
HSBC. Krishnan, who works eleven to twelve hours a
day, is married and has a ten-year-old son. His wife, a
management graduate, has given up her job and is now
a full-time housewife and mother. Krishnan admits that
the way work is structured in many organizations, the
executive takes care of his job and his wife must perforce
take care of everything else. However, this is not
something that he is unduly concerned about as he
believes it is the executive who can and must decide
how much family time he is willing to sacrifice, for
what rewards.

He believes that people must accept that and that,
with regard to work–life balance, ' the world is not
going to get easier, that is simply not going to happen,
so responsible organizations must see that they do not
push their people too far. The individuals concerned
must strike a balance between work and family life
that is acceptable to them and their families. They have
to decide how much they are willing to sacrifice for
what benefits.'

Can Employees Decide what Work–Family Balance They Want?

There are many who believe that every employee must take a call on what he is willing to give up, for what gain, almost as if the workplace were a supermarket where one decides what one can purchase and at what price. Is this really the case? This presupposes there are any number of less lucrative jobs, which demand less of the employee's time and commitment, and then there are top-end jobs where you are handsomely rewarded for the sacrifices you make in terms of time and commitment. This clearly is not the case. Small, private companies often have the most exploitative working conditions of all. People work long hours and they work intensively for meagre rewards.

> Ranjan Kumar has a brand new job. It gives him twice his earlier pay in an FMCG major. The catch: his new job is at a call centre. He leaves home at 4 pm and returns along with the milk and the morning daily at 5 am. It's early days and he's enjoying himself . . . 'Even in my regular so-called nine to five job, earlier, I barely got an evening to call my own. You always had to be at the beck and call of the employer,' he says, 'And even if you are not needed, you must be in office late because others are there. If you are missing, you lose out in the promotion sweepstakes. In India, there is no concept of work life balance' ('Balancing Act', the *Telegraph*, 2004: 1).

What Do People Want?

What do people want in today's world? Is career progression valued more than work–life balance? Are material rewards in cash or kind more attractive to employees than time with family, or simply more control over their time? Asking organizations about this does not get one any answers. Organizational and HR heads admit that the very in-depth employee satisfaction surveys undertaken by them do not check this out. Organizations do not have the answers, because they have not thought to ask these questions. The effect of a work culture that demands a disproportionate share of the employee's time and energy is clearly apparent. What is still unknown is what value people give to the rewards that accrue from work and how much they value personal and family time.

Are People Being Pushed to Want Certain Things?

In my survey of young singles, I found that young singles faced considerable peer pressure with regard to what it was acceptable to aspire for. 'One is pushed to wanting to be VP at thirty-two, to retire by forty', as one MBA student put it. Siddhartha Mukherjee, vice president of Cognizant Technologies Solutions India Pvt. Ltd. also believes that in India there is unusual peer pressure to keep moving up the ladder. 'In the US, many people are happy being programmers all their lives, here there is tremendous pressure to keep moving up', he says.

Interestingly, in 'Values and the MBA: The Implications of Gender' by Fran Siemensa, published in the March 2004 issue of *Management Review* brought out by IIM, Bangalore, which has research on MBA students in India and Australia, the respondents voiced many concerns that also came through in my interviews. The lack of enthusiasm for a hire and fire culture with high rewards and quick terminations is very evident here as well, with a perceptible distaste for the new 'economic rationalism', which was no longer about 'how to motivate and get the best out of the people', but involved a new style of manager: a 'hit person' who organized voluntary departure packages with 'no apologies'. Here too, as I found in my conversations, young people were divided in their opinions. Some idealistically believed that it would be possible to have work–life balance. For others, the concept of a 'family-friendly employer' was dismissed as 'an oxymoron'. Some young people who had worked for or had trained in companies that were lauded for being sensitive, and employee-friendly claimed that such reputations were not based on reality. 'We are asked to get on to the basket ball court, or in the canteen, when important guests or the media come visiting! All your boss actually wants of you is work, and more work!'

Indeed, in my experience, most people expressed the view that work–family balance did not exist. Working conditions were taken as somehow unalterable, all that an individual could do was to find ways to cope with the new work culture through stress releasing activities like yoga, meditation, walks, exercise, weekend getaways or other methods of relaxation.

A news item quantifies the dissatisfaction with work-family balance many employees experience:

The Working Wounded

Do you carry work home?
Always -15 %
Sometimes -54%
Never-31%

Does your job leave you with enough time for yourself?
No-66%
Yes-32%
Can't say-2%
('The Working Wounded', the *Telegraph*, 2004: 1).

Clearly, many employees are facing a problem. Yet, it is also true that if organizations actually faced difficulties in attracting and retaining the kind of talent they wished to, they would change their policies to become more family friendly. In this country, with so many people and so few jobs, left only to market forces, a change does not seem likely in the near future.

What is the Rationale for Long Working Hours?

Eight hours for work, eight for rest, eight hours for what we will (Labour movement anthem of the 1880s, quoted in Hayden, 1999)

It is ironic that the civilized world went from long working hours to the eight-hour day and is now slowly going back to long working hours. In India today, much of the action is taking place in companies with an American connection and is influenced by US mores in this sphere. In the US, achievement and success are considered far more important than work–family balance. Europe is governed by a great deal of legislation to protect the interests of the family, while countries such as Sweden are leagues ahead in trying to achieve true gender equity by actively supporting the involvement of fathers with childcare. Closer to home, one is getting reports that the Philippines is introducing a four-day work week.

Over and over again one hears how time permeates the management of work. 'The culture is that you get credit for long hours. Working long hours is the thing to do. There is no forty-hour week. If you are not doing at least fifty you are not a team player. It's a sign of dedication [and it] doesn't matter if there's work to do.' Time is also viewed as infinitely available. 'The only way to attack the problem is with hours and hours of work'. And only people who put in time are seen as slated for career success. 'It's not that someone who isn't is not being a good performer, but they are not seen as aggressive in wanting to move up the company. And so in general, they don't [move up].'

The underlying assumption seems to be that employee time belongs to the company, a notion reinforced by the company's evaluation and promotion practices. Yet, other voices acknowledge the irrationality of this cultural norm: 'If there are two people of equal performance, the promotion will go to the one who has put in overtime. But that means it took that person longer to get to the same level of performance, so the other guy is the better one. It makes no sense' (Bailyn, 1993: 80-81).

Lotte Bailyn is the T. Wilson Professor of Management at the Sloan School of Management at

MIT. She is an authority in the area of work-family balance. In *Breaking the Mold*, Bailyn explains how much of the conflict that arises in managing work and family life stems from an organization's pre-conceived notion of how a valued and valuable employee must demonstrate commitment to the organization.

In this context, though the software and other, more progressive, companies do care less about input and are more focussed on output, 'companies are not so gullible as to be impressed merely by long hours when they wish to measure productivity', says Ramnath Krishnan (of HSBC). However, even he conceded that if two people showed an equal measure of performance, the one who put in the longer hours would have an extra tick in the box!

It was interesting to note that while the MNCs who brought in the culture of working long hours have now moved on to the work-from-home option, and in some cases have done away with the attendance register altogether, Indian corporate houses and public sector companies have now adopted the culture of long hours.

Time at the Workplace is Still Valued

Even though the workplace clearly requires quite different skill sets and job requirements, over the years, a culture has evolved based on 'industrial values' stemming from work that is largely manufacturing-dominated. In an industrial environment, the longer the plant was functional, the greater was the output. Industrial workers were therefore valued for working overtime and were paid for extra hours. In many of today's jobs, extra hours bring in absolutely no additional benefit to the employer. A person who needs to network, for instance, would not only be far better off personally, but would also bring the employer greater benefits if he or she was out in the real world, meeting people. Creative people may actually work best outside the four walls of an office. Yet this does not seem to matter.

Employees across the spectrum were categorical that an employee who put in noticeably fewer hours than others in the organization, was treading on very thin ice indeed. Organizations were equally categorical that they were very keen that employees have time with their families. They also said that they have sophisticated appraisals in place for assessing the worth and contribution of individual employees and that 'face time' and long hours were irrelevant in determining career progression. However, in scores of conversations with organizational heads and HR managers, a request for the names of employees who were in senior positions, or likely to get there, who did not work after office hours, drew an embarrassed silence. Either such a creature did not exist, or it was considered awkward to have someone so identified. Saying a particular employee, or a particular team had worked around the clock to meet a set of objectives was praiseworthy. Clearly, identifying a person or a group having done the same, working only the stipulated hours, was not.

One Way of Demonstrating Commitment

In an uncertain job environment, the one thing an employee can do to show commitment is to work long hours. Is this linked to his vulnerability? In interview after interview, men and women who did not wish to be named said that it was. 'No one wants to leave while the boss is still in the office. No one wants to be known as the person who is the first out, of course one is often hanging around, even if there is no work.' 'Since everyone stays late, work only kicks into full gear in the afternoon.' 'Earlier in the public sector, one worked official working hours, now a culture of working late has crept in.' If you are still not convinced consider this nugget of information: In the UK, research has found that fathers who have dependent children work longer hours than fathers who do not have dependent children do. A Joseph Rowntree report on research by Dr Charlie Lewis and Wendy Langford of Lancaster University says that fathers respond to the birth of a new child by working longer hours. Though his wife would undoubtedly welcome more help at home with the baby, the man responds to the additional responsibility by putting in longer hours at the workplace!

Are Some Professions More Family-Unfriendly than Others?

The very nature of the job in some professions dictates irregular working hours and stressful work conditions. The medical profession is one where emergencies may arise at any time of day, the armed forces and the police force too cannot expect to have 9 to 5 timings, nor can news reporters. And in most professions, especially in the service industry, people have to be prepared to respond fast when a situation that needs their attention arises. Siddhartha Mukherjee of Cognizant, for instance, points out that though in Cognizant, as in most other software companies, teams enjoy a large degree of flexibility in deciding their schedules, 'a programme that was running perfectly till yesterday may suddenly crash. This would mean that the personnel involved would have to drop everything and rectify it. Having more software engineers on hold is not likely to help in the case of malfunction of one team's programme.'

Can Hiring More People Help Solve the Problem?

While hiring more people is unlikely to help solve the problem in the careers just mentioned, in many other industries, the stress is clearly due to being understaffed. In the drive to cut flab, some organizations have downsized right to the bone. The new equation famously being hire one person, pay the salary of two and extract the work of three. Not only has the downsizing in such circumstances caused unnecessary pain to those who were laid off, it also complicates the lives of the survivors.

A More Intensive Work Culture

'We don't encourage people to hang around the office unless there's actually work to be done. People put in long hours because there's a genuine requirement for this, we are actually working every minute of the time we are at office', say some senior executives in apparent self-justification. According to research on work–family balance in the US, this more intensive work-style is actually even more detrimental for the family than merely putting in longer hours. For when parents come home after working intensively, they are emotionally and physically worn out, wanting only to unwind and relax and have little energy to respond to a child's needs, or indeed to anything else.

Impact on Relationships

When an employee is pressed for time, it is likely that he (or she) is going to be too exhausted to do justice to other roles that require attention. A senior executive I interviewed who worked an eleven–twelve-hour day, six days a week, admitted that he tried to make some time for his school-going children, but admitted that 'I soon lose my temper, because I don't have that much time, and sometimes it seems that they take just too long to understand'. He is not very happy about the way the children are turning out, but he does not see what he can do about it. He also feels some guilt about not being able to visit his parents who live at their ancestral home in a small town, but again feels his schedule leaves him no option but to be a son who can only act when there is an emergency situation.

But perhaps even more alarmingly, the new dynamics of the workplace leave little time to form new relationships. Increasingly young people find that there is little time or energy to meet new people socially. Not everyone is comfortable with the lottery of the arranged marriage system, though it has undeniably worked very well for generations. However, for those young people who wish to find their own marriage partners, today's all-consuming workday is a real problem. New concepts such as speed dating where people meet and evaluate a series of partners in the course of one evening, spending no more than three minutes with every person are attempts to allow men and women to work long hours and also fulfil their need for companionship. Of course, once a connection is made, time will still be required to nurture the relationship, so we have to see how one can fast forward that process!

All relationships need nurturing, but the high-pressure demands and long hours of most jobs today make work the centre and indeed, the very purpose of existence. It was interesting to note that almost all the executives interviewed, who had been handpicked from companies that were considered enlightened, all worked either eleven–twelve hour days, or had been unable to take vacations.

Impact on Health

Stress-related illnesses such as hypertension, obesity, spondylitis are almost considered a by-product of today's work-intensive culture. Most companies try to help employees cope in various ways. It is common practice for top-end companies to call in yoga experts or to send executives to spas or other relaxation courses on company expense. But, of course, in many ways they are treating the symptoms rather than the cause.

Time was when a slight attack of influenza meant a few days in bed with tomato soup or khichdi, to give the whole system a rest. Now, people tend to work right through, keeping the temperature in check with analgesics. However, 'employment researchers', and employers themselves, are increasingly acknowledging that 'having sick employees stumble in to work and slog through the day, a phenomenon they call "presenteeism"— is not just painful for the employees, but can also hurt the company . . . "Presenteeism" is twice as big as absenteeism in America and accounts for two-thirds of the losses that occur at work, says Ronald Kessler, a professor of healthcare policy at Harvard Medical School' ('Caught a Cold?', the *Telegraph*, 2004: 20).

As with so many other contemporary corporate practices, good old common sense behaviour has been replaced by behaviour patterns that are clearly good for neither employer nor employee.

The Implications of a Shorter Work Week

Much of the pressure on time and energy today's employees in the corporate sector face is because of being short-staffed.

Might this not be the time for a shorter work week as an alternative to downsizing? This would meet the needs of women and men in the childbearing years and people throughout life as they continue further training, education and work. This would help older people who would welcome a less rigid schedule. Could it also meet the needs of employers who prefer today to hire temporary or part-time workers if we fight to have such work covered by pro-rated benefits?

We have to have new thinking about competitiveness, new thinking about the bottomline, new thinking about benefits, new thinking about work in terms of time and family, and new definitions of success if we are going to build a better paradigm (Friedan, 1963).

The key question is that while it may be excellent logic for more people to have both work and leisure, would this be acceptable to employees? Are people willing to work less for less money?

What is the Problem this Mindset Creates?

Most of the young people I interviewed for the chapter on young singles were very comfortable with the punishing hours they had to work at their institutes or jobs. They saw this as a problem that would affect them only when they got married and had children, or when they had to look after elderly parents or other dependent relatives. While interviewing single career women and men, I came across many who said that the workplace itself provided them with an opportunity to socialize. Indeed, in an era where the variety of jobs available make it possible for most people to be in jobs that excite them, the adrenaline of being in a high-pressure job is itself fairly exhilarating.

'Let's be honest: there's something addictive about a newsroom, especially at night. The rush of deadline can be far more exhilarating than helping your kid with her history paper' (Eisner, 2001). There were any number of women, and this includes mothers, who were candid that it was easy for them to get completely caught up with the world of work, which in some ways repaid effort the way the responsibilities at home never would. One father, who had an off day on Saturdays while his wife did not, confessed that he found Saturdays to be the 'toughest day of the week'.

Working from Home

When family responsibilities make coming to the workplace difficult, one option is to work from home. Few people who have been confined to the house would actually argue that being at home is in any way easier or pleasanter than being at office. Housework was found to be monotonous by almost every housewife interviewed. Looking after young people or, indeed, old people, again, is stressful at the best of times. So though there is a small minority of people who work better from home for any number of reasons, they are the exception rather than the norm. The work-from-home option is then, more of a way of finding a solution for people who have to cope with multiple responsibilities. A parent can work with far greater peace of mind if able to keep an eye on the child, than if he or she is located miles and hours away from home.

But the work-from-home option does offer substantial benefits. It can be far more time efficient as one is spared the expense and discomfort of long commutes. It enables people to do with part-time help rather than

296　The　Great　Indian　Family

full-time help, which is considerably more expensive and difficult to organize. And, though this may appear trivial, it cuts down on laundry costs as one can work dressed in an old pair of jeans on any day of the week!

But the most compelling reason for a work-from-home option is that it allows people who would otherwise be unable to work, because of 'carer' responsibilities, to do so.

For the organization, having some employees work from home may reduce the need for office space, which, considering the high cost of office space in commercial areas, could lead to substantial savings. In the British Council office in London jobs are shared to save on office space, says Sujata Sen, the director of the British Council, Eastern Region, India. Working from home, or even switching to flexible timings, would also ease rush hour, or 'office traffic' in any metro city of the country, with substantial benefits for both the environment and for the nerves of commuters of every variety!

Are Employees Becoming One-Dimensional?

In an environment where such great store is set by work, it is highly likely that the workplace does indeed fulfil many of the needs earlier met by friends and family. Niroop Mahanty, who was Vice President , HR, Tata Steel when I interviewed him, rues the fact that increasingly when you interview young people they seem to have no interests or passions that are not job related. Mahanty does, however, admit that one reason for this could be that the atmosphere has become very competitive in the new era of liberalization and globalization. 'Our company is seeking to re-create [a plant of the size of] Jamshedpur at Orissa.' It is a mammoth task and Mahanty is concerned as to how employees will be able to retain adequate work–life balance while trying to meet this challenge.

It is also true that working long hours, and working intensively, is something some people enjoy, more than they perhaps themselves realize. Especially in an environment where one's energies have been trained for just this from early childhood. But we need to think about who really benefits by having people who are so one-dimensional? It is quite ironic really that on the one hand, organizations handpick individuals with social skills and multi-faceted interests, and then promptly put them into environments where the most important discriminator is the difference to the bottom line in the last quarter.

The only way change can be effected according to Mahanty is through 'role modelling', when top management shows by example what the company really values. Tata Steel has facilities for a wide range of sports and activities at Jamshedpur, including a full-fledged adventure sports division headed by mountaineer Bachendri Pal. Mahanty believes that not just the individual, the organization would also benefit if these facilities were properly utilized. However, he is hopeful about the future as he sees younger employees are more interested in family time. 'They see their wives as companions and are keen to spend time with them.'

Family-Friendly Measures

International Norms on Work and Family Life Differ

The United States differs from Great Britain and Sweden both ideologically and institutionally. Both differences are anchored in the following cultural assumptions. (In the United States): 1. Families/children are in the private domain. The choice to have children is entirely personal . . . 2. The care of children and elders is rightfully the province of women . . . 3. In an individualistic, achieving society, balance between work and personal life is not seen as a high priority goal. Career and work success are more important (Bailyn, 1993: 72).

As opposed to the United States, where the effort has been to allow women to meet male demands, and to Britain where the emphasis has been on accommodating work to the needs of mothers, the effort in Sweden has been to equalize gender roles. Balance between work and family is encouraged for both men and women; men are urged to be more involved with the family and are supported in this effort . . . Swedish men find it more ideologically appropriate to spend time at home. But the response is selective, since career rules for moving up have not changed significantly (ibid: 76).

One Reason Why There is a Difference

European countries, unlike the US, have had strict immigration policies and therefore rely on their own citizens to meet labour force demands. Thus their investment in policies conducive to fertility, and also to the quality of the next generation, relate not only to family well-being but also the labour market (see Moen 1992: 10).

As mentioned elsewhere in the book, especially in the developed world, but even in Asia, women are marrying later, or not at all, and more young people now choose not to have children. The workplace is so structured that it is difficult to fulfil one's responsibilities at home and also take care of the commitments at work.

The way work is organized has meant that qualified women, even from the premier institutes of management, who have shown uncommon promise and should have been able to command top-drawer salaries and positions, are unable to stay the course.

An interesting analysis of the American situation has recently concluded that the present design of work is, in the legal sense, discriminatory. The argument states that the many presumed requirements of high-level work are actually not job related but merely 'corporate convenient'. For example, 'long hours or excessive travel may not actually be necessary for a given task; there may be other ways to get the work done. But it is more convenient to continue to impose these "requirements" than to re-think what is actually necessary for the job at hand. The trouble arises because such demands are prejudicial to one particular group, namely, women. It is this combination that fits the legal definition of discrimination' (Bailyn, 1993: 77).

It is undeniable that though being an 'equal opportunity employer' is politically correct these days, the way the workplace is organized and the way

300 The Great Indian Family

employees are assessed makes it impossible for a large proportion of women to remain in the workforce. A survey conducted by the Confederation of Indian Industry shows that even in fields such as travel, media and advertising, banking and IT-enabled sectors, which appear to be more women-friendly, the representation of women at the top varies from 10 to 29 per cent though they account for 20–35 per cent of the employee strength and, of course, even more importantly, though they comprise 50 per cent of the population!

Women in the boardroom are still a rarity; the government is trying to change the Companies Act to mandate a minimum percentage of women on a company's board. The Securities and Exchange Board of India is also trying to do this under the umbrella of corporate governance. How far legislation will help more women to get on board is yet to be seen. A survey of women from the class of 1982 from IIM, Ahmedabad, conducted several years after graduation shows findings that are a stark commentary on the challenges working women face. Only 5 per cent of them were still in the corporate world (most of them were in senior positions), the majority 70 per cent were running their homes! Twenty-five per cent had turned entrepreneurs and were successfully managing their businesses.

In this respect, the position in India is similar to the position in countries such as the US where only 13.6 of the directors of the *Fortune 500* companies are women. Even in Sweden, which has some of the most women-friendly work practices in the world, few women hold managerial posts (Kristindottir). Norway has said that company boards must comprise at least 40 per cent of each sex or face legal action. ' "There is no slack," industry minister Ansgar Gabrielsen said . . . Most companies are far from the goal . . . Unless firms reach the quota by mid-2005, the centre-right government will impose affirmative action to ensure more equal representation' (report by Inger Sethov, the *Economic Times*, 27 April 2004, p.11).

So, though 'family-friendly' is a catchphrase of our times, very few organizations are aware of quite how family-unfriendly they really are. Requirements such as emergency leave, or job sharing are still regarded as exotic, alien concepts. Some companies do offer employees the option of flexible timings, but overall the norm is to work even longer hours. The picture is far from comforting anywhere in the world. The slowdown in the economy has seen a drop in the number of organizations offering flexitime in the US. And while developments such as the Philippines introducing a four-day work week are heartening, on the whole, the picture is bleak. Most women continue to leave the labour market to care for young children, leading to downward mobility in terms of job status and income on return.

In such an environment, do people have real choices? Undoubtedly, many young people are totally focussed on success at the workplace. Others are clear that they wish for work–family balance. Those who want a family life, as also a job, would do well to look at careers that allow greater flexibility. People are more likely to make exceptions for employees who are seen to offer something that is not easily replaceable. This is also possible in fields where a certain degree of flexibility is possible. Jobs with a creative content generally fall into this category on both counts. Jobs in fields where customer interface is essential, as in the hospitality industry, are going to be most demanding of 'face time', and require the employee's presence at the workplace.

Feminists would, of course, be outraged at the idea of jobs being categorized as more or less compatible with family responsibilities. The apprehension would be that jobs that are 'family-friendly' will be predominantly done by women, and identified as 'soft jobs' and be less well paid than others are. This would lead to gendered employment opportunities, institutionalizing the inequitable family responsibilities women continue to shoulder even today. This is possible. And would be regretable. But it is also entirely possible that men may choose such jobs. Indeed, till policies at the workplace change, it may be worthwhile for those (of either gender) who wish for greater work–family balance to understand what pressures they may encounter depending on the career choice they make. In the case of women, considering the high drop-out rate even of women from a career-oriented and extremely competitive institute such as IIM, Ahmedabad, this awareness may help them to not only get, but also retain, their jobs.

Organizations are Trying to Create a More Woman-Friendly and Family-Friendly Environment

The realization that women are conspicuous by their absence in the workplace has many organizations actively seeking to identify suitable women for the fast track. It is entirely possible that other things being equal it is the woman employee who will get the promotion ahead of the male employee.

There is also a willingness to look at issues like the effect of a transfer of an employee on the family, especially in a dual-career family.

'As a firm we are keen to provide an environment within which women can thrive. We appreciate the talent that is present in women and are very keen to fully tap into it. We also recognize the challenges women face, especially after they start families. To support women, in addition to the normal maternity leave, we offer a leave of absence, we offer flexitime and also allow them to work part-time. We understand about allowing them to work from home when required and when possible', says Janmejaya Sinha, Director, Boston Consulting Group.

Ramnath Krishnan describes HSBC as a family-friendly organization that encourages work–life balance. 'It is mandatory to take twenty days leave in a year, of which ten days [not including weekends] must be taken at a stretch, so you are off for about a fortnight at a time', he says. The company also has ten days paternity leave in addition to maternity leave. HSBC also allows people not to relocate if they do not wish to do so. Such employees may however, have to accept a slower track with regard to job progression.

PricewaterhouseCoopers also tries to ensure that the organization is able to retain balance. 'We would not bid for assignments that would require employees to work 24/7. We have a five-day week, and I think eight hours a day is adequate', says Joydeep Datta Gupta, director, PwC. He himself, however, works a ten-hour day. But he goes on to share other forward-looking measures. 'There is no attendance register at PwC, and there is no mechanism to track and monitor when employees come in and leave'. Other family-friendly initiatives at PwC include paternity leave and the option to log in rather than report to work physically. If a woman employee, for instance, wants to work from home for a while after her maternity leave is over, she may do so. PricewaterhouseCoopers also has an errand service through which theatre tickets and the like can be organized by the company at a highly subsidized rate!

Siddhartha Mukherjee, vice president, Cognizant Technologies Solutions India, says that though his company is very open to people working from home, and some often do, such arrangements are not completely problem-free as network connectivity and infrastructure are still not up to the mark. Another problem with the work-from-home option is that jobs that require teamwork are not possible.

At ITC Sonar Bangla Sheraton and Towers, Ranvir Bhandari, the general manager, says that he always tells employees that at any given time one is juggling different balls: 'If you drop the career ball, you can always pick it up again, but if the family ball breaks, you have a problem'. 80 per cent of the employees at ITC hotels are in operations. 'To ease their work–life balance, they are free to leave the hotel and attend to their personal jobs when work is likely to be slack', he says.

Flexibility Encourages Work–Family Balance

Flexible working hours was cited by almost every woman interviewed for the chapter on working women as something that would immeasurably help bring in work–family balance. There is research to show that flexible working conditions permit individuals to substantially improve productivity. And interestingly, the men in the study benefited even more than the women!

Flexibility Eases the Impact of Long Hours

'Finding an Extra Day a Week: The Positive Influence of Perceived Job Flexibility on Work and Family Life Balance' was a study of IBM employees conducted in July 2001. This study was unique in that it almost quantified the relationship between flexibility and work–life balance. The hypotheses tested by researchers Jeffrey Hills, Alan Hawkins, Maria Ferris and Michelle Weitzman was that, given the same workload, those with perceived job flexibility will have less difficulty with work–life conflicts and will be able to work longer before having problems with work–life balance. Both were found to be true. Of those working forty–fifty hours per week, 46 per cent who were not allowed to either alter their starting or ending times, work a compressed work week, or work from home, had trouble balancing work and personal life compared to only 28 per cent of those working the same hours with flexibility. For men with pre-schoolers, the flexibility advantage was even more impressive: 59 per cent without it had problems compared with 38 per cent who could work flexible hours. The business benefit was greatest in the case of women with pre-schoolers who could work from home; they could put in forty-three hours a week without experiencing a lack of balance, and women not allowed to work from home reported balance problems with a thirty-two-hour week. The researchers concluded, 'in a heavy workload environment, perceived flexibility in the timing of work enables the employee to work an extra day a week before work–family balance becomes difficult' (see http//findarticles.com, Work and Family Newsbrief)

There are other examples. A study by Brigham Young University researchers has shown that workers who believe they have flexibility are able to work eight hours more a week and still feel they have work–life balance.

Flexibility, however, demands real commitment from the organization (Bailyn, 1993: 117).

Understanding real equity for women, or for any individual who has another responsibility, means that the organization completely change the way it views such matters. *Breaking the Mold* gives the real life example of a woman executive in a large manufacturing company who had an arrangement that she leave the office at 5.30 p.m. One day, she was at a meeting that was scheduled to end at 5 p.m. but which continued far beyond that time. At 5.30 p.m. the woman executive left to pick up her child from a daycare centre, regretting that she could not be there till the meeting ended. Senior management was understanding and reassured her that they understood her situation and did not mind the fact that she had to leave midway. Only one senior manager understood that continuing the meeting without the woman executive signalled that 'her presence was less necessary than that of others and that real equity could only be served by stopping the meeting'.

This is the kind of shift required in the mindset of employers if organizations are to demonstrate real sensitivity to the other responsibilities of their employees. This is the change that will translate into concrete support for the family. Organizations that have introduced flexibility recognize this but are also aware that such changes are problematic. Janmejaya Sinha of Boston Consulting Group says, 'As far as possible we would like to introduce family-friendly policies in the workplace. We are open and happy to try out new things. However, we are a client service business and our clients come first. Our work requires high-energy people who can reach innovative solutions to difficult problems quickly. This can create situations where people working part-time face pressures in meeting client deadlines, which vary from their work schedules. Or when meetings are suddenly called for. Also case teams in which some people are part-time or working from home can result in situations where they are not immediately available. This requires people running the teams to plan their work better. People working full-time may also feel they bear an increasing brunt of the work pressure due to the absence of some case team members. As one experiments with new solutions challenges always arise. I guess these are challenges for all of us in an increasingly competitive work environment where the pace of change is ever increasing and time is getting squeezed.' Sinha is absolutely on track when he says, 'the point is not to give up too easily but to try a little harder'.

Flexibility needs to be both in terms of timings as also in terms of allowing employees to take time off or reduce workload and commitment for longer and shorter periods of time to enable them to better handle the demands of their personal lives. In a very limited way, we can see how this might work with a greater freedom in organizing work time and time off.

The new concept of 'trust holidays' has been imported from the US, where accounting firms, law firms and advertising firms have all adopted the idea.

Under the scheme, managers allow staff to decide among themselves how much time they want off, so long as between themselves they get the job done. Each employee's performance is assessed at the end of the year to ensure that they are performing up to standard. In the US where employees rarely get two weeks holiday a year, one executive took six months paid leave after completing a deal that had required him to work without a break for the previous eight months . . .

There are only two conditions [to taking leave]: customers must not suffer and all holidays have to be agreed to by their immediate colleagues. Everyone who has requested leave has so far been granted it. David Brooks, the co-founder of Inbucon, a human resource consultancy from

Richmond, south west London, said most staff were taking more time off than before the scheme was introduced, but work had not suffered (Bamber, 2004).

Clearly, it is now time for companies to deal innovatively with old problems. Sadly, instead of inventing new ways to work that are as able to take care of the special needs of individuals at differing points of their life cycle, some companies have decided that the old are the problem.

The Bias Against Age

Many older employees are being pushed off the corporate ladder and being replaced by younger colleagues. Earlier, organizations effectively discriminated against youth by putting great store by experience. Today, it often seems organizations are biased against age. Everywhere one hears that 'this is a lean organization', and then with even greater pride, 'it's a young organization'.

Ageism Will Soon Be Illegal

Ironically, even as India is adapting an 'ageist' fad it has inherited from the West, in the Western world, indicating a preference for young employees will soon be illegal. The European Union is formulating proposals, effective from early 2006, whereby phrases such as 'young and enthusiastic' will be banned from job advertisements. Lawyers fear that many employers will face 'ruinous claims' (Judge, 2005).

The rationale for favouring young employees over older employees is perhaps based on the premise that it is easier for younger people to adapt to rapidly changing business environments and also that younger people when promoted to senior positions will be at the head for a long time thus allowing continuity in policies. Also, in an environment where some young people are in a position to get top jobs and top salaries, perhaps it has become more difficult to retain promising people with a more conservative growth path.

These assumptions are suspect on a number of counts. They are also particularly unfortunate from the point of view of work–family balance. Men and women in their thirties are likely to have young children and therefore would normally have far greater commitments to the home. That is when the organization will also demand high energy and commitment. Later, when they are in their late forties and fifties, the children are likely to have grown up and commitments to the home have reduced. They are now in a position to give their best to the job, but are no longer wanted at the workplace. Incidentally, there is research to show that most employed men are only able to integrate work and family concerns in the third decade of their employment.

Evans and Bartolome, in their study of successful male European managers showed that the first career decade was more highly organizationally oriented, but during the second decade, managers were more likely to turn their attention to their families. Only in a third decade, with career and family both well established and the immediate demands from both somewhat lessened, did these managers find it possible to integrate the two domains. A prerequisite for future success is primary commitment to work and career, which creates obvious difficulties in a period of life that is usually associated with starting a family of one's own (Bailyn, 1993).

How Young People Will Pay the Cost for the Bias Against Age

Some people believe that this is not an issue for us as India is a young country. This is only partly true. 'Youth Brigade Growth Stagnant, 30-49 Age Group Dominates Population, India's Not All That Young, It's Bulging in the Middle', says a report in the *Economic Times* (Ananthnarayan, 2004: 1). The report quotes the latest census figures to point out that 'the youth in India as a proportion of total population is either stagnant or even declining. India is getting fatter in the middle, and a growing number of people are being added to the sixty-plus age group. Kids in the 0-4 age group have grown just 8% between 1991 and 2001, which is the lowest among all age groups, they also account for just over a tenth of the total population of 110 crore, down from 12% a decade ago. If this continues, the lower growth in the number of infants will have a spillover effect on subsequent age groups too.' One outcome which is causing concern in the West is that since people are retiring, or rather, being forced to retire earlier, people who are fit and able to work will, instead of contributing taxes to the government, be supported by the taxes paid by younger colleagues, who will be working overtime to support them!

And How Older People Will Also Pay

For a man, being a breadwinner has its own stresses and anxieties, especially in a changing world. He faces a threat both from younger men as also from women. 'An economic revolution equivalent to the Industrial revolution is pitting mature men against younger, computer savvy digerati. Experience may no longer count for as much in marketplaces focused on the now . . . The rules of the game have changed. You used to be able to count on the corporate father—the far-seeing, benevolent giver of rewards and reprimands. Now the corporation is a virtual father—amorphous, nonhierarchical and you can never know where you stand' (Sheehy, 1999: 6).

As jobs become contractual arrangements rather than long-term relationships, employers and employees both constantly reassess the fit. 'If you're going to be opportunistic in your choice of employees, they're going to be opportunistic with regard to you', points out Dr Leena Chatterjee, professor of Behavioral Science at IIM, Calcutta. Dr Chatterjee believes that many organizations undertake performance surveys at the end of which those who are chronologically older seem to be eased out. 'People are not always very good at conducting these surveys', and they can cause a lot of damage not only to those who are asked to leave but also to those who survive. 'There is the guilt of a survivor; sometimes people [who remain] are clueless as to why they were retained and other colleagues were asked to go. It's not very healthy'. This experiment of picking people with potential and giving them great responsibility at a very young age is still fairly new. It is yet to be seen how they cope in the long run. 'If you peak early, you are hungry for more, and there may not be that much more', Dr Chatterjee cautions.

If such practices complicate a young employee's life and career, they have even graver implications for older employees. With rising life expectancies, people are not only living longer but also staying fitter longer both mentally and physically. Yet, a fifty-year-old employee who may be in his prime, with his family responsibilities now in control, who has the experience and skills to really contribute to the organization, often finds himself unemployed.

A new survey of senior executives by ExecuNet (www.execunet.com), a career networking and job-search service found that 82 per cent consider age bias a 'serious problem' in today's workplace, up from 78 per cent in 2001. A startling 94 per cent of managers in their forties and fifties said that they believed that their age had resulted in their being cut out of the running for a particular job, although this was virtually impossible to prove. This is strange when you consider how rapidly the US population is ageing: according to the Census Bureau, the proportion of Americans who are at least fifty-five years old will grow by 46.6 per cent between now and 2010, making them 38 per cent of the population and the fastest growing segment.

Such large numbers of fifty-plus managers have already been put out to pasture through layoffs and early retirement programmes that the only people left to make hiring decisions in many companies are young enough to think fifty is older than dirt. But the main culprit is the rotten job market: 'when job seekers outnumber the available jobs, employers use age as one way to quickly screen out candidates' (Fisher, 2004: 46).

This is particularly unfortunate as there is considerable evidence to show that this generation is not only perfectly capable of adapting to changing times and changing circumstances, they perhaps are embracing change, seeking adventure and fulfillment, perhaps more than any other single age group.

> There is no evidence that older cohorts are rigid, set in their ways and incapable of change . . . if public opinion at large was shifting, change characterized the older cohorts as well' (Cutler, forthcoming).

> Just as Baby Boomers once set the tide in motion, so now they will respond to new currents set by the emerging generation. A classic study of the parents of boomer high school graduates in the 1960s and early 1970s showed they were much more flexible than the researchers anticipated, changing their views along with their children (Cutler, forthcoming).

In the UK, the over-fifties are the single largest age group to go in for adventure holidays, or socially relevant projects. 'Over-50s were becoming more adventurous in their choice of holidays. The trend for adventure and fulfillment is demonstrated by a survey by Saga which shows that nearly two thirds of over-50s would consider travelling around the world. Half of 55-to 64-year-olds are planning a far-flung holiday. They are also taking part in far more exciting activities: white water rafting, elephant trekking, even scuba diving' (Womack, 2004: 20).

For reasons difficult to fathom, organized industry is burdening younger employees who must juggle active parenting responsibilities with increased demands at the workplace while ignoring an older workforce who has the time, energy, and as it turns out, the zest for new challenges from contributing in the way that they might, in a manner that would be beneficial to both.

Flexibility Encourages Innovation and Creative Thinking

The real benefit of flexibility is to allow the development of a multi-skilled, multi-faceted personality where individual employees can effortlessly cross-reference from a wide variety of experiences and activities. In an era where innovation is likely to be more important than ever before, encouraging parents, and even older employees, to move in and out of employment at different stages of their life cycle may be an effortless way to introduce fresh and original thinking. That it is also family friendly could be regarded simply as an added bonus.

The Value Family Life Brings to the Workplace

Not too long ago, organizations were involved with the personal lives of their employees. An employee grappling with a crisis at home could hardly be expected to contribute very effectively at the workplace, this was common sense. In the recent past, the view that your personal life was your own, to be dealt with as you thought fit became accepted wisdom. Slowly the pendulum is showing signs of a shift. In the book, *Successful Innovation*, brought out by the *Economist*, interviews carried out by the authors show that the influence of family life is the most powerful, by far, in senior mangers' perspective of their role at the workplace.

Among the factors taken into account, the first is where the individual's partner has a direct professional knowledge of the sector or company and can provide expert advice from a non-partisan standpoint. The second type of influence is the 'get real' factor, expressed to the senior managers by their wives and older children. The third influence which is the ability to transfer inter-personal relationships in family life to inter personal relationships at work. But most interesting of all is the viewpoint of many women who feel that bringing up children provides a formative experience that directly relates to managing of staff . . . 'I always found that I was two or three steps behind my children's evolution and that is often the case with managing organizations. People move on from where you think they are and you can often miss significant changes in their needs and aspirations when you are working on out of date assumptions' (Syrett and Lammiman: 2002: 29, 30).

Perhaps this is exactly what today's employers must also consider. What is the best way to address the concerns of the heterogeneous work force that will enable more people to have a job and also a life?

Work has become more important to an individual's life then perhaps ever before. In a highly competitive global environment, the opportunities for growth are both lucrative and exciting. However, work–life balance is declining, as is job security.

The very long hours and the intensive nature of work create problems for individuals who wish to lead full, multi-faceted lives. Innovative ways to work may address many of the issues that arise due to current work practices.

Future Trends

Looking Ahead

By 2020, it is expected that both the family and the workplace will show significant change. In 1999, when I first read the projections a British bank had made about the future, that women would be the major breadwinners and that there was likely to be a return to the multi-generational family living under one roof, with domestic help again in evidence, it seemed a fairly unlikely scenario. Today, in both UK and the US, though men still receive more pay than women do, men's salaries are showing a decline, while women's salaries are rising. In her book *Beyond Gender*, Betty Friedan says that while the income of white men is dipping, the salaries of women shows an imperceptible rise. Interestingly, even Japan has seen more men becoming house-husbands while more women are in paid employment. A survey published in the *Economic Times* shows indication of what could well signify a reversal of roles. The number of men listed as dependants stood at 80,108, more than double the number of 40,000 seven years ago. The number of dependent women fell by one million in the same period. Japan remains a traditional society with many more dependent women than men. However, as the title of this news item states, 'The Times They are a Changin', (the *Economic Times*, Kolkata, Saturday, 18 September 2004, p. 1).

> Projections for Britain 2010 show more single people, a booming consumer market for over 50s and a major expansion of home workers—key trends highlighted by Economic and Research Council (ESRC) Foresight Programme, a UK-wide initiative that brings together business, the science base and government to develop and act on the shared base of the future (the British Journal of Administrative Management, 2000).

There is also research to show that parents in the West are now much more open to living in the same house with their adult children, so the multi-generational family is already in sight. In *Changing Families as Societies Age*, quoted in 'The Great Baby Shortage' in the *Sunday Times*, London, Sarah Harper points out that the great majority of European countries are seeing striking increases of twenty-somethings still living with their parents (for Italian eighteen to twenty-four-year-olds the figure has now reached 95 per cent) Research in India too shows that young singles like the idea of living in a joint family because they think the presence of grandparents will have a beneficial effect on their children.

Since the manufacturing sector is declining in the developed West, and many jobs in this sector have been automated, there will be a rise in jobs in the services sector, the real increase in demand may be for 'carers' for the very young and the very old. We have already seen a demand for nurses and teachers from India in the UK and in Europe.

For Indians who are in their twenties right now, the world should open up most attractively. It is likely that by 2020, Indian executives may be as much in demand in these countries as software professionals were earlier.

There will also be a rise of single people, and of older people, who will have more spending power than they have had in recent times. The impact of this is already visible in the proliferation of shopping malls in urban India and the boom in consumerism that is apparent everywhere. Higher disposable incomes and the rise in the number of working women makes eating out a routine activity. Experimentation with cuisine from other regions of the country and the world, has brought the pizza and tortilla, as well as more exotic delicacies such as sushi, into the consciousness of the middle-class urban Indian who now has the awareness, the inclination and the wherewithal to sample these hitherto unattainable delights.

Working from home will become an increasingly common option. A new generation of Indians will experience the pleasures and pains of not having to go to office, of never having to leave the house.

Epilogue

Work has had a powerful impact on family life. Job induced migration made the home mobile and had a profound effect on the equation between generations as parents often had to live with adult offspring rather than the other way around. The change in physical location often spelt a fairly dramatic break with the past. Women's paid employment has similarly changed forever the notion of male provider and female homemaker and with it the traditional equation between the sexes.

To deal with the new realities of the dual-career family, working people want flexible working conditions. The need for this is especially urgent in homes where the mother and mother-in-law may also be working and there is no relative to take care of the very young and the very old. People are likely to pace their work to accommodate the requirements of their lives. And working from home will become increasingly commonplace. As we look to a future where women are slated to be bigger earners and where the population of older people is likely to be higher than ever before, it may make excellent sense to do so.

Will the great Indian family survive? Will the home continue to nourish and nurture future generations? It is we who will determine this by the decisions we make today. The future is in our hands.

Bibliography

Ananthnarayan, Ravi, 'Youth Brigade Growth Stagnant, 30-49 Age Group Dominates Population, India's Not All That Young, It's Bulging in the Middle', *Economic Times*, ET Intelligence Group, 11 October 2004, p.1.

Bailyn, Lotte, *Re-Thinking Time and Autonomy, Breaking the Mold, Women, Men and Time in the New Corporate World*, 1993, Free Press.

Bamber, David, 'Trust Holidays to Keep Jack on Toes', the *Daily Telegraph*, published in the Telegraph, 5 April 2004, Kolkata.

Barlow, Jim, 'Work and Family, Fathers in India More Socially Connected to Family than US Dads', News Bureau, 2001, University of Illinois at Urbana Champaign.

Basham, A.L., *The Wonder That was India*, 1993, Picador (first edn. 1954).

Bennis, Warren G. and Robert J. Thomas, *Geeks and Geezers. How Era, Values, and Defining Moments Shape Leaders*, 2002, Harvard Business School Press.

Birla, B.K., *Swant Sukhaya*, 1991.

Bose, Sajal, 'Corporate Philanthropy Better Living, Parivar is Changing the Lives of the Street Children of Calcutta', *Business India*, 5–18 July 2004.

Chanana, Karuna, 'Introduction', in A.M. Shah, B.S. Baviskar, E.A. Ramaswamy (eds), *Social Structure and Change in Indian Society*, Vol.2, 1996, Sage Publications.

Cherlin, Andrew J., *Marriage, Divorce and Re-marriage*, 1981, Harvard University Press.

Clinton, Hilary Rodham, *Living History*, 2003, Simon and Schuster.

Clinton, Hilary Rodham, *It Takes a Village*, 1996, Simon and Schuster.

Coontz, Stephanie, *The Way We Really Are*, 1997, Basic Books.

Coontz, Stephanie, *Coming To Terms With America's Changing Families*, 1997, Basic Books.

Cooper, Cary L. and Roy Payne (eds), *Causes, Coping & Consequences of Stress at Work*, 1988, John Wiley and Sons.

Crompton and Sanderson, in Julia Evetts (ed.), *Women and Careers: Themes and Issues in Advanced Industrialised Societies*, 1990.

Cutler, Stephen, 'Aging and Social Change', in Jeffrey Michael Clair and Richard Allman (eds), *The Gerontological Prism: Developing Interdisciplinary Research and Priorities*, forthcoming, Baywood Press.

Eekelaar, J.M., and S.N. Katz, *Marriage and Co-habitation in Contemporary Society*, 1980, Butterworths.

Eisner, Jane, 'Job vs. Life. The New Equation', *Columbia Journalism Review*, September / October 2001.

Engels, Fredrich, *The Origin of the Family, Private Property and the State*, 1884.

Evetts, Julia (ed.), *Women and Careers: Themes and Issues in Advanced Industrialised Societies*, 1990.

Fisher, Anne, 'Older, Wiser, Job-Hunting', The Bias Against Age, *Fortune*, 9 February 2004.

Freidan, Betty, *The Feminine Mystique*, 1963, W.W. Norton and Co.

Friedan, Betty, *Beyond Gender: The New Politics of Work and Family*, 1963, Johns Hopkins University Press.

Ganesh, Kamala, 'Diverse Forms, Plural Structures and Multiple Perspectives: A Contemporary "Take" on the Family', paper presented at the CIF International Conference on 'The Evolving Family in the 21st Century: A Social Work Challenge', Goa, 2003.

Giddens, Anthony, Reith Lecture broadcast by BBC Radio 4 in 1999 and published in *Runaway World*, Profile Books.

Girling, Richard, 'The Great Baby Shortage', *London Sunday Times*, 15 February 2004.

Government of India, Ministry of Home Affairs, *Census of India*.

Greer, Germaine, *The Change, Women, Aging and the Menopause*, 1991, Ballantine Books.

Greer, Germaine, *The Whole Woman*, 1999, Doubleday.

Gulati, L., 'Women and Family in India, Continuity and Change', *Indian Journal Social Work*, 1995 (56), pp.134-54.

Hayden, Anders, *Sharing the Work, Sparing the Planet. Work Time Consumption and Ecology*, 1999, Pluto Press.

Herman, J. B. and K.K. Gyllstrom, 'Working Men and Women: Inter- and Intra-role Conflict', *Psychology of Women Quarterly*, 1, 319-333.

Hill, Jeffrey E., Alan J. Hawkins, Vjolica Martinson and Maria Ferris, *Fathering*, 2003.

Hindustan Times, Kolkata Live, 'Rejected Job Seeker Stabs Woman in Office', 2 December.

Houseknecht, Sharon, Suzanne Vaughan and Anne Stratham, 'The Impact of Singlehood on the Career Patterns of Professional Women', *Journal of Marriage and Family*, 49 May (1987): 353-366.

Jennings, M. Kent and Richard Neimi, *Generations and Politics: A Panel Study of Young Adults and Parents*, 1981, Princeton University Press.

Judge, Elizabeth, 'UK Gears Up for New EU Age Laws', the *Times*, London, reprinted in the Statesman, 1 January 2005, Kolkata.

Kanter, R.M., *Men and Women of the Corporation*, 1977, Basic Books.

Kliger, Deborah S., 'The Effects of Employment of Married Women on Husband and Wife Roles: A Study in Culture Change', doctoral thesis, Yale University.

Kristindottir, Gudrun, *Swedish Women and Employment: The Absence of Careers*.

Laslett, P., 'Introduction', in P. Laslett and R. Wall (eds), *Household and Family in Past Time*, 1972, Cambridge University Press.

Lala, R.M., *The Creation of Wealth*, 1981, IBH.

Levinson, D.J., *The Seasons of a Man's Life*, 1978, Alfred A. Knopf.

Majumdar, Jaideep, 'New Life for Homemakers', Kolkata Live, *Hindustan Times*, Sunday, 27 June 2004, p. 12.

Majumdar, R.C, H.C. Raychaudhuri and Kalinkar Datta, *An Advanced History of India*, 2001 (first edn. 1946), Macmillan

Mansfield, Penny, *The Good Life*, 1998, Demos Collection.

Manu, *The Laws of Manu*, translated by Wendy Doniger with Brian K. Smith, 1991, Penguin.

Millet, Kate, *Sexual Politics*, 1969, Granada.

Moen, Phyllis, *Committed. Women's Two Roles, A Contemporary Dilemma*, 1992, Auburn House.

Moses, B., *Career Intelligence—The 12 New Rules for Success*, 1999, ACVE.

Rao, Vijay Rukmini and Sahba Husain, 'Invisible Hands—the Women Behind India's Export Earnings', in Nirmala Banerjee (ed.), *Indian Women in a Changing Industrial Scenario*, 1986.

Roopnarine, Jaipaul L., 'Study on the Sex Roles Titled Paternal Involvement in Childcare as a Function of Maternal Employment in Nuclear and Extended Families in India', *A Journal of Research*, May 1999.

Roy, Nilanjana S., 'The Last Word', the *Telegraph*, Kolkata, Sunday, 11 April 2004.

Salisbury, Joyce, *Encyclopaedia of Women in the Ancient World*, Foreword by Mary Lefkowitz, 2001, ABC Clio.

Seth, Leela, *On Balance*, 2003, Viking.

Sheehy, Gail, *Passages, Predictable Crises of Adult Life*, 1976, Bantam Books in association with E.P. Dutton and Co.

Sheehy, Gail, *Passages in Men's Lives*, 1999, Simon and Schuster.

Siemensma, F., 'Hopes, Tensions and Complexity: Indian Students' Reflections on the Relationship of Values to Management Education', *Journal of Human Values*, 5 (1999).

Siemensa, F., 'Values and the MBA: The Implications of Gender', *IIM Bangalore Management Review*, March 2004.

Sonawat, Reeta, 'Understanding Families in India: A Reflection of Societal Changes', *Psicologia: Teoria e Pesquisa*, 17 (2), Brasilia, May/August 2001.

Smart, Carol and Bren Neale, *Family Fragments?* 1988, Polity

Soondas, Anand, 'Indians Break Taboos, But Play Safe: Survey', the *Telegraph*, Wednesday, 2 June 2004, p. 6.

Syrett, Michel and Jean Lammiman, *Successful Innovation: How to Encourage and Shape Profitable Ideas*, 2002, Profile Books.

Tata, J.R.D, *JRD Tata Letters*, 2004, Rupa and Co.

Toynbee, Polly, 'Happy Step Christmas', *Good Housekeeping*, December 2001, p.108.

The *Telegraph*, Jobs, 'Balancing Act', Tuesday, 18 May 2004, p.1.

The *Telegraph*, Jobs, 'The Working Wounded', an *Economic Times* survey carried in the *Telegraph*, Tuesday, 18 May 2004, p.1.

The *Telegraph*, 'Caught a Cold? Better Skip Office' by Denise Difulco, New York Times Service, 2004, p.20.

Uberoi, Patricia (ed.), *Family, Kinship and Marriage*, Oxford in India Readings in Sociology and Anthropology, 1993, Oxford University Press.

UK Government, *Supporting Families*, consultation document, 1999, UK Government.

Varma, Pavan, *The Great Indian Middle Class*, 1998, Viking.

Williamson, 'Status Zero Youth and the "Underclass": Some Considerations', in R. Macdonald (ed.), *Youth, the 'Underclass' and Social Exclusion*, 1997, Routledge.

Womack, Sarah, 'Gap from the Grind for Grown-ups', the *Telegraph*, 10 August 2004, p.20.

Index

absenteeism, 293
accomplishment, 113, 236
adjustments, 67, 76, 79–81, 217
adoption, 9
adult children, 82; with parents vs. parents with adult children, 65–66; relationships in joint family, 48
age bias, 309–11; impact on older people, 312–15; and the young, 311
age of consent, 16
alienation, 109
ambivalence, 250–51
anachronism, 19, 23
attitudes and practices, 9, 18–21, 67; changing, 10, 29, 61, 71–72, 131, 154, 197; amongst Indian young singles, 230–31
Australia: work-family balance, 34

behaviour pattern, 64, 254–55, 293

belief systems and culture, 101
Bengalis, chauvinism, 57
bonding, bonds, see emotional bonding
British family, 21, 23, 26; changes, 24–25; marriage, 23, 25–27; longevity, 32; remarriage, 28; stepfamily, 28; traditional values, 25
businesswomen, 147

capitalist system, oppression of women, 101
career: preference over family, 257, 267–68; preference to marriage amongst young women, 262–67; affects a working women's marriage, 170–71
caring and sharing, 71, 79
caste, caste system, 46, 49; prejudice, 273; and social security, 48
childcare, childrearing, 98–99, 130, 208; burden of, 96–97; involvement of father, 189, 286; support of

husband, 172–74; and the job, 88–89, 92; lack of facilities in India, 92; role of joint family, 40, 53, 66, 71, 72, 78, 80, 82, 86, 94, 175; facilities at workplace, 125; and working mothers, 128; concern of young singles, 249

children, children and young adults: negative behaviour pattern, 205; do not long for parents and family, 102–03; perception to father's role, 187–88, 200–02; perception to mother's role, 187, 200–02; phenomenon of the invisible father, 194; rights in the traditional family, 20

class, 131

cohabitation, cohabitational relationship, 23, 28–31; fathers' rights, 29; split in comparison to marriage, 30; women in disadvantaged position, 29

community, sense of, 61, 96, 102, 110

Companies Act, 300

companionship and compatibility, love, 12–13, 63, 109, 292

competition, competitiveness, 193, 214, 228, 232, 249, 270, 272, 276, 280–81, 297

compromises, 74

Confucius, 5

consciousness, 189

conservatism, 25, 79

consumerism, 91, 94, 102, 198, 224, 227–28, 239, 319

contraceptives, 23

corporate India, insensitive to an individual's personal needs, 148–49

crèches, 145

crime and family problems, relation, 30

crisis management, 111

cultural, culture, 8; clash, 51–52, 68; dissonance, 232; mores, 221

dampati, 4

daughter-in-law, 63–65, 67, 73, 79, 81–82; in the joint family, 11–12, 39–40, 51, 52, 57–59, 61, 75; pre-determined, traditional role, 12, 66; *see also* mother-in-law

decision-making process in a joint family, 70

depression, 91, 147, 156

divorce, 1, 9, 17, 32, 68, 139, 152, 171, 217, 232, 253; impact on children, 217

domestic help, 103, 131, 139, 145, 147, 174, 208, 295–96, 317; job uncertainty, 100; unreliability, 99–100, 159

domestic management programme, 87–88

domestic services, work, 100, 107

domestic violence, 15, 17, 18

domesticity, 102, 106, 264

double standards, 182

double-income-no-kids (DINK) syndrome, 140–41

downsizing, 183, 241, 290, 293

dowry, 18; in ancient times, 7; deaths, 16, 123; Prohibition Act, 17

drug abuse, 17; and family problems, relation, 30

dual-career family, 40, 69, 124, 133, 139, 158 , 144, 147–48, 150, 199, 220, 251, 260, 268, 303, 320; attitude to children, 247–48; roles of father and mother, 199

East and West, cultural difference, 231

economic divide, widening, 215–16

economic independence, 172

economic rationalism, 284

economic revolution, 312

economic slowdown, chastening effect on young singles, 240–41

egalitarian society, 271–73

ego, 57

emotional bonding, fulfillment, 17, 21, 40, 51, 55, 62, 70, 105, 130, 189, 198, 210, 233, 237, 266

empathy, 51, 71

employee-employer relationship, 154, 244

employment shift, 7, 134

equality, 19, 88

Europe, European: decline in birth rate, 134–35; marginalization of fatherhood, 190; work culture, 244

European Union: ageism, 309

expectations, 219

extended family, 41–42; break up/decline, 34, 88

family background, 272

family in India, family life, 7–21; changing, 10–14;— negative, 17; economic role, 20, 41, influence at work, 315–17; an institution, 8; kinds 9–10; reflects the value system of a patriarchal society, 234–35; perspective, 21–24; reforms, 15–17; support system, 233–34, 235; traditional, 19–20

family-owned business, 40

father, fatherhood, 186–90; and child bonding, 191–92; role, biological more than parental, 203; historical and religious viewpoint, 190–92; role in joint family, 42; modern perspective, 192–93; role model, 210; sense of security for children, 200; stay-at-home, 195, 199, 206–07

father-in-law, 58

female infanticide, 16, 17, 123

feminism, 101

filial duty, 49

flexibility, 221

foreign postings, impact on spouse's job, 209

frustration and resentment, 108, 178; of jobless young singles, 242; of losing job, 212–13

Full Time Mothers, 98

gays and lesbians, 31

gender, gender roles, 83, 85, 101, 104, 132, 187, 195, 272, 283; discrimination, divide, 18, 98, 299; equality, equity, 182, 269, 286; equations, 90, 154; justice within family, 16

Generation Next and the joint family, 76–83

globalization, 114, 273, 297

grandparents, 80, 97, 224, 318; and grandchildren relationship/influence on, 48, 80, 82, 231

grihapati, 4

hatred, 213

hierarchy in family, 12, 46, 195, 271

household, residential aspect, 8

housekeeping, household responsibilities, 78, 80, 90, 94, 111, 208, 210, 295; support of husband, 172–74

housewife, housewives, 172, 210, 214, 220, 263–64, 266, 268, 295; children's performance in comparison to the children of working mothers, 153–54, 160–61;

contributions, no monetary value, 91; downgraded role, 176; impact of being housebound, who have worked previously, 92–95; identity, 90, 218; insecurity and inadequacy, 106; not having a life of her own, 119–20; loneliness and boredom, 93, 110, 164, 177–78, 193, 263; loss of financial independence, 89, 92, 120–21; maintained male workforce, 101; and mothers, 2–3; responsibility of men, 210–11; lack of self-fulfillment, 91; skills, 110–13; stress, 100; versus working wife, 208–11

human relationships, 34

husband: stay-at-home, 195, 207, 317; sharing household responsibility/ domestic work, help, 131, 132, 140, 172–74, 188–89; unwillingness for, 107, 128, 139–40

identity, 18, 90, 218

Indian father connected to family and children, 197–99

individualism, 21, 41, 65

industrial revolution, 34, 312

inequality, 108, 130, 132

infants, and the working mothers, 154–58

information technology, impact on work culture and working hours, 34–35

inheritance, 9
interpersonal relationships, 64

Japan: concept of house-
     husbands, 317; traditional
     society, 318
job: aspirations and
     compulsions; and family, 2,
     10;—and spouse posted at
     different locations, impact
     on family, 176–79; loss,
     effects on men, 213; related
     mobility, migration, 40,
     320; precedence over family,
     13 security, 3, 114, 195,
     243, 270, 277, 316; related
     separation, coping with,
     116–17; uncertainty, 277,
     288; attitude of young
     people, 251–53; see also
     career, work
joint family, 2, 9, 10, 20, 70–
     71, 73–75, 165, 214, 218,
     220, 231, 237;
     accommodating, 83; role of
     father, 42; role of mother,
     42; role of elderly relatives,
     42–43; multi-generational
     family, 82; moving to
     nuclear family, 70; in the
     past, 48–49; practical
     considerations, 73; sheer
     necessity, 82; and the next
     generation, 76–83; power
     structure, 58; loss of
     privacy, space and freedom,
     80; repression, 39; and
     social security, as a safety
     net, 48, 75; source of
     stress, 53–54, 83, 95, 175;

as a support system, 175;
     today, 50–51; traditional
     and urban, 40–41, 43–45,
     58, 76
juvenile delinquency, 17

legislations against social evils,
     16–17
liberalization, 193, 227, 297
lifestyle, lifestyles, changes,
     219–26, 232; difference,
     impact on family, 215–18;
     see also middle class
local community, traditional
     bonds, 34
loneliness and boredom: of
     elderly parents, 2, 63; of
     housewife, 93, 110, 164,
     177–78, 193, 263; of stay-
     at-home father, 207
long working hours, see
     working hours
longevity, impact on marriage, 32

male dominance, 132, 135,
     137
man, men: attitude to career,
     221; experience nostalgia
     for the past, 214–15;
     housework, 128; insecurity,
     132; marriage and
     fatherhood, 195–96; in the
     middle, 66–67; provider,
     320; see also husband,
     father
man-management, 111
Manu, 5–6, 47
marriage, marital relations, 1–
     2, 5, 9, 12, 23, 32, 67,
     106–07, 133, 143, 199,

216, 219, 220, 234;
arranged, 13, 108, 216–17,
218, 254, 255–56, 291–92;
break-up, 88, 114–16; in
Britain, 23, 25–27; affects
the career prospects, 129,
149, 170–71, 184–85; and
cohabitation, comparison,
30–31; emotional trauma of
children, 115; fragility, 14,
256–58, 263, 264; security
to women, 13; impact of
spouse posting at different
locations, 176–79, 251–53;
impact of work, 180–83;—
long working hours, 139–
40; and women's interests,
28–31
masculinity, 195
materialism, 21, 78, 227–28;
led greater selfishness
amongst the young, 228
middle class, urban middle
class, 2, 3, 8, 10–11, 32,
46, 179, 192, 196, 208,
216, 220, 228, 272, 273;
changes in the family, 21;
consciousness, 319; joint
family, 40–41; women, 14–
15, 77, 92, 99, 102, 124,
128, 143, 199;—education,
88; young, 243, 250, 254–
56
modern age compulsions, 62
monogamy, 103
mother, motherhood, 1–2,
112–13, 186; break from
career, 248–49; child
interactions, 161; rejecting
equality in workplace and

prefer to become
housewives, 97–98; role in
joint family, 42; of special
children, pressures, 113–14;
see also working mother,
working women
mother-in-law, 61, 71–72, 77,
81; accommodating, 73;
and daughter-in-law, friction
and differences, 67–68;
dominance, 55–57; relevance
in modern lifestyle, 62–63;
role model, 75; in waiting,
72–75; working, 320
multiculturalism, 225
multi-generational family, 35,
317, 318; see also extended
family, joint family

non-governmental
organizations (NGOs), 16
NRI syndrome, 75–76
nuclear family, families, 9, 10,
21, 22, 23, 40, 43, 45, 50,
51, 66, 70, 74, 78, 79, 82,
90, 93, 95, 144, 238;
oppression of women, 101

occupational attainment, 151;
and marriage, relation,
129–30
occupational structure, 271
old-age homes, 222
One Plus One, United
Kingdom, 25, 27, 30
out-of-work fathers, 199
outsourcing, 104, 106, 226

parents, 20; and adult sons,
relationship, 51; control

over adult children, 46; as domestic help, 46; elderly, 21, 45, 63, 92, 165, 209, 210, 221, 251, 294;—adaptation to change, 222;—loneliness and neglect, 2, 63; and young singles, 235, 237, 238

parents-in-law, 131, 175, 251; how young singles feel, 235, 237

parent-teacher committees, 162

paternal identity, 198

paternity leave, 33, 304

patience, 82

patriarchal family/society, 20, 39, 47, 50–51, 52, 67, 125, 234–35; source of gender discrimination, 18

peer pressure, 227, 246, 283

personal desires and family responsibilities, balance, 78

personal relationships, 142

personality clash, 218

Philippines, four-days a week, 34, 286, 301

politics, 101

polygamy, 15

population explosion, 272

power equations of family dynamics, 58, 74

pragmatism, 72, 233

presenteeism, 293

progeny, 5

proximity problems, 65–66

public consciousness, 153

racism, 225

rapport and understanding, 74

relationships, 8, 78, 154, 216

religion, 5

religious festivals, ritual and ceremonies, role and knowledge of women, 62

resentment, see frustration and resentment

respect, lack of in young people, 88

role models, 85

rural to urban, shift, 7

sacrifices (yajna), 5

same-sex marriages, family, 22–23, 25, 29

sati, 16

school demands on parents, 162–63

secularization, 24

Securities and Exchange Board of India (SEBI), 300

self, self-esteem, 91, 110–11, 156, 172, 199, 207, 271

selflessness, 47–49, 78, 82

self-sacrifice, 85

sense of belonging, 54

sense of family and community, 61, 64

servant problems, 99

sex amongst young singles, 253–55

sexual abuse of children, 15, 16, 18

sexual equality, 18

sexual harassment at workplace, 179–80

sexuality regulation, 18

single mothers, 25

single women, 132; working and the work environment, 137–38

single-parent homes, 3, 22, 30
social behaviour, 254
social evils, 18
social life, 192
social mores, 253
social norms, values and
    structures, 17
social policy reforms, 130
social power, 106–07
social security, 3, 19, 48, 239
social transition, 218
social welfare organizations, 21
socialization, 17
societal pressures, 154, 256
soft jobs, 302
spouse posting at different
    locations: impact on
    children, 202–03; impact on
    marital relations, 176–79
stereotypes, 64, 126, 229;
    reinforced by religion, 85
stress, 172, 213; caused in a
    joint family, 53–54, 83, 95,
    175
support system, 11–12
Swayam, Kolkata, 115
Sweden: gender equity, 286;
    norms on work and family
    life, 298; welfare policy
    initiatives, 130; women, 29

technology and housework, 103
transferable jobs, 144; impact
    on women, 95–109, 114,
    121
trust holidays, concept of, 308

United Kingdom; demand for
    Indians, 319; divorce, 32;
    fatherhood, 196;—role of

income provider, 198;
    gender bias, 317; marriages,
    26–27, 258, 263; norms on
    work and family life, 298;
    single mothers, 19; stay-at-
    home fathers, 206; working
    hours, 289
United States of America,
    ageing population, 313;
    conservatism, 23–24; father
    and children, interaction,
    197; gender bias, 317; hire
    and fire, work culture,
    243–45, 284;
    marginalization of
    fatherhood, 190; marriage
    and sexuality, 23–24; norms
    on work and family life,
    298; stay-at-home fathers,
    206; trust holidays, 308;
    women, 267; workplace,
    gender discrimination, 299
urban family in India, 16

values and traditions, 11, 94,
    154, 205
Vedic times, family, 4–5
voluntary retirement scheme
    (VRS), impact on an
    employee, 211–13, 222;
    frustration of losing job,
    212–13

West, Western 3, 97;
    contemporary family, 24–
    27; decline of
    manufacturing sector, 319;
    marriage, 2; mores, 257;
    society, 82; women, no
    ideological baggage, 87;
    work practices, 194

Westernization, 214
widow, widows, 47; re-
    marriage, 14, 16
wife, 123, 129–31; earning
    more than husband, 171,
    182, 215; stereotypical role,
    139; see also housewife
woman, women: attitude to
    work, 221; changing role,
    61–62, 214; characteristics
    as codified by Manu, 5–6;
    crimes against, 123;
    education, 19; interests
    within a marriage or
    outside of it, 28–31;
    marriage and motherhood,
    196; middle-aged, 71;
    oppression in family, 18–
    19, 101; potential and
    performance, dichotomy,
    123; public consciousness,
    124; rights in the
    traditional family, 20; roles
    and responsibilities, 125–
    26, 129, 168–69, 220;—
    dual, 126, 133; self-
    development, effect of a job,
    172, 196; sense of loss,
    104; status, 29, 86, 88,
    90;—in ancient civilizations,
    6–7; lack of tolerance, 184;
    traditional support to
    family, 11–12; subservience,
    86, 88, 128; vulnerability,
    116; Westernized career-
    oriented, 64; more
    comfortable at work rather
    than home, 294–95
women's lib, 98

work, work culture,
    workplace, 11, 112, 243–
    45, 283–86; adjustments,
    220; aspirations of people,
    282–83; change, 110, 154,
    233; childfree woman, 138–
    40; commitment, 288–89
    40; competitiveness, 280–81;
    employees becoming one
    dimensional, 296–97;
    impact on family, 20, 32–
    34, 110, 133, 204, 208,
    218, 220, 246, 254, 274,
    278, 279, 282, 285–87,
    288–89, 291, 297, 299,
    305–09, 320; family
    friendly measures, 284,
    289–90, 298, 307;
    flexibility, 301–02, 305,
    320;—encourages
    innovation and creative
    thinking, 314;—eases the
    impact of long hours, 305–
    9; flexitime for women,
    303; future trends, 317–19;
    gender divide, 98; impact
    on health, 292–93;
    hierarchy, 134; lack of
    homogeneity, 279–80;
    inflexibility, 92, 121, 125,
    169–70, 184; more
    intensive, 290–91; impact
    on marital relationship,
    180–83; new focus, 273–
    75; psychological
    importance, 271; ; impact
    on relationships, 291–92;
    sexual harassment, 179–80;
    implications of shorter
    work week, 293; effect on

single working
professionals, 136–37;
stress/pressure, 246, 278–
80, 289, 292–93; things
getting better or worse,
183–85; related travelling,
158–60, 167, 210;
uncertainty, 277; and
women-friendly, 302–05

work and family life/work and
home: adjustments, 164;
balance, 14, 59, 117, 122,
125, 127, 133–34, 135,
146, 148, 153, 164–67,
184–85, 187, 192, 203,
204–05, 208, 214, 220,
246, 258, 260, 265–66,
270, 275, 278, 281, 282,
284–87, 297–02, 304–05,
310, 317; change, 193–97;
choice, 1, 2, 113, 163;
conflict, 101, 192, 256,
264; international norms,
298; for young singles,
224, 233, 245–46, 250–51
work-from-home option, 280,
287, 304
working conditions, 125, 193,
279, 282, 284
working couples, 3
working father, 200; lack of
family time, 202–06;
handling of responsibilities,
149–50; long working
hours, 204, 208; paternal
involvement, 205; stress,
204–05
working hours, long, impact
on the family, 32–34, 204,
208, 218, 220, 254, 274,
278, 279, 282, 285–87,
288–89, 291, 297, 299;—
on children, 246; people's
choice for, 141–42; and the
workplace flexibility, 305–
09
working men, 200
working mothers, 29, 118,
142–43, 187, 195, 189;
behavioural problems in
children, 131, 160; and
childcare, 143–48, 150–51;
children's reaction, 151–54;
an expert juggler, 143–48;
who have greater control
over timings, 163–66; guilt
of not taking care of
children, 150, 154, 156–58,
160–62, 163; pressure to
have their children excel at
academics, 160–62, 184
responsibilities, 149–50;—in
comparison to full-time
mothers, 184; role conflict,
200; single, 248; should get
special considerations at
workplace, 137; stress,
154–56, 158, 165, 168
working wife, wives, 208–11,
220; understanding, 181,
184
working women, 60, 66, 84,
91–92, 99, 109, 172, 214,
259–61, 263; best time of
the day, 167–69; childcare
and household
responsibilities, 172–74;
disadvantaged in
comparison to men, 169;

economic independence, 129, 184; and the joint family, 52–54, 80, 83; sacrifices at the career front, has to give up job, 88–90, 92, 120, 126, 132–33, 146–47, 159, 166–67, 168, 178, 208–09, 220, 250, 252, 281; single, 195, 199, 294;—and the work environment, 137–38; stress, 175, 193; dual responsibility, 193–94

young people, young singles, 283; bitterness of jobless, 241–42; job aspirations, 275–76; and joint family, 77, 79, 82; living on credit, 229; comfortable with long working hours, 294; attitude to marriage, sex and family, 232–34, 237–38, 253–55, 292; men, preference for working women, 259–61; perception about parents, 236–37; and their peers in West, commonality, 229–30; prefer security, 243–46; selfishness, 228; stress , 232;—from the pressure to excel, 249–50; women, 261–62, 267–68;—preference of career to marriage, 262–67; attitude to work amongst men, 239–40